# PHalarope Books

PHalarope Books are designed specifically for the amateur naturalist. These volumes represent excellence in natural history publishing. Each book in the PHalarope series is based on a nature course or program at the college or adult education level or is sponsored by a museum or nature center. Each PHalarope Book reflects the author's teaching ability as well as writing ability.

BOOKS IN THE SERIES

*The Curious Naturalist*
JOHN MITCHELL and the
MASSACHUSETTS AUDUBON SOCIETY

*The Amateur Naturalist's Handbook*
VINSON BROWN

*The Amateur Naturalist's Diary*
VINSON BROWN

*Nature Drawing: A Tool for Learning*
CLARE WALKER LESLIE

*Outdoor Education: A Manual for Teaching in Nature's Classroom*
MICHAEL LINK, Director,
Northwoods Audubon Center, Minnesota

*Nature with Children of All Ages: Activities and Adventures for Exploring, Learning, & Enjoying the World Around Us*
EDITH A. SISSON,
Massachusetts Audubon Society

*The Wildlife Observer's Guidebook*
CHARLES E. ROTH,
Massachusetts Audubon Society

*Nature Photography: A Guide to Better Outdoor Pictures*
STAN OSOLINSKI

*A Complete Manual of Amateur Astronomy: Tools and Techniques for Astronomical Observations*
P. CLAY SHERROD with THOMAS L. KOED

*365 Starry Nights: An Introduction to Astronomy for Every Night of the Year*
CHET RAYMO

*The Art of Painting Animals: A Beginning Artist's Guide to the Portrayal of Domestic Animals, Wildlife, and Birds*
FREDRIC SWENEY

*At the Sea's Edge: An Introduction to Coastal Oceanography for the Amateur Naturalist*
WILLIAM T. FOX

*Nature in the Northwest: An Introduction to the Natural History and Ecology of the Northwestern United States from the Rockies to the Pacific*
SUSAN SCHWARTZ

*The Fossil Collector's Handbook*
JAMES REID MACDONALD

*The Crust of Our Earth: An Armchair Traveler's Guide to the New Geology*
CHET RAYMO

*Exploring Tropical Isles and Seas: An Introduction for The Traveler and Amateur Naturalist*
FREDERIC MARTINI

*Suburban Wildlife: An Introduction to the Common Animals of Your Back Yard and Local Park*
RICHARD HEADSTROM

**Susan Schwartz** is a writer, editor, and teacher of scientific writing. She was formerly a reporter for the *Seattle Times*, where she covered environmental issues. She has written two other books on natural history, as well as several articles.

# NATURE IN THE NORTHWEST

## An Introduction to the Natural History and Ecology of the Northwestern United States from the Rockies to the Pacific

## SUSAN SCHWARTZ

### Photographs by Bob and Ira Spring

A SPECTRUM BOOK

Prentice-Hall, Inc., Englewood Cliffs, New Jersey 07632

*Library of Congress Cataloging in Publication Data*

Schwartz, Susan H. (date)
    Nature in the Northwest.

    (A PHalarope Book)
    "A Spectrum Book."
    Bibliography: p.
    Includes index.
    1. Natural history—Northwestern States.    2. Ecology—
Northwestern States.    I. Spring, Bob (date)
II. Spring, Ira.    III. Title.
QH104.5.N62S38    1983        508.795        83-4468
ISBN 0-13-610394-4
ISBN 0-13-610386-3 (pbk.)

This book is available at a special discount when
ordered in bulk quantities. Contact Prentice-Hall, Inc.,
General Publishing Division, Special Sales, Englewood Cliffs, N.J. 07632.

1  2  3  4  5  6  7  8  9  10

ISBN 0-13-610394-4

ISBN 0-13-610386-3 {PBK.}

Map on pages xiv-xv by John and Helen Sherman
Cover photo: Sunrise on Glacier Peak from Image Lake,
Glacier Peak Wilderness, Washington.

Editorial/production supervision by Kimberly Mazur
Cover design by Hal Siegel
Manufacturing buyer: Christine Johnston
Page layout by Diane Heckler Koromhas

Prentice-Hall International, Inc., London
Prentice-Hall of Australia Pty. Limited, Sydney
Prentice-Hall Canada Inc., Toronto
Prentice-Hall of India Private Limited, New Delhi
Prentice-Hall of Japan, Inc., Tokyo
Prentice-Hall of Southeast Asia Pte. Ltd., Singapore
Whitehall Books Limited, Wellington, New Zealand
Editora Prentice-Hall do Brasil Ltda., Rio de Janeiro

# Contents

# Preface

The Northwest corner of the United States, from the continental divide to the Pacific Ocean, is the most diverse natural landscape in the nation.

It includes rain forest, rugged coast, fiords and islands of an inland sea, deserts, mountaintops locked in permanent ice, a violent volcano, and the deepest canyon in North America.

Man has changed much of this landscape only slightly. Six national parks and more than a dozen wilderness areas and wild rivers have been set aside to preserve its most spectacular features. Much more is kept nearly natural in national forests, recreation areas, monuments, and wildlife refuges; state parks and wildlife areas; and other official reservations.

All of this public land, as well as the simple pleasure of seeing natural beauty from towns and highways, is available to you. This book aims at helping you understand and enjoy what you see.

A book like this one cannot take the place of field guides that help you identify rocks, fish, birds, mammals, and the like. (The better ones also summarize life histories, areas and habitats where things may be found, and other information.) Some of these field guides are listed in the bibliography at the end of the book. Take some along as you travel through the Northwest. They will make you feel at home in nature and open your eyes to detail you would otherwise miss.

Besides giving things names, though, we like to know why we see the things we do. Why does the Northwest have mountains in one place and plateaus in another? Why are some areas rainsoaked and others parched?

Why do specific kinds of plants and animals live in some places and not in others? Why are certain species so often found together? Why do living things behave the way they do? How do they divide up the nutrients and energy available in their surroundings, and how do they harm or help one another?

This book partly answers these questions. The answers are partial first because the book covers a large area, and so omits much detail, and second because not all the answers are known. Geologists, for example, have revolutionized their ideas in the last decade or so, raising new questions about how the Northwest was formed almost as quickly as they have answered old ones. Biologists have described what most of the Northwest's living things look like and what they do. Questions remain about *how*: How do species compete with one another? How are behaviors like hibernation controlled? How do plants use chemicals to influence one another?

The Savage Mountains in the northern Idaho "panhandle"— just one of many Northwestern landscapes.

It hardly matters whether your favorite outdoor activity is tending your garden, taking a Sunday drive, walking on a beach, gathering wild mushrooms, climbing rocks and glaciers, or kayaking in white water. Understanding the how and why of things you see will add to your enjoyment.

If you want to know more about specific topics, the bibliography lists a few of the many books available. This short list is only a start. A good way to find information on a subject is to look at the bibliographies of recent articles and books on that topic. Remember that books lag several years behind science—really keeping up requires searching through highly technical and specialized journals. Nonscientists can get a grasp of current knowledge in general fields with popular magazines such as *Natural History*, *Science 83*, and *Discover*.

At the end of each chapter, this book suggests some ways in which you can deepen what you know about Pacific Northwest nature, and how you can enjoy it more. Some outstanding places are mentioned, such as major wildlife refuges and easy-to-reach highlights of national parks. As much or more, though, can be gained by exploring lesser-known spots, including your immediate surroundings.

A few of the many Pacific Northwest guidebooks to specific areas are listed in the bibliography. They are updated and new ones are published frequently. I recommend a visit to a public library or bookstore before you take a trip. (If you live at a distance and are planning a trip to the Northwest, look at a bookstore's catalog of books in print and order a guidebook or two well in advance.)

## A NOTE ON NAMES

Because this book is written for nonexperts, it avoids technical terms wherever possible. In general, both Latin and common names of plants and animals are given. Two exceptions to this are: (1) where the reference is extremely general, such as "deer," or "conifer," and (2) names of birds, as birds have widely used common names clearly restricted to specific species. (The American Ornithological Union checklist is the "official" list of these names.)

We need Latin names not just to free scientists from the difficulty of translating names into different languages, but also to clarify what we mean in our own. Easterners talking about "skunk cabbage," for example, mean *Symplocarpus foetidus*. Westerners mean the similar-looking but only distantly related *Lysichiton americanum*.

Two-word Latin names usually are enough to specify what plant you are talking about. The first of these is the genus, a group of related plants or animals. The second is the species—roughly defined as a set of organisms sharing a unique set of inherited characteristics, passing them on to their progeny, and not interbreeding with others.

By custom, genus and species names are written in italics. The name of the genus is placed first, and capitalized. The species name is second and is not capitalized.

Individuals and groups within a species can differ considerably. All human beings, for example, belong to a single species, *Homo sapiens*. Scientists sometimes designate a subgroup with distinct characteristics and confined to a specific geographic area as a subspecies or variety. This name, also in italics, is written after the genus and species names.

Genuses are grouped into broader categories: families, orders, classes, phyla. Sometimes these are further grouped into such categories as suborders and infraclasses. The coyote, *Canis latrans*, for example, is a member of the Canidae, or dog, family; of the suborder Fissipedia, or land-living meat eaters; of the order Carnivora, or carnivores; of the infraclass Eutheria, or mammals with placentas rather than pouches; of the class Mammalia, or mammals; of the phylum Vertebrata, or animals with backbones. In the few places that this book uses proper names for these broad categories, their names are capitalized but not written in italics.

Learning Latin names won't do much for your party chit-chat. It will, however, tell you a lot about how living beings are related to one another, along with tidbits of history, vivid description, and even poetry.

Twinflower, a common groundcover in Northwest woods, was the favorite flower of Carl Linnaeus, father of the modern system of biological names, and it is named *Linnaea borealis* for him.

A great many Northwest plants, for example, carry the names of the region's explorers. Steller (of Steller's jay, *Cyanocitta stelleri*) was a physician and naturalist with Vitus Bering, who died while exploring the Bering Strait and Aleutian Islands for Russia in 1741. Archibald Menzies (*Menziesia, menziesii*) was a physician and naturalist with Captain George Vancouver (*Vancouveria*), first explorer of Puget Sound, in 1792. *Lewisia* and *Clarkia, lewisii* and *clarkii*, honor Lewis and Clark, leaders of the first overland expedition to cross North America, in 1805. David Douglas (*Douglasia* and *douglasii*) braved hostile Indians, storms, and near starvation, botanizing for England's Royal Society in the 1820s and 1830s. The still-young Scot met his death soon afterwards, falling into a wild boar trap while collecting in Hawaii. Nat Wyeth (*Wyethia*) was an adventurous New England businessman who failed to crack the Northwest's fur trade in the 1830s. Thomas Nuttall (*nuttallii*) and John Kirk Townsend (*Townsendii*) were prominent Philadelphia naturalists who traveled with him, as well doing important collecting and identification on their own. The journals of these and others make fascinating reading.

The many species dubbed *oregonensis* and *californiensis* remind us that these names once denoted much larger areas. "Oregon," for example, denoted Washington and Idaho as well until the 1840s.

Other names are graphic. Examples are *fluviatilis*, riverside; *parviflorus*, few-flowered, *cyano-*, blue; *leuco-*, white; *flava-*, yellow. *Sterna hirundo* means the tern like a swallow, for the seabird's forked tail and nimble hunting on the wing. "*Lotor*" is Latin for "washer." *Procyon lotor*, the raccoon, is thus the animal that washes (its food).

*Spilogale putorius*, the spotted skunk, needs no translation—it even sounds like a spewing of foul odor. One could guess that *Oplopanax horridum* was something unpleasant even without knowing that it was devil's club, the spiny bane of damp Northwest woods. On the other hand, what more appropriate name for a water lily than *Nymphaea odorata*—meaning the fragrant water nymph?

## THANKS AND APOLOGIES

Hundreds of technical books and journal articles and thousands of man-years of research by experts make possible a general book like this one. I am sorry that I cannot give credit to the many naturalists and scientists whose work I have drawn upon. I am grateful for all they have done to enrich my knowledge and enjoyment of nature, and I hope I can thank them by passing some of their gifts along.

The responsibility for errors and misinterpretations, of course, is entirely my own.

# THE
# PACIFIC NORTHWEST

| 0 | | 30 | | 60 | | 90 Miles |
| 0 | | 48 | | 97 | | 145 Kilometers |

# 1

# The Young
# Northwest

## THE GEOLOGIC REVOLUTION

Pacific Northwest Indian legend has it that Mt. Rainier, the tallest of the Cascade volcanos, was once married to Mt. Baker, the second volcano to the north. When Baker took up with a younger peak, Rainier rumbled south to her present home.

Volcanos did not gad about, but the way the nation's most spectacular corner really came to be is hardly less surprising. The revolutionizing theory of plate tectonics is sketching a Pacific Northwest history in which, for much of geologic time, the region did not exist. Details are still speculative and controversial, but the history emerging includes tropical islands bumping into Idaho, the glacier-carved North Cascade Mountains as a former separate mini-continent, and the gentle Coast Ranges of Oregon trundling 60 miles or so westward to their present position.

Most significantly, perhaps, the new insights hold out hope for understanding the previously bewildering comings and goings of mountains, seas, and climates.

Like many scientific revolutions, this one is possible now largely because of improved technology. The idea that the continents were once connected has been around since at least 1620, when Francis Bacon noticed

**Figure 1-1.** A wild couple: Mt. Rainier (top), at 14,410 feet the Northwest's highest mountain, in Indian legend was once married to Mt. Baker (bottom), the 10,778-foot volcano 140 miles to the north.

that the New World being mapped by explorers fit rather neatly against the old one. But only the current generation of geologists has the tools to test the theory. For example:

1. Elaborately equipped research vessels can detect ocean canyons and undersea volcanos, evidence that sea floors are spreading away from rising molten rock.

2. Increasingly sophisticated magnetometers can show how rocks were oriented with respect to the pole when they cooled. Seismic waves, gravimeters, and instruments that measure heat flow can map local differences in earth's interior.

3. Improved chemical techniques can analyze rocks quickly and efficiently. Measurements of radioactive isotopes, showing how much of various kinds have decayed, make it possible to determine the ages of rocks and organic materials.

The vast amount of information gathered by traditional field geology also is corroborated by kinships among fossils and living species on different continents. The weight of all this evidence makes the case for continental drift overwhelming.

## HOW CONTINENTS WANDER

To understand how the Pacific Northwest came to be the fiery, rugged land it is today, we have to understand the varied and violent history of our earth's surface.

Briefly, plate tectonics theory holds that fairly rigid plates form the continents and sea floors. These plates, called the lithosphere, glide over a less rigid, very hot layer called the asthenosphere, about 70 miles beneath them. They move at about the rate your fingernails grow—roughly one to six inches a year. What drives them is uncertain. It may be convection—the rise of hotter matter and the fall of colder. This is the same thing that happens when warm air rises and cold air falls in a room. The force driving the plates also may be gravity, pulling on the edges of sea floor that has grown cold and dense and has moved away from rifts where rising magma forms new hot ocean floor.

Whatever force is driving them, the moving plates collide with or scrape past one another. In the process they are broken, stretched, compressed, wrinkled, forced one above the other, or partly welded to the plate they meet.

This process has not always gone on—the plates' composition and the way they are driven must have changed as the young earth cooled. For more than 600 million years, though, back into the shadowy Precambrian era when only very simple life forms existed, continents, including most of today's great land masses, have moved about on the globe. At times they have assembled and at times they have broken apart. Oceans, meanwhile, have come and gone. They have widened as magma rose, cooled, and formed new crust in sea-floor rifts, and they have vanished as their floors were swallowed beneath continents.

Thus, we have to throw away our mental map of the globe to envision plate tectonics. Most of the Pacific Northwest did not exist when our story opens—nearly 600 million years ago. In geologists' time scale, this was the dawn of the Cambrian period which opened the Paleozoic era, in which animals like corals and sponges—fairly complex sea animals that still lacked backbones—developed.

## THE PACIFIC NORTHWEST
## BEFORE DINOSAURS

At this dawn of the Cambrian, North America probably lay "sideways" across the equator. The continent's edge ran a bit west of the Idaho-Washington border, detoured inland around Oregon, and continued into Nevada. This is where the thick, stable, continental basement rock ends, and the much thinner, younger crust that underlies most of the Pacific Northwest begins.

For hundreds of millions of years, sediments from this coast had washed, probably northward, into a shallow sea whose floor subsided under the debris. This may have been a proto-Pacific—a young ocean recently formed when North America was torn from some other land mass. But the size of that ocean is a mystery—we cannot tell the age of the Pacific because all of its crust older than about 190 MYBP (million years before the present) has been swallowed beneath continents.

The sediments washed from this coast formed limestone, sandstone, and shale. Much of this rock later metamorphosed to marble, quartzite, and slate. Today these beds of Precambrian sediments, three to four miles thick, have been eroded and uplifted to become much of western Montana's rugged Glacier National Park and the gentler green mountains of Idaho's northern panhandle. The sediments laid down before the Cambrian period edge into northeastern Washington, not quite reaching the southward-flowing Columbia River there. Younger Paleozoic sediments, similar except that they hold fossils of more highly developed animals, stretch as far as Republic in northeastern Washington's Okanogan Highlands, and sprawl across the mountains of southeastern Idaho. Thus, the continent continued to erode slowly into the sea.

The early Paleozoic sediments that washed onto the then continental shelf, though, show that climates were changing as the continent moved. Limestone, sandstone, and shale show that the shelf was covered at times with rich algae, perhaps from tropical oceans, and then with barren sands as it reached the dry "horse latitudes" about 30° from the equator. North America and the other continents were coming together to form the supercontinent Pangaea, which lay mostly in the Southern Hemisphere.

## THE VIOLENCE OF GROWTH

At an unknown distance off the Pacific Northwest, certainly by Ordovician times, when the first animals with backbones developed in the sea (that is, about 500 MYBP) arcs of volcanic islands lay at an unknown distance off the Pacific Northwest. They may have been somewhat like the many islands off today's Southeast Asia.

To understand the origin of the islands and volcanos, we have to visualize the way subduction—that is, one plate overriding another—takes place. The leading edge of a continent, as it grinds over the sea floor, typically is not dry land but a submerged "toe," the continental shelf. This toe ends at a trench created by the downward slope of the sinking ocean plate. As ocean floor is forced beneath it, the continent's leading edge acts as a scraper. Rock and sediment from the ocean plate pile up above it and at the same time jack it up from below. In this way part of the continent's leading edge is raised. Sometimes it emerges as an arc of islands. The Aleutian Islands and many of the islands of Southeast Asia are examples. Volcanos often rise above the point where the ocean crust, sloping down beneath the continent, meets the hotter asthenosphere. These volcanos are the source of the Pacific Ocean's "rim of fire"—the volcanos of Southeast Asia, eastern Siberia, Japan, the Aleutians, the Pacific Northwest, Mexico, and South America.

Subduction can have complex consequences. Sea-floor plates eventually can be swallowed beneath continents. This seems to have happened beneath Alaska. Colliding plates sometimes are completely or partly welded together—the Philippines, for example, contain bits of several island arcs and of Southeast Asia. Moving with the ocean crust are submerged plateaus that may be fragments of continents, and undersea volcanos that erupted above more or less stationary "hot spots" in the earth's interior. Like islands, these submerged mini-continents and seamounts can collide with land masses. They can clog the trench where sea floor has been sinking, and change the location or even the direction of subduction.

All of these complex interactions seem to have affected the Pacific Northwest. Most of the history of the region is one of progressive growth as

**Figure 1-2.** Four volcanos of the Pacific Northwest's "rim of fire": From left, Mt. St. Helens, Mt. Rainier, and Mt. Adams, in Washington, seen from Mt. Head, in Oregon.

bits of sea floor, seamounts, volcanic islands, and even mini-continents widened northwestern North America.

One of the earliest signs of this violent history is former sea floor thrust eastward over the continent's former edge. Such skins of older rock are found overlying older ones from California's Mojave Desert almost to the white-water Salmon River in central Idaho. The clash, or clashes, took place roughly 400 million years ago, as amphibians and spore-bearing plants were appearing on land. What caused the violence, however, is uncertain.

## THE ALIEN MOUNTAINS

Crescents of former islands and sea floor lie in the Klamath-Siskyou Mountains, the low ranges that span the westernmost part of the California-Oregon border. These arcs were welded to the continent one after another, as reptiles, insects, and cone-bearing trees developed on land, and the world moved into the age of dinosaurs. The oldest of these collided arcs is in California, at the range's southeastern edge. The youngest is in Oregon, to the

**Figure 1-3.** Running Oregon's wild Rogue River takes the adventurous person past ancient islands and sea floor that collided with North America.

northwest—white-water enthusiasts running the Rogue River pass through it. Although the Klamaths now edge the Pacific, ending at spectacular headlands above beaches of black sand, magnetism in their rocks and their neat fit against the Sierra Nevada indicate that they probably once lay much farther east, north of the present Sierras.

Part of the evidence for this history of collision is that types of rocks that form only on deep ocean floors now are high in the Klamaths. The range contains large outcroppings of serpentine, a greasy-looking, greenish rock that forms when water infiltrates the heavy rocks of lower layers of lithosphere. Serpentine contains concentrations of trace elements that poison many plants. Thus, the red soil that weathers from the green, deep-sea rock makes part of the dry Klamaths still more barren. Two elements usually concentrated in serpentine, and rare elsewhere, are nickel and chromium. The Klamath area is one of the few in the United States where both have been mined.

Another chain of former islands and adjacent sea floor today is cut by Hells Canyon, at 7,900 feet the deepest canyon in North America. (Its rapids roar where Idaho, Washington, and Oregon meet.) The evidence is bits of deep-sea-floor rock, volcanic rocks, limestone reefs, and fossils that were part of these islands. These remnants are strung on a broad southwest line through the mountain masses on both sides of the Snake's awesome rapids. They run from the dry Seven Devils Mountains of west-central Idaho through northeastern Oregon's piney Wallowa and Blue Mountains, roughly to the John Day River.

In the Cretaceous period, between about 135 and 65 MYBP, most dinosaurs mysteriously became extinct. In the Pacific Northwest the Cretaceous has another mystery: the appearance of the North Cascades. This highest, most rugged part of the range rises in north-central Washington, west of the Okanogan Highlands. Much of it is a jumble of rocks, thoroughly folded, faulted, and thrust at odd angles during this late age of dinosaurs.

Sandwiched between the spectacular, glacier-studded North Cascades National Park and the rolling Okanogan Highlands to the east are sediments from the highlands. These light-colored sandstones, pushed up and crumpled by pressure from the two adjacent ranges, are now the Pasayten Wilderness and the Methow Valley. Their gentler, rather regular folds differ strikingly from the jagged, dark North Cascades, which consist mostly of ancient rocks greatly changed by heat and pressure. Like a leaf of lettuce in this sandwich, a slice of former deep-sea floor crops out along the edge of the North Cascades,

**Figure 1-4.** The north side of Mt. Shuksan in Washington's North Cascades: a rugged, icy range that may once have been a separate mini-continent.

running along Ross Lake (a national recreation area) and cupping the south end of the North Cascades east of Wenatchee, Washington. (Here is found another serpentine area, with outcroppings of the greenish rock born on deep-ocean floors.)

One theory is that the glacier-studded North Cascades was a mini-continent rafted against the then west coast. Another, based partly on similarity of sediments west of the North Cascades to those east of them, is that the mountains originally lay south of the Okanogan Highlands. According to this idea, the Cascades moved north and west along huge faults like those found further north. There, a section of Pacific Ocean floor called the Kula Plate was moving north, helping to build Alaska.

Whatever its history, the mixture of older rocks that is the North Cascades seems to have been rather promptly "hit on the head" by Vancouver Island. This big, lush British Columbia island, like Alaska's Wrangell Mountains and the former islands of Idaho, seems to have been born in the tropics long before—about 200 MYBP, about the time dinosaurs and flying reptiles first developed. Perhaps it began as a slice of South America.

Thus, by the end of the age of dinosaurs, about 65 MYBP, alien lands had moved the coast of North America considerably westward. But while these collisions went on, changes beneath the continental plate, where the Pacific floor slid into the hot depths of the earth, also altered the way the continent grew.

## MOUNTAIN BUILDING
## AND THE CONTINENTAL SPEED-UP

By about 200 MYBP, the supercontinent Pangaea, which had included the Americas, Europe, Asia, Australia, and Antarctica, was breaking up. The Atlantic Ocean and the Gulf of Mexico opened and began to spread. As the widening Atlantic pushed North America westward, the west coast began to slide more quickly over the Pacific plate. The change was dramatic: For about 100 million years, into the Cretaceous period when dinosaurs became extinct, western North America near its margin was aflame with volcanos. Huge amounts of molten rock also were trapped beneath the surface. They cooled there to form batholiths—vast masses of granite and related plutonic rocks. These now are the roots of the Sierra Nevada range of California, the Klamaths of California and Oregon, and the Blue and Wallowa Mountains of Southeastern Washington and Northeastern Oregon. Largest is the immense Idaho Batholith, 250 miles long and 100 miles wide, that underlies much of mountainous Central Idaho, including the rugged Salmon River and Sawtooth Mountains.

**Figure 1-5.** McGowan Peak in Idaho's Sawtooth Mountains—
one of many ranges whose roots are the Idaho Batholith.

About 80 MYBP, not long before the sudden extinction of dinosaurs, another step in the breakup of continents again speeded subduction of the Pacific. (Such changes are inferred by comparing the locations of plates with those of fixed or slow-moving "hot spots" in the earth's interior. The positions of the hot spots are shown by chains of volcanic islands or submerged volcanos that erupt above them.)

The effect of this second speedup was quite different from the first. About 70 MYBP, all along the then west coast, the volcanic activity that had formed the roots of ranges from the Sierra Nevada into Idaho first shifted inland and then all but ceased. Well inland, though, mountain building continued. In western Wyoming and adjacent southeastern Idaho, a shallow skin of younger rock was forced eastward over older rock. Part of this thin skin forms today's oil-rich "Overthrust Belt," where pumps nod among the sage brush. In southeastern Idaho, slices of continental crust were pushed together so that the edges of one overlapped the next. This is the origin of the area's rows of nearly parallel mountain ranges with long, regular valleys between them. At that time the crust had not yet warped downward to create the dry Snake River Valley with its many small volcanos. Hence, the more northern ranges of this type—the Beaverhead, Lemhi, and Lost River Ranges north of the Snake—probably were continuous with the geologically similar Snake River and Caribou Ranges farther south and east.

In other parts of the wide mountainous belt today called the Rockies, as the age of reptiles gave way to the age of mammals, and ancestral horses and cattle appeared, the continent buckled. Blocks of the old continental basement, running roughly north and south, were pushed together. They rose, sank, or tilted and rotated. The younger sedimentary rocks above these blocks were pushed into covering drapes and folds. This was the origin of many of today's Rocky Mountain ranges, including the Beartooth, Bighorn, Teton, and Wind River Ranges of Idaho, Montana, and Wyoming. The Rockies did not reach their present height until a second, later uplift, not long before the Ice Age. But their beginning, as large blocks running north and south, explains their distinctive features: their lack of foothills, their often plateau-like summits, and the fact that peaks within a single range are often of nearly uniform height.

The uplifting of the Rockies also moved the Continental Divide. A large section of Montana and Idaho that had previously drained eastward became part of the Pacific Northwest. Idaho's spectacular Salmon River, for example, flows northeast for 100 miles, following its old course toward the Missouri and the Mississippi, the great rivers of the East. It then abruptly turns more than 90° to flow west toward the canyon that makes it one of the nation's official Wild and Scenic Rivers. After the Rockies rose, a "pirate" stream eroded from its headwaters back into the Salmon. (Most rivers cut back from their sources in this way.) The "captured" Salmon then turned to flow westward via this stream to the Columbia, the great river that drains most of the Northwest. The enlarged Salmon carved today's white-water canyon. Deeper than Grand Canyon, it was called by Indians the River of No Return. It turned Lewis and Clark back to try another route, when in 1805 they became the first non-Indians to cross the continent.

The cause of all these changes in the Rockies probably was North America's rate of movement over the Pacific Plate. Volcanos seem to erupt where sinking ocean lithosphere meets the hotter asthenosphere. When the continent overrode the ocean very quickly, Pacific lithosphere may not have had time to sink to those depths. Instead, it may have scraped against the underside of the continent, crumpling it into the ancestral Rockies.

**Figure 1-6.** One of the quieter stretches of Idaho's
Salmon River, a river that ran east to the Missouri
before the uplift of the Rocky Mountain ranges.

## REKINDLED FIRES
## IN THE EARTH

This interruption in the pattern of volcanic eruptions near the coast did not
last long. Still rather early in the age of mammals, shortly before the
beginning of the Eocene era, subduction beneath the continent is thought to
have slowed again. From about 60 to 40 MYBP, as hoofed grazing mammals
were becoming common, a wave of rekindled volcanic eruptions swept from
north to south across the Pacific Northwest. Eruptions formed ranges
including the dry, red-brown Absaroka Mountains east of Yellowstone
National Park, and central Oregon's Ochoco Range. Volcanic rock almost a
mile thick was laid down in central Idaho.

Trapped magma, too, was part of this wave of volcanism. (Magma is
molten volcanic rock.) Directions of magnetism show that older rocks in
northern and central Idaho and northern Washington were remelted.
Minerals, circulated in part by vast hydrothermal systems—giant hot
springs—concentrated in cracks and weak points in the reheated rocks. Ores
often are concentrated in this way by the heat and pressure near the edges of

batholiths, and by deep circulation of hot waters. So formed the veins that would bring pioneers rushing to these mountains in search of gold and silver. (Gold that miners wash from streams has been eroded from such veins and concentrated by its weight in specific areas.) This also was the origin of the real "pay dirt"—lodes of copper, lead, and zinc that have supported the mineral industries of northern Idaho and northeastern Washington to the present.

For the first time, in these Eocene eruptions, a line of craters rose in what is now the Cascade Range—where volcanos still grumble and occasionally, like Mt. St. Helens, explode. Thus, the coastline was still shifting westward. Vast deltas, rather like the maze of channels at the Mississippi's mouth, fanned into what are now the lowlands west of the Cascades, including Washington's Puget Sound and Oregon's Willamette Valley. Plants that flourished there in a warm, moist climate died to become coal that would fuel transcontinental railroads.

As in the Rockies, this only began formation of the range. The Cascades' modern volcanos, for example, were built during the Ice Age or later. The basic force building the mountains, though, remained the same: the clash of the North American continent with the Pacific floor.

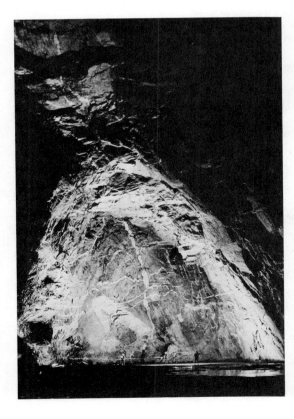

**Figure 1-7.** Heat and pressure, remelting rock deep within mountains, concentrated minerals like the copper dug from this gigantic ore cavity in the Holden Mine, in the Northeast Cascade Mountains of Washington.

# MOUNTAIN BUILDING
# AND NORTH AMERICA'S LIFE

The immense and sudden flare-up of rekindled eruptions was short. By about 40 MYBP, the main wave of volcanism had died out. Erosion was wearing the tops off the early Rockies and Cascades and burying their bases as it filled valleys.

Life around us today, though, was strongly affected by these ancient mountains. Mammals had replaced giant reptiles as rulers of the earth. A lush forest of broad-leaved flowering trees also had spread across the continent, taking dominance away from the older cone-bearing evergreens. As the Rockies grew high enough to wall off the continent's interior from moist Pacific winds, this uniform forest was divided. East-coast and west-coast forests from then on evolved more or less separately. Thus we find pairs of similar species, one on each side of the continent. Two of the many examples are sugar maple (*Acer saccharum*) in the East and broad-leafed maple (*Acer macrophyllum*) in the West; Nuttall's dogwood (*Cornus nuttalli*) in the West and eastern dogwood (*Cornus florida*) in the East.

**Figure 1-8.** The rise of the Rockies and drying of North America's interior divided Nuttall's dogwood (*Cornus nuttalli*), shown here, from the similar Eastern dogwood (*Cornus florida*).

The growing dryness in the center of the continent encouraged grasses and wildflowers. These smaller plants, which evolved even later than flowering trees, were particularly adapted to survive annual dry spells because they could become dormant or survive as bulbs or seeds. Thus, the dry, open areas in the Rockies' lee meant more food for the grazing mammals coming into prominence: ancestral bison, antelope, camels, horses, deer, and elk.

Later, the slow rise of the Cascade Mountains cut off the flow of moisture to eastern Washington and Oregon, just as the Rockies had dried the Great Plains. Drought-adapted plants that had evolved near the Mexican border migrated east of the Cascades. They included shrubs, grasses, and sunflower-like composites similar or identical to today's.

The mild, moist climate that had prevailed across the continent thus was gradually isolated in a narrow strip edging the Pacific. In this way, the coastal forests of California, Oregon, and Washington have become a refuge for trees found nowhere else in the world. Some of these are the giant sequoia, Port Orford cedar (*Chamaecyparis lawsoniana*), red-barked, glossy-leaved madrona (*Arbutus menziesii*), and fragrant "Oregon myrtle" or California bay (*Umbellularia californica*).

## THE WESTERNMOST MOUNTAINS

The North Cascades, of mysterious origin, end roughly at Washington's Snoqualmie Pass, east of Seattle. South of this, volcano after volcano erupted and was worn down. They built a mountain range so slowly that the Columbia, the river that drains most of the Northwest, was able to maintain its course through the mountains, cutting its gorge down through 4,500 feet of rock.

Big volcanic cones are built from many layers of often-loose lava. Thus they are eroded much more easily than hard metamorphic rock like that in the North Cascades, and because of this the Cascades look like, and are, two mountain ranges. The North Cascades are higher and more rugged. The Cascades from Snoqualmie Pass south are lower and gentler, except for the towering youngest cones.

The forbidding Olympics, most of them now in Washington State's most westerly national park, seem to have an origin somewhat like the Klamaths. That is, they are a series of eastward-curving arcs of oceanic lava and sediments, growing progressively younger from a core on the eastern border of the range, near Mt. Constance.

As the Cascades rose, scrapings from the ocean floor, being drawn under the continent some 50 miles farther west, began to push up the continent's seaward "toe." About 40 million years ago, in the Eocene epoch— about the time the Rockies began to rise—a group of massive basalt

**Figure 1-9.** The gentle folds of Washington's Southern Cascades beneath Mt. Adams are the remnants of ancient volcanos.

seamounts—undersea volcanos—apparently was drawn into this subduction system, jamming it. The trench where the seafloor started its descent "jumped" west of these masses, roughly to its present position. By the Oligocene epoch—about the time ancestral apes were developing in the Old World, some 30 million years ago—continued subduction began to push and crumple the seamounts and sediments up to form the future Olympic Mountains and the lower, more rounded Coast Ranges of Washington and Oregon.

The origin of the coastal mountains can most clearly be seen along Oregon's rocky coasts and Washington's, north of Grays Harbor. These shores, among the most beautiful in the world, alternate crescent-shaped sandy bays with prow-like capes and headlands. Waves have carved the capes into pinnacles, arches, rocks shaped like ships and whales, and sea caves that thunder and spout like geysers.

Most of the sandy beaches are worn from rather young sedimentary rock. Layers of these sediments, folded and tilted, can be seen in many bluffs back from the beach. Other bluff rock though is a contorted jumble called *melange*, formed when continents scraped against a sinking sea floor. Most of the headlands, by contrast, are basalt—the remains of volcanos that erupted mostly beneath the sea. Harder than the sediments, and so better able to resist the waves, they remain as jutting capes—like Washington's Point Grenville,

**Figure 1-10.** Natural bridges, pinnacles, and jutting headlands like these, at Twin Rocks on the Oregon coast, are mostly erosion-resistant remnants of old undersea volcanos.

whose promise of a harbor led two Spanish exploring ships, captained by Bruno Heceta and Juan Bodega y Cuadra, to make the first landing by non-Indians in the Pacific Northwest, on July 14, 1775.

The rise of the Coast Range and Olympics left the former continental edge, a gentle plain of sediments, as a sheltered north-south running lowland between the Cascades and the new mountains. Today this lush sag holds Washington's Puget Sound and Oregon's Willamette Valley, and is the home of the region's largest cities.

## PLAINS OF LAVA,
## WINGS OF FIRE

What caused the next great changes in the shape of the Northwest is a matter of mystery and debate.

They began about 17 MYBP, as flowering plants reached their full modern development, and ancestors of dogs and bears appeared. From Northern Mexico to the high lava deserts of Eastern Oregon, the crust of the earth stretched, grew hotter, and warped upward a kilometer or more. The

**17**

**Figure 1-11.** Hart Lake, below the steep western edge of Hart Mountain, Oregon, shows typical basin and range topography: Mountains are sharply tilted blocks of the earth's crust, and the flat valleys between them trap unexpected lakes.

strained continent cracked into long blocks. Some dropped; others were raised or tilted. So was born the Basin and Range topography of today's Great Western Desert: Block-like mountains rise gently on one side, then drop like cliffs at the edges of long valleys. In the valleys, trapped snowmelt often forms surprising lakes in the desert. In Oregon, Steens and Hart Mountains, Harney, Warner, Klamath, and Goose Lakes are typical examples.

The Precambrian continent had an embayment that kept it out of Oregon. Oregon's Coast Range and Cascade volcanos apparently had risen paralleling the old northwest–southeast trending indentation in the coast. Now, as the West stretched, these mountains seem to have rotated clockwise at least 17°, as if about an axis near the Oregon-Washington border. (The move is shown by directions of magnetism. They differ in the mountain rocks and in nearby rocks of the same age, showing that the two were not always oriented the same way with respect to the poles.)

Perhaps because of this move, the Oregon Cascades actually have dropped relative to surrounding territory. Only the outpouring of volcanic eruptions has kept this sinking block a mountain range.

In Northern Oregon and Washington, the crust was not stretched in the same way. Instead, beginning at about the same time, swarms of rifts opened in what is now southeastern Washington, northern Oregon, and southwestern Idaho. Thin molten basaltic lavas flowed quietly out of these fissures, in quantities matched in few places in the world. A single flow, the Roza, contained three times as much lava as the world's largest volcanic cone. But because basalt is thin, and contains little gas under pressure, these gigantic fissure volcanos formed not mountains but a plateau. Some flows rolled more than a hundred miles, even crossing the Cascades at the Columbia Gorge. In all, 120,000 cubic miles of lava poured onto the earth, covering about 85,000 square miles.

The lava pushed the Columbia River north and west against the mountains, into the half-circle course it follows today. They created a distinctive plateau, called the Columbia Plateau for the river. Where today's Columbia Plateau is cut—for example in stream canyons—you can see the distinct layers of lava flows. Some are separated by soil: Between flows, forests grew and lakes formed. Cooling, the layers of basalts often shrank into vertical, straight-sided columns, topped with a more jumbled layer called an *entablature*. Throughout the area of flows, you will see large and small cliffs of these columns, like angular organ pipes. Often they are bright spots in a gray desert: The basalt, usually weathered from its original black to brown, is dotted with orange, ocher, and chartreuse lichens.

**Figure 1-12.** Angular, often six-sided basalt columns, like these in Moses Coulee, Washington, formed where flows of basalt cooled quickly but evenly.

Where it flowed into lakes, the lava sometimes hardened around water-soaked trees and even animals, creating casts. An example is the Blue Lake Rhino cast, north of Lenore Lake in Central Washington.

Rockhounds have reason to be grateful to the lava flows. The slow deposit of minerals in pockets in the basalt created "thunder eggs," agates, and other semiprecious gems. Often these survive after the softer lavas wear away. They then are washed downstream as river and beach gravels. Hence the concentration of semiprecious stones on some watersides.

As the basalt flows tapered off about 14 MYBP, another wave of volcanism began on the Oregon-Idaho border. Thin basalts, followed by the thicker, gas-filled, more explosive lavas that form most volcanic cones, created the Owyhee Mountains in Idaho's southwestern corner. Deeply circulating hot mineral waters, part of these eruptions, deposited the rich silver lodes that miners of the 1860s found on the Owyhees' dry, juniper-pungent slopes.

From this time to the present, similar volcanic activity has spread like wings—northwest across Oregon to Newberry Crater south of Bend, and northeast along Idaho's Snake River Valley into Yellowstone in Wyoming.

Lying along these wings are some of the most unearthly landscapes in the world. Newberry Crater was used to train astronauts for lunar landings. The Craters of the Moon area in Idaho is studied by astronomers to understand volcanos on Mercury and Mars.

Oregon's fresh young lava fields, like Jordan and Diamond Craters, can be risky—you could break through a thin lava crust into a sinkhole that once contained gas or lava. Such flows built Oregon's High Lava Plains, desolate country of sand and sage broken by dramatic lava formations. Stockade-like Fort Rock rises southeast of Hole in the Ground, an almost circular crater one mile across and 500 feet deep. Both were created by sudden, explosive eruptions: Hole in the Ground, for example, was blasted when water-soaked gas and lava exploded violently up through the Ice Age lake.

Newberry Crater, north of Fort Rock and Hole in the Ground, is the youngest of several calderas along this Oregon wing of fire. (In fact, Newberry's youngest eruptions are only about 1,300 years old.) A caldera forms when a volcano empties its stores of lava so thoroughly that its roof caves into the emptied magma chamber, leaving a broad crater. Newberry's crater holds two lakes, East Lake and Paulina (named for a warlike local chief, not a woman). The 500-square-mile volcano and nearby volcanic formations are a three-dimensional encyclopedia of types of lava, with many examples open to the public and well-explained on short nature trails or displays. You can see fresh cinder cones, fissures, lava caves, domes, and corrugated flows of obsidian, silica-rich lava that chilled quickly to glass. The Northwest has little flint; Indians traveled here and to other obsidian flows for stone to chip into knives, axes, and arrowheads.

**Figure 1-13.** Lava River Caves near Bend, Oregon. Tube caves formed where the exterior of a ropy lava flow cooled, while the still-molten interior flowed on or was blown out by volcanic gases.

The eastern wing of eruptions followed the sinking crescent that became Idaho's Snake River Valley—a hostile desert that became the worst leg of the old Oregon Trail, used by trappers and pioneer wagons because it at least provided a lowland route through the Rockies.

Here, successive layers of lava pushed the Snake River south. The Big and Little Lost Rivers enter the jumbled lavas from the north and disappear. They work their way 50 miles underground beneath the parched plain, foaming out again in the area called Thousand Springs, just above the Snake River west of Twin Falls. (Irrigation has greatly reduced their flow today.)

Hundreds of small volcanos spit and belched lava and cinders onto the Snake River Plain. Many of the buttes jutting from this desert are remnants of older cones, partly buried by younger flows. Usually the eruptions took place along rifts—long fissures in the earth. Along these fissures, lava formed broad, low cones called *shield volcanos,* low-rimmed lava lakes, ropy flows, and small cones of spattered lava and cinders. (Volcanic cinders, like volcanic ash, are fragments of lava "blown to bits" when gas, trapped in the magma underground, is released from pressure and expanded explosively at the earth's surface.)

**Figure 1-14.** Small volcanos, like these spatter cones at Craters of the Moon National Monument, Idaho, often formed as lava was thrown out of volcanic rifts.

At Craters of the Moon National Monument, lavas are so irridescent and cones so fresh that they look as if they are still hot. Some rocks are so light they float—the lava "froze" with a froth of gas bubbles. Black tongues of lava hide winding lava tube caves—former channels whose outside cooled and solidified, but whose insulated interior remained molten and flowed on. Some of these caves are floored with ice, their ceilings hung with "lavacicles" spattered by molten rock. Such tube caves are common in areas of young lava flows—pioneers in Oregon and southern Washington, as well as in Idaho, used them as natural ice makers and for cold storage. Most are dangerous, but some are open to tours—at Idaho's Crystal Ice Caves, for example, visitors explore an ice cave that takes them into one of the immense rifts that poured out the Snake River lavas. The rift is 62 miles long; spelunkers have explored it down to 600 feet.

Along this wing of fire, as in Oregon, cones exploded and collapsed to become calderas. Island Park Caldera, marked by a semicircle of hills north of Ashton, near Idaho's eastern border, is 1.3 million years old. Yellowstone Plateau is a caldera that exploded twice: about two million and about 600,000 years ago. The 100-square-mile collapsed volcano cradles Yellowstone Lake, the largest freshwater lake in the United States outside the Great Lakes.

Yellowstone Canyon, with its spectacular falls and pinnacles cut deep in the colorful stone that named the area, is also a volcanic creation: Hot, mineral-laden waters circulated by volcanic heat weathered the lavas so that they eroded easily, and gave the weathered rock its sunset yellows and reds.

# HOT SPRINGS AND GEYSERS

The hot springs scattered throughout the Pacific Northwest show that the earth has not yet cooled beneath this and other volcanic areas. At Idaho's Soda Springs, pioneers on the Oregon Trail could stop for a welcome soak and a naturally fizzy drink before starting the hot, dry pull down the Snake. (The route led from Wyoming's Green River down Idaho's Bear and Portneuf to the Snake.) The most dramatic hydrothermal systems, of course, are those of Yellowstone National Park. There, liquid magma still stored beneath the caldera heats fantastic geysers, hot springs, and bubbling mud pots; and chemical reactions and strange algae stain the earth and water rainbow colors.

    All these are the result of hot water circulated by convection—the familiar rise of hot matter and the fall of cold. Rain and snowmelt, percolating downward, reach levels where the water is heated and begins to rise again. In simple terms, where hot water simply bubbles to the surface, a hot spring appears. Chemical reactions with the rock it passes through load some of this water with minerals or bubbles of gas.

    Where the water contains acids that dissolve surface rock to silt or clay, you find a bubbling mudpot. Where the hot water works its way through limestone or related rocks, it can dissolve their carbonates and deposit them on the surface as a fairyland of travertine terraces. Finally, if the hot water's rise meets a funnel-like block, the result often is a geyser—a periodic eruption, like Old Faithful's. Water deep in the earth is under considerable pressure from water and rock above it. Trapped beneath a partial block, however, it eventually becomes so hot that it boils despite the pressure above it. This boiling further lessens the pressure, and the water flashes spectacularly into steam. When the very hot water has "erupted," the cycle starts over again.

# WHY THE NORTHWEST STRETCHED

No model proposed so far satisfactorily explains these earth-stretchings and volcanic eruptions in the Northwest's interior. They may, however, be related to another change in the pattern of the continent's interaction with the Pacific —one that also profoundly affected land nearer the coast.

For millions of years, while a portion of the Pacific floor called the Farallon plate disappeared beneath the west coast, another ocean plate, called the Kula Plate, had been moving north into what is now Alaska. For millions of years the boundaries of these two plates with the rest of the Pacific had been getting closer to North America. About 55 MYBP, the last of the Kula Plate joined, or disappeared beneath, Alaska. This left a very large Pacific plate moving north-northwest, and only a small Farallon plate still moving eastward. This change may have slowed subduction and rekindled the volcanism that spread southward from Canada about 50 MYBP.

The Farallon Plate's junction with the Pacific Plate was not a straight line. Rather, it was and is a zig-zag of ridges and fracture zones, whose seams are clearly traced by locations of submarine earthquakes. About 27 MYBP, an easterly part of this Farallon-Pacific junction bumped into California. Soon after that it contacted Canada north of Vancouver Island. Now only a remnant, called the Juan de Fuca Plate, was left moving east beneath Northern California, Oregon, Washington, and Southern British Columbia. Along the rest of the coast, the immense Pacific Plate was grinding northward, bringing new strains to bear against the continent.

This change is thought to be the reason the Juan de Fuca Plate's eastward movement slowed to its present rate, less than an inch a year. A sign of this slow subduction may be the unusually shallow trench seaward of the continent's submarine "toe," about 250 miles off Washington and Oregon.

Farther south, a sliver of North America became welded to the Pacific Plate and began moving northward with it. So Baja California was born, opening the Gulf of California behind it; and so the San Andreas fault system, source of California's great earthquakes, began. Pacific Northwest quakes are less severe—perhaps because the Juan de Fuca lithosphere, generated just offshore, is still thin and hot as it sinks beneath the continent. Hence, it may bend or break before strains become too great.

Volcanos along the California and Canadian coast ceased to erupt as the Pacific floor no longer sank beneath them. Today, snow-capped cones of both dormant and active volcanos, like Mt. St. Helens, are found only from Mt. Lassen in northern California to Mt. Garibaldi in Southern British Columbia—in the zone where the Juan de Fuca plate is still sinking beneath the continent.

Two theories regarding the heating and stretching of the crust in the Basin and Range area, far inland, are tied to these changes of the last 20-odd million years. One is that hot asthenosphere rose into the "hole" that was left as remnants of the Farallon Plate continued to move east under California, Nevada, and Utah, while the Pacific Piate moved north. The second theory is that the continent was stretched by the pull of the northward-moving Pacific Plate.

These ideas are not mutually exclusive. Other factors also may account for some or all of the changes. Spreading of the crust, or just the Snake River Valley-Yellowstone volcanism, may result from North America's moving over a hot spot deep in earth. Alternatively, the Basin and Range area may have been created by the same mechanisms that produce basins behind island arc systems.

One possible scenario, however, is that the "hole" in ocean lithosphere beneath North America, or the strains created by the north-moving Pacific Plate—or both—stretched, heated, and thinned the crust as far north as Oregon. This could account for the Basin and Range stretching, and for the rotation of the Oregon Cascade and Coast Ranges on its western border.

Northeast from Nevada to well into Montana, along the wing of volcanism that follows the Eastern Snake River Plain into Yellowstone, recent magnetic studies show a possible weakness in the continent's crust. A "tear" along this weakness and a smaller, symmetrical rip northwest into Oregon may have relieved the strain of the pull on the crust. This could account for the volcanic eruptions along the wide "V," and for the lack of stretching of the crust farther north, in the area of the Columbia basalt flows.

## TODAY'S BIG VOLCANOS

The Miocene stretching of the continent was succeeded by another period of mountain building. In the Pliocene epoch, which followed the Miocene and preceded the Pleistocene, or Ice Age, the Rockies and Cascades reached roughly their present height. The stretched, compressed, crumpled collage of alien rock that is the Pacific Northwest was thus basically in place by the time the Ice Age began, about two million years ago. Today's Cascade volcanos, though, did not yet tower above the other peaks. Their cones were built during the Ice Age and later.

The pre-Ice Age Cascades had other giant volcanos. Hikers can see this from eroded but impressive remains such as Washington's Goat Rocks and Fifes Peaks. Volcanos, though, are short-lived compared to other mountains. Their layers of loose lava erode easily. Their own heat and chemicals help weaken them. Sometimes they blow themselves up.

Today's Cascades volcanos have differing histories, but a summary of things volcanos tend to have in common can help in understanding them.

Magma, the rock that forms volcanos, can be classified by the amount of silica it contains. (Lava is simply molten magma.) Silica, the most common element in continental crust, affects magma in two important ways. First, it makes lava thick and sticky. Silica-rich magmas build up, instead of flowing away. Second, silica-rich lavas tend to contain more moisture. This tends to make them explosive, as the force behind a volcano's most violent eruptions is simply steam. Water in magma far beneath the earth is kept liquid by intense pressure. At or near the surface, the pressure is released. The liquid expands explosively into steam, shattering rock and propelling it with tremendous force.

**Figure 1-15.** Island Lake (above) in the Absaroka-Beartooth Wilderness, Western Montana. Like much of the Rockies, which reached their present height in the Pliocene, these peaks have plateau-like summits showing their origin as tilted and rotated blocks.

**Figure 1-16.** Mt. Rainier's summit from the air—the ant-like dots are mountain climbers. The Pacific Northwest's modern volcanos are young mountains, built during and since the Ice Age.

Rhyolite and dacite lavas are high in silica. Too stiff to flow, they erupt as giant domes, or explode destructively. Once cooled, they often take on pastel colors—yellow, pink, tan, or gray.

Andesites, intermediate in silica content, can erupt quietly, as slow-flowing lava, or explosively, often as so-called ash—fine fragments of exploded lava. Darker than rhyolites but lighter than the black basalts, andesites often are dark red, green, gray, or brown. Stiffer than basalts, they build tall cones—the Cascades' modern towering volcanos are mostly andesite.

Basalt, the type of lava that erupts beneath oceans, contains little silica. Molten basalts are thin liquids that thus travel long distances. They usually flow quietly out of the earth, building plains like the Columbia Plateau or very broad, low cones called shield volcanos, which look rather like upside-down saucers.

The textures of erupted magmas also differ. Lava that contained large amounts of steam may fragment to ash, cinders, or breccia—terms for increasingly large angular pieces of exploded rock. Magma can freeze with bubbles still in it. This is the source of the lava fields' bubbly, lightweight boulders you can toss with one hand, and the fragments of pale, fine-grained pumice fragments covering miles of Cascade volcano slopes.

**Figure 1-17.** Near Two Captains Rock, on the Columbia River near Wallula Gap, Washington, the "layer-cake" structure of the Columbia Plateau's basalt flows has been exposed by the river's cutting.

Heat·can cement fragments ·together again as tuff, a rock that looks welded. Molten lava may contain solid rock, from house-sized boulders down to tiny crystals that give lava a starry look. (Such lava often has a lovely sheen, and is called *porphyry*.) Lava that is very dry and cools quickly can form obsidian, a black glass that Indians chipped for tools.

Because volcanos are formed from many layers of eruptions, usually of different kinds, you will find many of these kinds of rocks, and more, as you explore a volcano's rocky slopes. This makes most hikes on volcanos colorful and varied, although some, like Crater Lake volcano, have pumice-covered slopes as bare as deserts.

A volcano often begins as a basalt shield. Later eruptions build an andesite cone above this. The last stage often brings dacite or rhyolite eruptions that ooze up into domes called plugs, or explode violently.

**Figure 1-18.** Mt. Washington from Little Belknap
Crater—a typical Oregon High Cascades landscape.
Remnants of a volcano's plugged neck rise steeple-like
above a shield volcano. Note the ropy tongues and shattered
blocks of the relatively young lava flows in the foreground.

Oregon's High Cascades show this progression. This plateau-like country is a platform of lavas, up to 4,000 feet thick and 20 to 30 miles wide, running north and south along the eastern edge of the older, deeply eroded West Cascades. The modern High Cascade volcanos began erupting in the Pliocene period, about four MYBP. At first, basalt built immense but rather low-shield volcanos. Three-Fingered Jack's shield, for example, was 10 miles across. Belknap Crater in the fresh lava fields around McKenzie Pass is a youthful example of a smaller-shield volcano, five miles in diameter.

Many shields were later topped with cindery cones and plugged with rhyolites. Mt. Jefferson, Oregon's second highest volcano, is an andesite cone built on a basalt shield. The dramatic pinnacles that rise from the otherwise gentle High Cascades—Three-Fingered Jack, Mt. Thielsen, and Mt. Washington—are the eroded remains of plugs.

The fate of Mt. Mazama—today's Crater Lake—is another kind of ending to a volcano's progression. Back in the Ice Age, Mazama would have appeared extinct. Its 13,000-foot andesitic cone had erupted dacite domes, and then had long been quietly eroded by glaciers. Then, about 6,700 years ago, the ice-clad volcano suddenly blackened the sky with a series of immense explosions. (Their ash can be recognized as far away as Saskatchewan, Canada.) Clouds of glowing pumice and gas avalanched down the slopes, incinerating all life. More than 10 cubic miles of rock was thrown from the volcano, and Mt. Mazama's summit collapsed into the empty chamber. The resulting caldera holds Crater Lake—at 1,932 feet, the deepest lake in North America. Mt. Mazama's story may not be over: Rising from this lake is Wizard Island, a cone perhaps less than 1,000 years old, showing that eruptions could begin again.

The big andesite cones of Washington's and Oregon's Cascades need not be symmetrical. A series of eruptions with different centers, for example, formed Southern Washington's humpy-looking Mt. Adams, with its flattish top. For the most part, though, assymetry in Cascade volcanos reflects erosion and lack of recent activity. Deeply eroded Adams' main sign of life is an occasional whiff of sulphur on the summit. (Sulphur deposits there are so large that there were mule-train attempts to mine them.) Glacier Peak in the North Cascades, also much gouged by ice, last erupted violently about 12,000 years ago. Pumice and a blanket of ash from this eruption reached Montana. Glacier Peaks' only signs of heat now, though, are a few hot springs on its flanks.

Mts. Baker, Rainier, and Hood, much closer to the "classic" shape of cone and summit crater, all have erupted in historic times. They sleep fitfully, keeping geologists alert for signs of major eruptions. Mt. Hood, considered a quiet, not very dangerous volcano, nevertheless has grown three new domes in the last 2,000 years. On higher-risk Mt. Baker and Mt. Rainier, avalanches of rock weakened by volcanic heat and moisture have repeatedly sent immense mudflows rolling down the slopes. These prehistoric, but

**Figure 1-19.** The "Phantom Ship" jutting from Crater Lake, Oregon.

geologically very recent flows reached areas where they would create human disasters today. Small cities including Enumclaw, Auburn, Sumner, and Orting, for example, are perched on such tongues of mud, giant flows believed to have carried much of Rainier's old summit cone to the lowlands a mere 5,000 and 500 years ago.

Mt. St. Helens, considered the most dangerous of Northwest volcanos even before her recent eruptions, has seen several hundred active years in each of the last four millennia. Pioneers saw small and large eruptions from her summit. After a few quiet generations, this most perfect of the Pacific Northwest's cones—a lovely woman in Indian legend—showed her power in the series of violent eruptions that began May, 18, 1980. Ash and steam boiled 60,000 feet high from St. Helens' summit, and the old cone collapsed into itself. Clouds of glowing gas and rock rushed down the slopes. Blocks of glacier were hurled six miles. Trees snapped like matchsticks. Boiling mud cascaded down the mountain and flooded the nearby Toutle River. A deadly blanket of gray-white ash buried all life in what had been one of the most perfect of Pacific Northwest landscapes—a serene cone reflected in the still green waters of Spirit Lake.

The volcano devastated about 200 square miles of timberland, resort lakes, and river valley, and killed more than 60 people. There have been several waves of smaller eruptions since. Much of the area around the mountain remains closed because of the danger of new explosions, earthquakes, and mudflows.

**Figure 1-20.** Mt. St. Helens from the north, before and two years after her 1980 eruption. The "lovely woman" of Indian legend exploded away her snowy summit and made a desert of the country around her, including serene Spirit Lake.

With the Pacific Plate still sinking beneath North America, Cascade volcanos almost certainly will continue to erupt. In fact, Northwesterners may have been lulled because the region became thickly settled during a period when the volcanos were unusually quiet. Early settlers described numerous eruptions through the 1870s. But before Mt. St. Helens' 1980 disaster, the last Cascade volcano to erupt was Mt. Lassen, in California, in 1915. Increased heat at Mt. Baker's Sherman Crater, rumblings beneath Mt. Hood, and Mt. St. Helens' eruption may mean another active period is on the way.

Volcanos pose many hazards. Molten lava, which flows rather slowly, is one of the least of them. Explosions and fast-moving clouds of glowing gas and rock are much more likely to kill. Ash can suffocate plants and animals. (Luckily, the Pacific Northwest's prevailing westerlies would be likely to carry most ashfall east, away from centers of population). Lesser, but still significant hazards include earthquakes and resulting rockfalls, snow avalanches, forest fires, lightning storms, and suffocating gases settling in valleys. Really large eruptions could block enough sunlight to cause widespread crop failures. (Mt. St. Helens' recent eruptions are not expected to detectably affect the weather, but future ones could.)

The greatest danger from Northwest volcanos, however, probably is mudflows. These walls of melted snow, volcanic ice, and weakened rock can move up to 40 miles an hour, and reach 30 or more miles down river valleys. If one poured into a filled reservoir, the resulting flood could cause disasters in the region's major cities.

New volcanos, of course, could appear. Eruptions are possible—though not likely—at the isolated cinder cones found here and there in the Cascades, at areas of recent lava flows like those around McKenzie Pass or between Mt. Adams and Mt. St. Helens, or even at one of the many spots where hot springs signal heat within the earth. (In fact, geologists have issued a mild "watch out for new volcano" warning for the area around Mammoth Hot Springs in eastern California.)

This doesn't mean you should refuse to visit the Cascades for fear of an eruption. Geologists keep watch on the high-risk peaks, monitoring such signals as subterranean heat and swarms of characteristic small earthquakes. Such signs can indicate that rising lava is building up pressure within the volcano, and that another eruption is on its way. Heed the warnings, and observe all the usual precautions of mountain travel on these giants of the Northwest. But don't worry unduly—the volcanos are too fascinating to miss.

## DOING IT YOURSELF

Get to know general kinds of rock. Field guides describing rocks are helpful, but accurate identification requires special cutting and magnifying equipment and chemical tests. Seeing and touching specimens generally are much more helpful than looking at pictures in a book. A university near you is likely to have at least a small natural-history display including local minerals. Some state and national parks also have such displays.

Here are some easy rules of thumb in identifying rocks:

• Sedimentary rocks: Sandstone, shale, and breccia or conglomerate generally look like what they are: layers of sand, mud, or loose gravel hardened into rock.

• Limestone, which is sedimentary rock consisting mainly of calcium carbonate, usually is light-colored and less clearly layered than other sedimentary rocks. (If such rock contains large amounts of calcium magnesium carbonate, it is called *dolomite*.) Most limestone is formed beneath the sea, through chemical reactions of water and bits of shell. As a result, limestone usually contains fossils.

• Igneous rocks: Lavas are produced by molten rock cooling at or near the earth's surface. Generally, the lighter the lava, the higher its silica content. Thus pumice is pale and basalt is almost black.

In addition, dark lavas cooled faster than lighter ones. This is why obsidian, which is silica-rich volcanic glass formed by sudden cooling, is nearly black.

• Lavas may be reddish, grayish, yellowish, or brownish. Lavas are generally uniform in texture, but that texture can vary greatly from rock to rock. Thus, lavas can be filled with large or small bubbles, air trapped in molten rock. They can consist of angular fragments of any size, welded together while the rock was still partly molten. One kind, porphyry, does not have a uniform texture; it is a glassy rock containing distinct crystals that grew and hardened before the rest of the lava.

• Granite and related rocks are produced by magma cooling slowly beneath the earth's surface. They have a uniform, unlayered texture, with small but distinct crystalline grains. They may be grayish, pinkish, or yellowish. Like lavas, these rocks grow darker as they contain less silica. Granite is light; diorite darker. Silica is abundant in the upper continental crust but scarce on sea floors. Hence ancient sea-floor rock, such as peridotite, is quite dark.

• Metamorphic rocks: Under intense pressure, rocks are transformed, or metamorphosed. Limestone and dolomite metamorphose to marble, with larger grains that will take a polish. Sandstone becomes harder, with its often colorful glassy crystals. Shale becomes slate, with a luster given by flakes of mica, one of the most common minerals. These flakes grow at right angles to the pressure on the rock. Thus, slate may have lines of cleavage that cause it to break across the old layers of sediments.

Under intense pressure, granite's grains and crystals must flow past one another. The uniformly textured rock thus changes to a finely layered one. It has mica plates aligned in the direction of flow, or shear. Such rock is called *gneiss*. (Intense pressure also can transform slate into gneiss.)

Look for clues to formation of the earth around you.

You can start with maps—contour maps or aerial photos if you have them. Look for patterns of parallel lines, such as ridges, streams, even roads where they follow valleys. These often show patterns of faults and joints—places where the earth's crust has cracked and shifted under strain.

Look for signs of pressures and tensions in the earth's crust. Layers of sediments had to be horizontal when they formed. If such layers are now warped or at an angle, they must have been warped or tilted later.

Rocks also are deformed by plastic flow—slow movement rather like that of toothpaste. Look for wavy lines that indicate this kind of flow.

A sharp break with sides that don't match probably is a fault—a place where the earth cracked under strain. If you can mentally move the two sides of a fault back together, with layers and other features matching, you can tell how the parts moved in relation to one another. (Sideways movement is called *strike*; vertical movement is called *dip*.)

Look for whatever doesn't fit the expected pattern. A dark streak running up through layers of rock probably means lava found its way through a weakness there, hardening into a dike. A dark cap on a gray granite peak probably is rock that lay above a batholith before both were uplifted and eroded.

From the general shape of a range of hills or mountains, try to imagine how they were formed. The Southern Cascades, for example, were arched upward. They have fairly similar slopes and foothills on both sides. Most of the Rocky Mountain ranges, on the other hand, were formed by faulting—one side generally is steeper than the other, and the ranges often lack foothills.


Visit outstanding geologic areas—though not just for the geology. Many river trips, for example, take you through canyons that slice through layers of sedimentary and volcanic rock (for example, the Columbia Gorge, Hells Canyon on the Snake, and the canyons of the Grande Ronde, John Day, and Owyhee Rivers in Oregon.) Others follow major faults (the Wenatchee River Canyon in Washington and parts of the Salmon and Clearwater Canyons of Idaho are examples).

The Northwest has relatively little limestone or marble. Hence it has few of the spectacular "Carlsbad Cavern" type of cave, created as the weak acids in ground water slowly dissolved this basic rock. A major exception is Oregon Caves National Monument—marble caverns near Cave Junction in Southwest Oregon.

Oregon's rocky coves, headlands, and beaches are an easily reached textbook in geology. From Tillamook Head south to Sea Lion Caves (the easiest place to see marine animals), the headlands are mostly remnants of old undersea volcanos. They are dramatically carved, and broken by "spouting horns" (near Depoe Bay) and the churning Devils Punchbowl. Flat terraces behind the beach are mostly old Ice Age beaches (see next chapter).

**Figure 1-21.** Oregon Caves National Monument is one
of the Northwest's few big marble (or limestone)
caverns.

Wilderness lovers can find the same geology lesson in a hike on the coastal
section of Washington's Olympic National Park.

    Mining booms that were the result of the Northwest's geologic history
left the region with some fascinating ghost towns. Among the best preserved
and restored are Silver City, in Idaho's Owyhee Mountains, and Monte
Cristo, in Washington's Northwest Cascades.

**Figure 1-22.** Silver City is a relic
of mining boom days in the
Owyhee Mountains of
southwestern Idaho.

Yellowstone National Park, of course, is the nation's most dramatic hydrothermal, or hot spring, area. But hot springs dot the Pacific Northwest—they make great destinations for walks, since tired hikers can rest their bones while getting first-hand experience of heat from within the earth.

The best places to tour young, fresh-looking volcanic eruptions are the Craters of the Moon National Monument and nearby rifts and caves in Idaho; and the country around Bend, Oregon. Both have plenty of well-interpreted short walks and drives to such things as lava caves, cinder cones, and fresh-looking flows. (Near Bend, start at the Lava Butte Visitor Center, on Highway 97, 6.7 miles south of town.) Ape Cave, south of Mt. St. Helens, is the nation's longest known lava tube cave (Contact Gifford Pinchot National Forest headquarters, P.O. Box 449, Vancouver, WA 98660 for information on whether areas around Mt. St. Helens can be visited.) Shoshone and Crystal Ice Caves, shown on Idaho state maps, probably are the most spectacular lava tube caves.

At Crater Lake National Park, you can drive to the caldera rim and hike or cross-country ski around it. Oregon's High Cascades, and the country between Mt. St. Helens and Mt. Adams, provide hundreds of easy hikes (and some challenging ones) through varied volcanic country. Hiking the high meadows of Oregon's Mt. Hood and the Round the Mountain trail on Mt. Adams give you a feel of the variety of eruptions that built big volcanic cones.

Oregon's John Day Fossil Beds National Monument is famous for its fossils, as well as its small "painted desert." One of the best displays explaining Columbia Basin geology is at Sun Lakes State Park on Highway 17 in Central Washington, near Indian rock shelters and a rhinoceros cast in lava.

**Figure 1-23.** In the Painted Hills in John Day Fossil Beds National Monument, Oregon, weathering has given pastel colors to layers of ash blown from old volcanos of the Cascade and Ochoco Mountains.

# 2

# The Ice Age: Giants in the Earth

## THE WORLDWIDE GRIP OF ICE

If the clash of continent and ocean roughed out the shape of the Pacific Northwest, the Ice Age sculpted its details.

Giants were on the earth in those days: glaciers a mile thick, lakes the size of Lake Michigan, huge mammals including mammoths, mastodons, and immense long-horned bisons. The giants are gone, but the Northwest is left with an outsized landscape that still dwarfs man and his works.

The cold that changed the world did not begin suddenly. The Pleistocene Epoch, or Ice Age, was the culmination of gradual, worldwide cooling that had built glaciers in Alaska 15 million years before—while basalts were pouring onto the Columbia River Plateau in Washington.

Most geologists date the opening of the Ice Age proper, though, at a mere 2 to 2.5 million years ago. The last ice sheets began a rapid retreat only around 14,000 years ago—some were still in the United States as recently as about 10,000 years ago.

Thus, in geological terms, the Ice Age was a short moment, and only yesterday. It was a cyclic event, not a single one. Isotopes and fossils from cores of ocean floor show that as many as 17 times, the climate became an average of about 9° F colder than it gets today—enough to grip the land in ice.

**Figure 2-1.** The Homathko Ice Field, British Columbia, Canada, shows how the Northwest must have looked when such glaciers flowed from Canada into Washington, Idaho, and Montana. As the photo shows, the highest peaks remained bare.

The cold periods, about 100,000 years long, seem to have given way rather suddenly to short interludes of 10,000 to 20,000 years when temperatures were close to those today. Since only about 11,500 years have passed since the last warmup, the world may be in one of those warm pauses now—with another long cold spell on its way.

On land, the ice's record is confused and controversial, partly because later glaciers ground away evidence of older ones. The number of advances recognized has grown steadily: recent studies traced nine in Yellowstone National Park, for example. Most geologists, though, group Ice Age glaciations into three to five major advances. Others are considered subdivisions because the ice did not move far or the intervening warm period was short.

Glaciers advanced and retreated at roughly similar times in different places. These moves carry local names, however: The last major glaciation, for example, is Fraser in the Olympics and Cascades, Pinedale in the Rockies, and Late Wisconsin in the Midwest and East.

During each icy period, glaciers flowed down from highlands near both poles. Spreading and coalescing, they seized all but the highest peaks in their grip. The Northern Hemisphere carried about 13 times its present volume of ice.

Earth had seen ice ages before, roughly every 250 million years. Many theories have been advanced to explain their cause. These possible causes include:

1. A decrease in the sun's output of radiation.

2. Changes in earth's magnetic field.

3. Changes in earth's tilt and the shape of its orbit, which could affect such things as the length of seasons and the time of year that earth is nearest the sun. Correlations have been found between ice ages and these regular variations in earth's relationship to the sun.

4. Changes in shape and position of continents. For example, Panama's becoming a land bridge linking North and South America may have changed ocean currents and hence weather.

5. Changes in the amount of solar energy reaching the land. For example, ash from major volcanic eruptions could block sunlight, or the increase in sunlight reflected from large fields of snow and ice could decrease the amount of heat absorbed by land and sea

6. A series of coincidences or a combination of the above factors. For example, an unusual number of large volcanic eruptions, or one of the periodic changes in earth's relationship to the sun, could bring on unusually cold winters. The snow and ice that accumulated would decrease the amount of heat absorbed by the earth, so that the cold would feed itself. Finally, so much water would be locked up in glaciers that precipitation would decrease. Incoming sunshine would increase. Glaciers would melt or starve.

# THE ICE AGE IN THE NORTHWEST

Each time the ice advanced, glaciers grew down and outward from Canada's Rockies and Cascades. They formed ice caps that radiated in all directions. Those marching south crossed the United States border as huge lobes that followed major lowlands and drainage patterns.

At roughly, but not exactly, the same times, smaller glaciers in the Pacific Northwest mountains flowed down valleys. Some formed local ice caps—for example, along Oregon's High Cascades, and in today's Yellowstone National Park. Some reached the lowlands below, and, in the north, joined the great Canadian ice sheets. The area covered by ice was vast. Continental ice sheets reached south of Olympia (and south of Puget Sound) in Western Washington; to about the southern end of Grand Coulee, the northern end of Moses Coulee, and the present city of Spokane in eastern Washington; to about Lake Pend Oreille in Idaho; and farther south to present Missoula, Montana. Very roughly, this is about 47° to 48° N latitude. The Canadian border is at about 49° N, and the southern borders of Oregon and Idaho are at 42° N. Thus, even including the local glaciers that gripped northwest mountain ranges, most of the region remained unglaciated.

The Ice Age's effects, though, went far beyond the land gripped by ice. Ice dams and heavy rains near the margins of the glaciers created immense lakes in the Pacific Northwest. Time after time, these lakes burst in floods that scoured and sculpted thousands of square miles of land.

The ice was so heavy that it depressed the continent. At the same time, the vast amounts of water locked in glaciers lowered the oceans. As a result, Ice Age sea levels bounced hundreds of feet up and down, radically changing the land along today's coasts.

After the glaciers were gone, winds went to work, piling their debris into dune-like hills. Finally, the Ice Age, directly and indirectly shaped the Pacific Northwest's modern animal life, including man's.

# MOUNTAIN GLACIERS AT WORK

All Pacific Northwest ice sheets, even the mile-thick ice cap that marched down from Canada, began as mountain glaciers. Since Ice Age glaciers and those remaining today behave in similar ways, you can see how the Ice Age worked by visiting modern ice fields. Roughly 200 square miles of glaciers remain in the United States outside Alaska. Of these, 77 percent are in Washington's Cascades and Olympics. Most of the other lingering glaciers also are in the Pacific Northwest—for example, in Oregon's volcanic High Cascades and in and near Glacier National Park.

During the Ice Age, every sizeable mountain range of the Pacific Northwest was glaciated—even remote Steens Mountains in the Oregon desert. As a result, even where glaciers have vanished, you can easily trace the Ice Age's signature on Pacific Northwest peaks. In your imagination, you can follow a glacier from its birthplace, in a patch of snow that barely survives summer.

Through warm days and cold nights, sunny and cloudy periods, winter and summer, water in this snow patch alternately freezes and thaws. Water works its way into tiny crevices in rock beneath the snow. There it freezes, expands, and chips bits of stone free. Rills of meltwater, alternating freezing and thawing, and small, creeping rockslides carry these particles to the lip of the depression and away. In this way, the snow patch deepens its own sheltering basin, steepening its sides and hollowing its floor. You might discover such tiny valleys if you scooped up snow patches near the snowline today. On a grand scale you find them throughout Pacific Northwest mountains: They are alpine bench meadows or cirque valleys—characteristic glacial valleys with three steep sides and gently hollowed floors, often cupping icy alpine lakes.

**Figure 2-2.** Mirror Lake, below Devil's Peak in the Seven Devils Range of western Idaho: Such cirque valleys, the birthplaces of Ice Age glaciers, remain even in isolated, dry mountain ranges.

Cirque valleys are thus the fossil cradles of glaciers. Study a contour map and you will see that they are most common on northern slopes—more snow lingers on shady north faces. In a given area, cirques also tend to be clustered at similar altitudes, stairstepping upward toward the dry east. This shows the ice age snowline.

Snow can erode mountains most quickly where it freezes and thaws most often. Thus, cirques and glaciers usually are born not on mountaintops, but lower down, at about the level where the year's average temperature is close to freezing. During the Ice Age, the summits of the highest mountains projected black and barren above the ice that gripped the slopes and valleys below.

Cirques are responsible for much of the spectacular scenery of high mountains. As glaciers enlarge their cirques, they work back into the mountain, forming sharp ridges. Meeting back to back, two cirques cut a scallop-like gap in such a ridge. Many mountain passes were born in this way. Three or more cirques meeting often form a horn or pinnacle. Thus steep, spurred ridges are another characteristic signature of glaciers.

The snow patch that started this process, of course, will have long since become ice. Skiers see this conversion. Fresh snow usually is light and airy because its sharp-pointed crystals keep flakes well apart. The points, though, suffer the first attacks of evaporation, melting, and sublimation (direct change from solid to gas). The snow crystals become more rounded and cluster together, forming the larger crystals of grainy firn, or corn snow. Packed down further, under their own weight and that of new snow, the crystals lose almost all the air space between them. This, by definition, makes them ice.

As masses of ice accumulate, gravity starts them flowing downhill. This flow is not steady. Glaciers may be stationary for years and then suddenly surge hundreds of feet. The ice moves in layers: Often a lower, more plastic layer is capped by a brittle one. Where a steep drop speeds up flow and stretches the layers, this brittle layer may crack into deep crevasses and jumbled icefalls, the bane of climbers.

Few sights are as dramatic as a glacier, and few forces are more powerful. Nevertheless, much of their work is done by smaller, hidden instruments. Walking in high mountains, you see many rocks cracked into layers or blocks. These show how frost, expanding in minuscule weak spots, wedges out pieces of mountain. The glacier's icy fingers then carry off these fragments.

Crescent-shaped chips and long scratches in rock often point out the direction of a vanished glacier's flow. These marks usually were made not by ice itself, but by pebbles or boulders in its grip. Even much of the polishing of rock and carving of potholes beneath ice were done not by glaciers, but by streams flowing beneath them, and by sand and pebbles in those streams. (The pressure of ice helps melt the water in these hidden rivers.)

**Figure 2-3.** Glaciers carving back into mountains left
characteristic knife-edged ridges and pinnacles like
these at Prusik Peak (above Gnome Tarn), in
Washington's Alpine Lakes Wilderness Area.

Gravity and greater supplies of snow and ice guide most glaciers down pre-existing valleys. Eroded by the glacier and its attendant forces, these valleys lose the V-profile cut by mountain streams. They become broad and semicircular, a profile that reduces drag, allowing the greatest amount of ice to flow with the least possible surface area. Broad, U-shaped valleys are probably the Pacific Northwest's most obvious and widespread sign of former glaciation.

A main glacier usually can cut into a mountain much faster than a tributary glacier can. Thus, the Ice Age left many tributary valleys "hanging" far above the floors of valleys that once held large glaciers. A plume of falling water often decorates the drop-off where the higher valley ends, far above the main valley's floor.

Where glaciers ride over a ridge, or join in an ice cap that completely covers a summit, they tend to round and polish the rock. Outcroppings become whalebacks, streamlined in the direction of the glacier's flow. Thus, while the Ice Age steepened the summits of high ranges—for example, the North Cascades—it left domes and gentle hills in low ones—for example, the rounded evergreen mountains of the Idaho Panhandle, around glacially carved Priest Lake, Lake Pend Oreille, and Lake Coeur d'Alene.

**Figure 2-4.** Throughout the Pacific Northwest, glaciers carved broad, U-shaped valleys like this one: McDonald Creek Valley in Glacier National Park, Montana.

**Figure 2-5.** Where they overrode rocks or peaks, glaciers rounded and polished, leaving smoothed surfaces like these at Robin Lake, below Mt. Daniel in the Washington Cascades.

Flowing ice carries rubble with it. Thus, boulders found miles from any similar rock—a hunk of granite on a lava plain, for example—often are signs saying "glaciers were here." Such rocks are called *erratics*.

Boulder and gravel debris collects along a glacier's sides and at its melting toe, forming ridges called *moraines*. Many of these moraines dammed large and small lakes that now show the former location of a glacier's tip. In Northwest mountains, you often climb many a rubbly ridge to find yourself looking into one of these lakes. In some cases, man simply made the moraine a bit higher and formed a reservoir.

**Figure 2-6.** Plowing away eroded sediments, the Ice Age glaciers steepened the characteristically flat-topped Rocky Mountain ranges. The debris pushed in front of the ice dammed moraine lakes like this one: Swiftcurrent Lake, below Mt. Gould, Glacier National Park, Montana.

Yet another kind of lake, the small and shallow kettle lake, formed where a block of ice was buried beneath insulating debris. When the big ice cake finally melted, it left a depression. Such potholes dot the northern part of Washington's Puget Sound country, where they are popular swimming or fishing holes. One example is Seattle's Green Lake, a heavily used city park.

Rubble carried along glaciers often built flat terraces along the sides of valleys. Their rocks and gravel washed from the glacier's sides, or were deposited by streams running between the ice and the valley wall. Orchards emphasize such terraces along lower Lake Chelan and the Methow Valley in eastern Washington where temperature inversions sometimes leave the high terraces warmer, and hence safer for crops, than the valley below.

Less common are meandering ridges called *eskers*, formed by streams running beneath the ice. When glaciers melted, the former stream gravels were left as a raised feature.

You can see the ice's signature in almost any Pacific Northwest range today. Even the Klamath Mountains on Oregon's southern border have cirques below 3,000 feet altitude, recording a snowline that came halfway down their highest peaks. Isolated, dry ranges, like Oregon's Steens Mountain, had glaciers at their highest altitudes: not far below cirques on such mountains, valleys lose the glacial U-shape, and show only the V profile of steam erosion.

The glaciers left an outsized, exaggerated landscape. They steepened peaks and deepened valleys. As they plowed away sediments that had choked valleys in the Rockies, they were a major force carving what had been a range of gentle hills, perhaps 1,000 to 1,500 feet from base to summit, into today's scarps, plunging 2,000 to 5,000 feet.

The tracks of the giants can be seen in valleys far too large for the streams running through them today—the valleys of the Skagit and Chehalis Rivers in western Washington are oversize in this way. Many white-water rapids, too, are outsized relics: They are "fossil" collections of boulders much bigger than today's rivers could move.

## THE CONTINENTAL ICE SHEETS

The immense lobes of ice that poured down from Canada differed from the local mountain glaciers mainly in scale. Mountain glaciers might be 40 miles in length and 2,000 feet thick. But the ice sheets stretched hundreds of miles. In western Washington near Bellingham, ice was 6,000 feet thick—more than a mile. Basically, though, continental glaciers behaved like alpine ones. They, too, flowed downhill, although "downhill" was in relation to their source—glaciers can ride over local rises the way a river flows over shallow spots in its bed.

Continental ice sheets left the characteristic glacial signatures, such as grooved and polished rock, boulder erratics, moraines, and kettle lakes. Giant examples of U-shaped valleys are Puget Sound's complex waterways, shaped by a mile-thick lobe of ice.

Some signs are particularly characteristic of the continental ice sheets. These signatures include snaky eskers and bumpy hills called *kames*, formed by rubble lowered to the ground in various ways as glaciers melted. Both kames and eskers often grew when glaciers stagnated in one place a long time—they are particularly common in northeast Washington, where the Okanogan Lobe lingered much longer than its counterpart west of the Cascades.

Drumlins, streamlined hills with something of a teardrop shape, are made by glaciers riding over gentle country. The hills of Seattle, Washington, have this shape. North slopes are steep because the advancing glacier dug into them. Long, north-south running valleys show the direction of ice movement. South slopes drop gently, because there the ice flowed on without resistance.

The hills, and the resulting ease of building north-south rather than east-west roads, influence traffic jams to this day.

The ice sheets also profoundly changed soil. Many a gardener has had reason to curse them. As far as about 15 miles south of Olympia, Washington, the western Washington ice sheet's farthest advance, the glacier packed down a hard-to-work clay called *till*. South of this, miles of sand and gravel washed from the tongue of ice, leaving soil that drains quickly. Instead of Western Washington's characteristic conifers, this well-drained part of the Puget Lowland bears scrubby oaks like those common much farther south and east.

Layers of gravel washed from glaciers also are found farther north, usually beneath the till. The gravel often alternates with layers of sand that settled when the ice sheets dammed Puget Sound at its north end, creating a huge lake. This layer-cake structure is a major contributor to local landslide problems. When the till is cut, either naturally by waves or artificially by man, the sand and gravel become water-soaked; then they slide.

Farmers west of the Cascades, though, have reason to bless the Pleistocene. Its giant rivers, white with rock ground fine as flour by the ice, deposited rich alluvial plains. Among them are Washington's sunny Skagit Valley and the the dairy lands that produce Tillamook, Oregon's famous cheese.

## ICE AND THE SEA

Under the weight of glacial ice, the continental plate sank as much as a third of the thickness of the ice. The worldwide increase in the volume of ice and snow also lowered sea levels an estimated 400 to 500 feet. Between glaciations, the sea rose again and the continent bounced back. But the rise and fall of sea levels was much faster than the land's sag and rebound— in fact, Pacific Northwest shores seem to be still adjusting from the last glaciation.

Thus, Ice Age sea levels bobbed up and down in a complex order that no one has yet untangled. Anyone, though, can see the results.

Many of Oregon's sea cliffs are stair-stepped into distinct terraces. These are wave-cut beaches formed by a much higher sea. On the southern coast, where Oregon's first gold rush was caused by paydirt in the black sands, miners have sifted the old beaches for the heavy minerals they contain.

After the Ice Age, waves went back to cutting and building today's beaches. Where a wider beach or old, gentle continental shelf was exposed, landward winds and sand from alongshore currents have formed dunes. Oregon's spectacular 140 miles of coastal dunes (Washington has only about a tenth the area) were built in this way.

**Figure 2-7.** Terraces on the bluffs at Otter Crest, Oregon, are old Ice Age beaches.

Many of the older dunes now are covered by forest. North and south of the Columbia River's mouth, and in other low spots on the Pacific Northwest coast, rows of such wooded dunes trapped shallow lakes between them—an ideal home for the cranberry farms that flourish there. Two of the largest such areas, the Clatsop Plains south of the mouth of the Columbia, and the long spit that encloses Willapa Bay to its north, were born as sand bars running north in the direction of winter currents and winds. Gradually, the marsh behind the bars would silt in, and another bar would form farther west. In this way, the Columbia River's mouth has moved far to the west since the Ice Age.

Oregon's rivers enter the ocean through long, narrow estuaries—welcome harbors on a rugged coast. When the sea level was lower, these rivers emptied further west. Coos, Alsea, Yaquina, Tillamook, and other bays were marshy river valleys. When the sea was higher, wave erosion enlarged the valleys. Now, though the westernmost river mouths remain "drowned," some of the bays are slowly silting in, on their way to becoming dry land again.

## THE GREAT LAKES

The continental ice cap, marching across the low mountains of northeastern Washington and northern Idaho, advanced farthest along the north and south running valleys of these ranges. The major drainage of the Pacific Northwest, though, is into the Columbia River and its tributaries, such as the Clark Fork, Pend Oreille, Coeur d'Alene, and Spokane Rivers. These run east and west near the ice sheets' former border.

Again and again, lobes of ice crossed the major rivers and dammed immense lakes. And again and again, the ice dams broke, sending floods whose size is almost beyond imagining down the Columbia River.

At today's Grand Coulee, the Columbia River was backed up into Glacial Lake Columbia. At today's Long Lake, the Spokane River was blocked, flooding the site of present Spokane. Modern Lake Coeur d'Alene is tiny compared to the 275-feet-higher lake dammed by another ice lobe, blocking the Spokane River farther east. Largest of all was Glacial Lake Missoula, 2,000 feet deep and 2,9000 square miles in area. Its frigid arms stretched far into Montana each time the ice cap dammed the Clark Fork River at Idaho's Lake Pend Oreille.

About 40 times, Lake Missoula's glacial dam broke. In the largest floods, an estimated 500 cubic miles of water roared down the Clark Fork River. Stripping the Clark Fork's channel, the wall of water raised glacial Lake Coeur d'Alene and Lake Columbia as much as 500 feet without a pause. Spilling over every low spot from Cheney to Grand Coulee, the flood rushed southeast across the Columbia Plateau, sometimes more than 1,000 feet deep.

The results still are obvious in these "channeled scablands" of eastern Washington. Walls of the dry canyons called *coulees* soar hundreds of feet. Dry waterfalls are more than two miles wide. Deep stream channels interlace on rock hundreds of feet above today's valley floors. Miles of basalts are stripped bare. Others are laced with giant deltas and gravel ripple marks 9 feet high.

**Figure 2-8.** Dry Falls, Central Washington, from the air: The abandoned channels and waterfalls were cut by huge Ice Age floods pouring across the Columbia Plateau.

The waters backed up at the Big Bend of the Columbia at Wallula, dropping a thick layer of gravelly sediments. Beyond the bend, they spilled deep into Oregon, from Pendleton almost to the Dalles. After crossing the Cascade Mountains at the Columbia Gorge, the flood backed up again into Oregon's Willamette Valley, making a lake 400 feet deep well south of today's Portland.

Such floods lasted months or years. When they had receded, winds began their work. For thousands of years, the prevailing westerlies blackened the sky with dust storms whipped from the flood's sediments on the scarred plateau. The dust settled in immense dunes on the lee side of the Columbia Plateau. Today, these are the Palouse Hills, extremely fertile and golden with wheat. Their slopes, steepest on the northeast, show that in the Ice Age, too, winter storms blew mostly from the southwest. Similar hills formed for similar reasons on the eastern end of the Snake River Plain, in Idaho.

South of the glaciers, another kind of lake formed. The Pleistocene's cold and rains filled the Basin and Range lowlands—the sunken blocks of continental crust between long, upraised mountains.

During the Ice Age, Oregon's desert basins filled with cold lakes that supported salmon and trout. Mastodons and giant musk oxen roamed their shores. Below massive Abert Rim, salty Abert and Summer Lakes were a single large lake, Chewaucan, once 300 feet deep. The Warner Lakes, a chain of jewels under cliff-like Hart Mountain, home of antelope and mountain sheep, were a single icy finger stretching into Nevada. Malheur and Harney Lakes, their swampy remnants today one of the world's great wildlife refuges, covered 920 square miles.

Some of the remnants of these Ice Age lakes today are alkaline and barren. Others have evaporated to whitish salt flats, or are marked only by plateau-like benches that mark their former shores. Fossil Lake, one of the Northwest's great troves of prehistoric bones, was found when homesteaders plowed the desert soil, and it blew away, taking their hopes with it. Almost the only reminder of the teeming Ice Age life are strange little fish—hump-backed suckers, chubs, and dace—found only in these desert basin lakes.

The two largest Great Basin lakes just touched the Pacific Northwest. Nevada's Pyramid Lake is a remnant of Lake Lahontan, a many-armed octopus the size of Lake Erie, that reached into California and Oregon. Utah's Great Salt Lake is a remnant of Lake Bonneville, largest of the Ice Age lakes. Almost the size of Lake Michigan, it sprawled across Utah into Nevada and Idaho. Lake Bonneville, like Lake Missoula, flooded catastrophically, leaving scablands and dry cascades near where it spilled into the Snake River, south of today's Pocatello.

Fishermen have reason to be grateful to Lake Bonneville, for it explains how fish reached isolated streams in the middle of deserts. The Great Basin of Utah and Nevada, for example, today drains only inward. The cutthroat trout found in isolated cold streams there today probably arrived via Lake

**Figure 2-9.** Fort Rock formed from ash that settled as a volcano exploded through one of southern Oregon's Ice Age lakes. Waves steepened the rock's sides—the broadening near the bottom shows the old shoreline.

Bonneville's flood into the Snake River—Cutthroat are known for exploring up streams. In turn, a Great Basin stream probably was "pirated" when a tributary of the Colorado eroded into it. This brought cutthroat into the Colorado River drainage. Thus, the popular sport fish are an Ice Age gift from the Pacific Northwest.

Deep, cold Bear Lake on the Idaho-Utah border is a curious fossil of the Ice Age. Remarkably, this 21-mile-long lake supports four very different species of whitefish (*Prosopium* spp.), three of them native nowhere else. The rare species are believed to have evolved in the Snake and Bonneville lake systems. These were joined to Bear Lake at different times by lava dams and floods. When the other lakes vanished, the local whitefish survived only in Bear Lake's high, cold waters.

## THE COLD CRADLE OF MODERN LIFE

Pre-Ice Age fossils contain few modern species of birds and mammals—though they generally contain close relatives, members of the same genus. By the end of the Ice Age, North America held almost all of today's species—including man.

The warm and cold cycles of the Pleistocene nurtured modern life in many ways. The ice caps, you remember, grew not from the poles, but from the mountains of Canada. Thus, while ice ground southward into today's United States, much of Northern Canada and Alaska remained ice-free. The Ice Age's lowered sea levels exposed a broad Bering Land Bridge. (The bridge also was exposed at earlier times.) In this way, man and other animals crossed back and forth between Asia and the New World.

Bears, chipmunks, beavers, modern bison, minks, and many others are believed to have entered the New World by this land bridge. The traffic was two-way—horses and camels, American natives, crossed to the Old World but died out in their original home. Some animals evolved in North America and stayed. They include pronghorns, skunks, badgers, lynx, kangaroo rats, and jackrabbits. Relatively few animals entered North America from the south, but raccoons and porcupines are among those that did make the trip up through Panama.

Given this melting pot, the Ice Age's changed conditions may have speeded up evolution in that many mutations or variant characteristics became useful, helping animals to survive and propagate. Thus, new genetic patterns spread.

Another spur to formation of new species may have been that, to survive the Ice Age, many plants and animals had to move or perish. Many became isolated in small "refuges" of suitable soils and climate. Mutations could spread and become established fairly easily in these small, isolated populations. When the animals or plants later expanded into larger areas, they carried the change with them. The three Western races of white-crowned sparrow (one familiarly known as the Puget Sound sparrow) are thought to

**Figure 2-10.** The "Puget Sound sparrow," singing plaintively on brushy shores, is one of the races of white-crowned sparrow that probably separated during the Ice Age.

have become established in such refuges. East-West differences between such close relatives as the western and eastern meadowlarks, and the lazuli and indigo buntings, are also thought to stem from Ice Age separations.

Amphibians and reptiles are "older" than birds and mammals—many of their modern species existed well before the Ice Age. But these cold-blooded animals had to move during the Ice Age. Their migrations, and their survival in refuges, accounts for much of their modern distribution.

The most dramatic change in Ice Age animal life, though, was the wave of extinctions that swept giant animals from North America just as the Ice Age ended. Among those that vanished were mammoths; mastodons; woodland musk-oxen; camels; horses; giant relatives of bears, bison, and beaver; giant land tortoises; dire wolves; saber-toothed cats; and huge vultures and eagles. Three factors make this swath of extinctions particularly mysterious. If the cause was the Ice Age's drastic climatic changes, why did nearly all the animals survive every Pleistocene cycle of cold except the last? Why were large animals struck down, leaving medium-sized and small ones— the animals of today? And why was the toll so much greater in America than in the Old World?

Evidence points to man as the culprit. *Homo sapiens* crossed the Bering Land Bridge repeatedly during the Ice Age and wandered south (probably through gaps between the Western and Eastern Canadian ice caps). Implements found in shallow caves show that man was in the Pacific Northwest before the glaciers had departed. With teamwork and crude stone-tipped weapons, man could assure himself of plentiful meat supplies by killing a mammoth or a giant, long-horned bison. The big predators—saber-tooth cats and dire wolves—may have perished when man robbed them of their prey.

This theory, however, also has weak points. Bone piles in prehistoric camps show that North America's early inhabitants depended heavily on mammoth and bison, but killed few of the other vanished grazing animals.

Thus, the cause of the Ice Age extinctions, that left us with our modern wildlife, remains almost as veiled as the cause of the Ice Age itself.

## SINCE THE ICE AGE

The grip of ice was not loosened by a steady warming trend. Although Ice Age glaciers began to retreat about 14,000 years ago, they paused and advanced in northwestern Washington about 11,000 years ago.

As the ice retreated, streams and rivers went back to cutting V-shaped canyons. Thus, in areas that were ice-covered, most such stream beds are younger than the Ice Age. There are some notable exceptions, though. One of the most dramatic is sunset-colored Yellowstone Canyon, in Yellowstone National Park. Each time the glaciers advanced, an ice-dammed lake filled this canyon with sediments before the glaciers overrode it. Thus the pre-Ice Age canyon was preserved. Once the ice retreated again, the Yellowstone River washed the sediments out again.

Forests crept back following the retreating glaciers—pioneering lodgepole pines first, and then spruces, firs, and others. The modern migrations of birds, of course, were established after the disappearance of ice.

Between about 6,000 and 4,500 BP (before the present), the climate was warmer and drier than it is now. Deserts and grasslands advanced farther into the Northwest than at present. The resultant dust storms boosted growth of the Palouse Hills. Human populations declined. Some plants that had been more widespread were isolated in mild, wet coastal areas. These include the beautiful madrona trees (*Arbutus menziesii*) and Pacific yew (*Taxus brevifolia*).

There have been extreme periods since—for example, a worldwide warm period between roughly 700 and 1100 A.D., when Indian farming societies expanded in North America while Norsemen colonized Iceland and Greenland. In the Little Ice Age that followed, glaciers advanced worldwide, the area cultivated by Indians shrank, and the Norse settlement in Greenland perished.

Recent trends are less clear. A general warming seems to have ended after the Dust Bowl years of the 1930s. Although glaciers in the Rocky Mountains are generally receding, some in Washington's Cascades and Olympics are growing, perhaps because these ranges are so well-supplied with rain and snow. Another Ice Age, or another warm period, could be on its way—or man, changing the atmosphere's cloud cover or insulating properties with his pollutants, may create one.

**Figure 2-11.** The Palouse Hills are immense dust dunes made of Ice Age debris that settled at the leeward end of the Columbia Plateau. Dust storms of the hot, dry interval roughly 6,000 to 4,500 years ago enlarged them.

## DOING IT YOURSELF

Look for evidence of glaciers near you. These may be U-shaped valleys, hills shaped like teardrops or snakes, or large boulders that don't match bedrock. If you don't find such signs, ask yourself why.

On hikes or drives through mountains, look for other signs of ice: sharp ridges and pinnacles, cirque valleys, large and small scratches on rocks that show direction of glacier flow, or ridges that probably are moraines.

Try to imagine the topography before the Ice Age, what land would have looked like under the ice, and which features post-date the glaciers (for example, most flat flood plains, spits and bars, and V-shaped valleys).

You can hike to glaciers, and climb on them, in Montana's Glacier National Park and Washington's Olympic National Park, and on Washington's Mt. Baker, Glacier Peak. and Mt. Adams, among other places. By far the easiest to see, though, are in Washington's Mt. Rainier National Park. This highest of Pacific Northwest mountains has 11 major glaciers and many smaller ones. The glaciers are up to six miles long. Fed by permanent snowfields, they snake down well below timberline. The main road to Paradise in the park almost touches the toe of Nisqually Glacier.

Remember, though, that glaciers can be dangerous. Thin snow can hide a crevasse. Ice caves can collapse unexpectedly. Mountain weather can change suddenly. Don't explore glaciers without proper clothing, experienced companions, and proper equipment, such as crampons, ice axes, and ropes.

In Washington, take the boat ride up Lake Chelan, a spectacular, glacier-carved lake in the North Cascades. The ferry from Seattle to Bremerton also takes you through glacially scoured fiords. The big lakes in Idaho's northern panhandle—Priest, Pend Oreille, and Coeur d'Alene—also show the elaborate sculpture of glaciers on the continents.

**Figure 2-12.** Glaciers are spectacular but dangerous, as is shown by this crevasse in Challenger Glacier, on Mt. Challenger in Washington's North Cascades National Park.

Visit central Washington's coulees and channelled scablands, remnants of Lake Missoula's great floods. Some of the most interesting are Moses Coulee, Crab Creek, Banks Lake, Lenore Lake, and Long Lake Wildlife Recreation Areas, managed by the state game department; and Columbia National Wildlife Refuge. At Lenore Lake, you can see rock shelters like those used by Indians, who had reached the Northwest by the end of the Ice Age. Nearby Sun Lakes State Park has an excellent geology exhibit. In the Oregon desert and along its rocky seacoast, look for old wave-cut beaches—flats above the present beach or valley floor. You can combine such visits with good wildlife watching at Hart Mountain National Antelope Range and at Malheur National Wildlife Refuge, which includes Harney and Malheur Lakes. Summer Lake, another remnant of a larger Ice Age lake, has an interesting state wildlife area.

How do you think the Ice Age would have affected native plants and animals? Would it have affected their ranges or habits? Do you see any such effects around you?

# 3

# Northwest Weather

Pacific Northwest climate begins with two powerful forces: the sun and the vast ocean. The sun is the driving force behind two great cells of moving air, one born at the equator and the other at the North Pole. In their cycles, storms or calm are born. The Pacific Ocean plays two parts. First, the Pacific's ancient geological clash with the continent shaped the mountains. They govern whether air flowing from the ocean creates rain forest or desert in the Northwest. Second, the ocean's water, fluctuating only a few degrees throughout winter and summer, tempers the air that flows over Washington, Oregon, and Idaho. This keeps their climates unusually moist and mild.

## GLOBAL FORCES AND WEATHER

To understand the role of the sun in Pacific Northwest weather, you must start far away—at the equator and the North Pole. Radiating most intensely on the tropics, the sun heats air that rises there, just as warm air rises in a room. From the equator, this air flows north and south. Cooled by the release of pressure, it drops its moisture as rain. (Cold air holds less moisture than warm air—that is why droplets form on a glass of ice water on a summer day.) At about 30° latitude, the tropical air, now dry and cold, begins to fall again.

As the air sinks, the growing weight of atmosphere above rewarms it. No more moisture is released. The resulting high-pressure area forms belts of desert that all but girdle the earth at these latitudes: The Sahara and the Kalahari in Africa; the Peruvian and Chilean deserts in South America; and the Sonoran Deserts of Mexico and the southwestern United States. When they move north from the desert latitudes into the Northwest, the tropical highs bring calm, sunny weather.

The polar cell is the reverse of this tropical one. Little of the sun's heat reaches the poles. Cold air there falls and flows toward the equator. Where it begins to rise again, at about 60° N latitude, it forms a belt of low pressures and instability, with frequent storms.

In the Northwest, the polar and tropical air flows meet. The two great cells are semipermanent over the Pacific. Their interfingering swirls of high-pressure air, blowing clockwise, and low-pressure air, moving counter-clockwise, flow eastward from the ocean across the land, like eddies in a slow river. They bring the region its alternate storms and calm, and a pattern of changeability. In the Northwest, neither extreme heat nor extreme cold last long.

**Figure 3-1.** Winds from the Pacific Ocean alternately bring the region calm and storms, like this one at Ruby Beach, Olympic National Park, Washington.

**Figure 3-2.** "Rain forest" beside the Hoh River in Olympic National Park, Washington.

The seasonal shifting of the great cells governs Pacific Northwest weather. As the earth's tilt on its axis brings more sunshine to the Northern Hemisphere in its summer, the high-pressure tropical air moves farther north, over the Pacific Northwest. In winter, the stormy polar cell moves south across the region. As a result, Pacific Northwest summers are warm and dry; winters are cool and wet.

## WHY IT'S THE *PACIFIC NORTHWEST*

Because the earth is wider at the equator than at the poles, air (and anything else) must travel faster at the equator than at the poles in order to complete a daily rotation around earth's axis. This difference in speed puts a slight "twist" (called the Coriolis effect) on winds or other currents traveling north or south. In the Northern Hemisphere currents are turned right. This rightward twist of air creates the prevailing northwesterlies of summer and the prevailing southwesterlies of winter, both carrying moisture eastward from the ocean in tne latitudes of Washington and Oregon. (Winds are named for their source—westerly winds blow eastward.) In this way, winds from the Pacific dominate the climate of the Pacific Northwest.

Over the Pacific, air takes on ocean moisture. It also grows closer to the ocean's temperature, which fluctuates much less than temperatures on land. This is the reason for the damp, cloudy, but extremely mild climate of the Pacific Northwest coast and nearby inland valleys. Precipitation, for example, averages 60 to 100 inches a year along the coast, with more than 150 inches falling in the wettest Olympic rain forests. This decreases to a still-substantial 30 to 50 inches in the valleys east of the Coast Range—Puget Sound country and the Willamette Valley. In the mild lowlands, nearly all this moisture falls as rain. The ocean coast gets only an inch or two of snow a year. Seattle and Portland average eight or nine inches, or about three snowy days a year.

Rainfall, of course, means clouds. Seattle and Portland get only about 45 percent of maximum potential sunshine. More than 200 days of the year are cloudy in both cities, and rain falls an average of 150 days each year.

The cloud cover further helps moderate the climate, by trapping and reflecting the earth's heat. Daily fluctuations in temperature average only about 15°F in Seattle and Portland; differences between the average temperatures of the warmest month, July, and the coldest one, January, are only about 20°.

**Figure 3-3.** Mist over Lake Lytle, a lake trapped between old, wooded dunes in northwestern Oregon: Moisture from the Pacific keeps weather in the coastal Pacific Northwest mild—but at the cost of frequent gray skies.

These are the basic reasons why Portland, Oregon, for example, has a climate so much milder than say, Minneapolis-St. Paul, Minnesota, or Bangor, Maine—which actually lie on more southerly latitudes.

The "moderating" Pacific influences, though, also contribute to a contrast between summer's drought and winter's rain and snow. In winter, the continent is cooler than the sea. Chilled by its contact with land, the maritime moisture condenses as rain and snow. In summer, Pacific Northwest land grows warmer than the ocean. Air flowing inland can retain its moisture, so little rain falls. The Pacific Northwest thus has a marked winter wet season, from October to April. West of the Cascades, nearly half the precipitation falls in the three winter months, December to February.

As Midwesterners know, the climate in North America's great interior is quite different. There, air heated by sun and earth in summer rises, cools, and forms drifting castles of cumulus clouds and sudden thunderstorms. In winter, skies are clear and cold. Thus, over the Great Plains and most of the Rocky Mountains, summer brings rain and extreme heat. Winter is dry but cold.

The Rockies, though, wall off most of the Pacific Northwest from the continent's interior. Air masses from the Great Plains, from Canada, and even from the Gulf of Mexico do sometimes cross the wall. When they do, they often bring the Pacific Northwest its greatest extremes of heat and cold. Oregon, for example, has seen temperatures ranging from $-54°$ F to $119°$ F.

The influence of ocean air, however, is much stronger. One reason, already described, is that the Pacific Northwest lies on the "storm track" of the prevailing westerlies. Another reason for the ocean's strong influence is that the Coast and Cascade ranges form only a broken wall against its winds. Pacific air can flow inland through the Columbia Gorge, and across the relatively low mountains of Southern British Columbia and Northern Idaho.

The passage of ocean air eastward thus is easier in the Pacific Northwest than it is either north in Canada or south in California. You can see the ocean influence far inland. Idaho's moist northern Panhandle has about the same total precipitation as the Puget Lowland. Farther east, in Montana, the glaciers that give Glacier National Park its name and distinction are fed by these same moist Pacific winds. Forests of the Rockies in the Pacific Northwest are closer kin to coastal forests than are the forests either north or south. For example, nowhere else do the Rockies have Western hemlock, Western larch, and whitebark pine, normally trees of the Cascade and Coast ranges.

The ocean air carries with it the cloudiness and wet-winter, dry-summer climate that distinguishes the Pacific Northwest. For example, northern Idaho, 300 miles inland, gets only about 50 percent of maximum potential sunshine. Only in extreme eastern Idaho does a high percentage of the year's (scanty) moisture fall in summer. Low passes there admit continental air just as they gave easy passage to pioneers along the Oregon Trail.

Unstable updrafts brings short-lived summer lightning storms to Pacific Northwest mountain ranges, as forest fires bear witness. But thunderstorms, as well as hail and sleet, are rare there compared to the Great Plains. Tornados are still scarcer: Washington, Oregon, and Idaho each average one a year or fewer. The Northwest's weather-related disasters are mostly the result of heavy mountain snows, which can cause avalanches or spring floods. The nation's most deadly avalanche, one of its greatest railroad disasters, was at Wellington Station just west of Stevens Pass in the North Cascades. In the early Morning hours of March 2, 1910, a slide crashed down on two snowbound trains, killing 96.

The distinctive Pacific Northwest climate has profoundly affected life in the region. To use just one example, before pioneer days, vast herds of buffalo, deer, and elk, shepherded by wolves and coyotes, wandered the Great Plains—but not the rangelands of Oregon, Washington, and Idaho. The huge herds depended on lush summer grass and light winter snow—results of dry winters and summer rain. West of the Continental Divide, deer and elk had to move to mountains for summer grazing. Buffalo perished in years of deep snow.

**Figure 3-4.** Bison in Lamar Valley, Yellowstone National Park, Wyoming. The Pacific Northwest's deep snows kept the great herds east of the Continental Divide.

Thus, the region is well named. More than other parts of the American West, then, the Northwest has a unity conferred by a single force: the Pacific Ocean. And its weather can best be understood by following Pacific air as it flows east and inland.

# THE FOOTPRINTS
# OF OCEAN WINDS

Looking up at clouds, you can see the ocean air moving onto the Pacific Northwest. Because clouds are made of water droplets floating on the air, their shapes show the direction of air currents. In the Pacific Northwest's coastal region, clouds are mostly stratus—layered clouds. They show the horizontal layers of air flowing inland. By contrast, the Midwest's towering cumulus clouds dramatize upward air currents.

The coast's frequent morning fogs also illustrate the inland flow of air. Warm ocean air moving inland at night meets a land colder than the sea. Water droplets condense as horizontal layers of fog, trapped under warmer air in a temperature inversion. It's curious that in the Northwest fog usually heralds good weather—by afternoon the sun usually has "burned off" the fog, and skies are clear.

In Southern Oregon, where the southern, high-pressure air cell holds sway longer, frequent summer fogs help counterbalance a long dry season. In a complex way, this is again due to the great air cells and the rotation of the earth. The prevailing winds, from the south in winter and from the north in summer, create along-shore currents that flow north in winter and south in summer. The rightward twist given currents in the northern hemisphere turns water away from shore in summer, from central Oregon down through northern California. As a result, very cold water wells up from deeper levels close to shore. This cold water chills the warmer ocean air, so that it forms fog droplets that drift in to land.

Air flowing onto the shores of Washington and Oregon must rise to cross the Coast Ranges and the Olympics. Rising, it is released from pressure, cools, and is forced to drop its moisture. (The change in air temperature with altitude, rising or falling, is about 10° in 6/10 of a mile. This is called the *adiabatic rate.*)

The result of this forced precipitation is the lush, ferny "rain forest" of the coastal mountains. These evergreen woods bear a heavier weight of plant matter per acre than any other conifer forest in the world.

On the lee side of the coastal ranges, and of any mountains, is a "rain shadow"—a relatively dry area where wrung-out air that has crossed the mountains is compressed and warmed as it falls. Most of the Coast Range is low—only about 1,000 to 3,000 feet—so the lowlands east of them, including

**Figure 3-5.** Stuart Island in the Washington's San Juan Archipelago, an island group kept sunny and dry by the rain shadow of the Olympic mountains.

Seattle and Portland, stay relatively moist. Northeast of the nearly 8,000-foot Olympic Mountains, though, rainfall drops to about 20 inches a year, a fifth of what it was on the ocean side of the mountains. Trees are scrubby. The nearby San Juan Islands bake golden in summer's drought.

The rain shadows are strongest northeast of the mountains, rather than due east, because of the the shifting cells and the twist caused by rotation of the earth. Winter storms, bringing the heaviest rains, blow counterclockwise off the low-pressure cell in the Pacific, and roar in from the southwest. As a result, the lack of their precipitation thus shows up most strongly northeast of a barrier.

All Pacific Northwest mountain ranges repeat this pattern: moisture on the west slopes of mountains and drought on the east. For example, precipitation on the west slopes of the Cascades is comparable to that on the coast. But from 92 inches at Stampede Pass, at the summit of the Central Washington Cascades, annual precipitation drops to 22 inches at Cle Elum, in the foothills just 20 miles eastward.

You can see the pattern of rising air being squeezed of its moisture in snowfalls, which average 400 to 600 inches on the high west slopes of the Olympics and Cascades. At Paradise Ranger Station on Mt. Rainier (elevation 5,500 feet) snowfall has reached 1,000 inches, one of the highest totals recorded in the United States.

You also can see the pattern of rising and falling air in clouds. For example, rows of flying-saucer-like lenticular clouds seem to hover above and downwind from mountain ranges. These flat-bottomed lenses form as air flows across the summit in waves, like water waves that form when the ocean encounters a beach. Moisture condenses in the colder, higher crests of these waves and evaporates in the troughs. The clouds, therefore, appear to stay still.

In vegetation, the results of the rise and fall of air crossing mountains are most obvious in the Cascades, although you can spot them in most Pacific Northwest ranges. Crossing the Cascades, you see a lush fir and hemlock forest replaced on the east first by pines and meadow, then by grassland and sage desert.

As more moisture is wrung from the air, the land grows drier from west to east. Most of the world's deserts are the result of the worldwide system of air cells. The Pacific Northwest's, however, are different. Shut off from moisture by the Cascades on the west and the Rockies on the east, they are the

**Figure 3-6.** Lenticular clouds skim like flying saucers across the summit of Mt. Baker, Washington (seen from Artist's Point).

result of mountain rain shadows. Precipitation, 150 inches a year on parts of the coast, drops to less than 10 inches a year in the driest areas of the Northwest—much of south central Oregon, the Columbia Basin in south central Washington, and Southern Idaho's Snake River Valley.

Even so, the dry areas retain the Pacific's cloudy influence: Only extreme southeastern Oregon and southwestern Idaho get as much sunshine as the Great Basin to the south or the Great Plains to the east.

The flow of air across the Pacific Northwest also brings two strange winds, one that leaves its tracks as ice, the other that strips slopes of snow.

Several times during most Pacific Northwest winters, Chinook winds sweep down slopes and into valleys. These actually are misnamed: The Chinook Indians lived at the mouth of the Columbia, and Hudsons Bay traders used their name originally for warm, moist winds that blew from the Pacific. The word came, though, to mean very different air: air that reaches the crest of mountains warm and dry, and then is heated still more as it flows down the leeward slope. Where they kiss the ground, Chinooks can melt snow in hours—saving the lives of cattle, or setting off deadly avalanches.

**Figure 3-7.** Christmas Valley, east of the Oregon Cascades, shows the extreme drying effects of the Northwest's mountain wall.

Chinook winds can come from the Pacific or the interior of the continents. The icy canyon wind of the Columbia River, however, comes only from frigid air that slips over the Rockies. It rushes, cold and dense, down the river's huge gorge. Rain falling from warmer air above freezes at this wind's touch, hanging the canyon's trees with ice. Spilling onto lowlands west of the Cascades, the canyon wind brings that mild country its hardest frosts.

## ELEVATION AND EXPOSURE

A pattern ruled by sun, slope, and elevation also is at work in Pacific Northwest climates. It is most evident where drought and cold are extreme.

Because rising air cools and drops its moisture, more snow and rain fall at high elevations than at low ones. This pattern of more moisture at higher elevation holds for the Cascades and Olympics, but it is most obvious in the drier mountains farther east. For example, the gentle Okanogan Mountains running east and west across Northern Washington bear evergreen forests, while the Columbia Plateau just to the south of them is gray sage desert. As the land rises again in extreme eastern Washington, western Idaho, and the Blue Mountains of Washington and Oregon, rainfall—and forests—rise as well. Thus the Blue Mountains with their grassy slopes and piney stream valleys were a relief to pioneers on the Oregon Trail. Even though they meant tough traveling, they were better than the parched, low Snake River Valley; the Columbia plateau; or the deadly Oregon deserts, which killed many members of one wagon train that tried to cross them.

Very dry mountains, like the Owyhees in Idaho, support trees only at higher elevations. Even then their forests are little more than scatterings of juniper, the most drought-tolerant of cone bearers.

Other effects of drought also show up most strongly in dry ranges. The sun, shining mostly from the south in the Northern Hemisphere, melts snow and evaporates water fastest on south slopes. Snow and rain runoff are lost quickly from steep, sunny ridges, but linger in valleys. Thus, dry mountains and desert slopes are likely to be greener on their north slopes than on the south. Fingers of trees often run up their canyons, while the ridges between stand brown and bare. You can see this pattern clearly in such dry ranges as the Blue and Wallowa Mountains of Washington and Oregon and the Lost River, Lemhi, and Beaverhead ranges of Central Idaho.

At subalpine and alpine levels, forests become scattered, then dwarfed and deformed. Finally, they yield to tiny cushions of plants clinging to crevices in rock. Shining mostly from the south, the sun warms and dries south slopes earliest. On any face of a mountain, snow lingers in valleys, but slides and melts from ridges. For this reason Indian trails across Northwest ranges followed ridges and not valleys, and at the upper limits of vegetations, trees and alpine plants usually find their highest toeholds on south slopes and on ridges.

# SMALLER PATTERNS OF WIND

Sun, land, and air interact to form smaller climates, down to the bit of warmth trapped by a stunted alpine fir, edged by wildflowers because its mat of branches has melted a patch of snow.

Interactions involving wind are perhaps easiest to see—and feel. Mountaintops, for example, are likely to whistle with wind. Air funneling over and between the peaks must speed up, just as a river does in a canyon. Sometimes you can see the result as clouds pile up on the windward side of a range, like standing waves in a rapid.

The rising sun strikes mountaintops first—snows turn pink and gold while light is still dim in green valleys. Sunward slopes heat quickly, as rays strike them almost at right angles. Thus warmed, the air near the peaks begins to rise, creating the up-valley breezes that blow toward the summits through many mountain days.

Such breezes can quickly change to short-lived thunderstorms, the result of an unstable rush of upward-moving low-pressure air. A Pacific Northwest mountain may experience about 7 to 14 such storms each year; the lightning that leaps from their sudden thunderheads is a major cause of forest fires. In dry areas, the sudden rains can send flash floods rushing down stream canyons.

Late in the day, the peaks cool quickly. Clouds that have piled up on their windward sides slip away. With little land to retain absorbed heat, thin mountain air cools quickly and begins to fall. Daytime's upslope breezes change to down-valley through the night. The cold air collects in valleys. Thus a seemingly protected hollow is likely to be a chilly campsite, several degrees colder than the slope above.

In the cold valley air, moisture often condenses as fog droplets. The morning sun's warmth on the peaks can trap such fog in a temperature inversion: Valleys often are gray with clouds until afternoon, while the slopes above are clear and sunny.

A similar pattern often prevails on seacoasts or even edges of large lakes. Breezes blow toward shore in daytime, when the land is warmer than the water. They blow away from shore at night, when the water is warmer than the land.

On the ocean, though, stronger winds often mask this pattern. Gales are common—on the Oregon coast, winds exceed 100 miles an hour almost every

**Figure 3-8.** Morning clouds fill the Soleduck Valley on Washington's Olympic Peninsula. (Mt. Olympus is in the distance). Such clouds usually vanish as sunshine heats the peaks.

year. You can see the force of such winds in the wind-sculpted lodgepole pines and Sitka spruces clinging to bluffs—some dramatically twisted, some "pruned" smooth as park hedges by the tiny particles of salt that bombard their needles or leaves. The ocean winds even reshape the land: Winter's southwesterlies sculpt eerie towers and steep northeast lee slopes in Oregan's dunes. These sand castles disappear in summer's gentler air. The lee slopes are steeper than those that meet the wind because sand settles on windward faces and cascades from the summit down lee slopes to the angle of repose. Because summer's sand is loose and dry, summer "slipslopes" cannot stand as steeply as those of winter, and sand towers collapse.

## DAY AND NIGHT

In the Coastal and Western Cascade areas, day-night differences in temperature are seldom extreme. Cloud cover and thick vegetation keep the air cool and moist during the day and trap heat at night. The resulting moisture and moderate temperatures probably are important to some deep-woods animals, such as grouse.

In desert and mountain areas, contrasts are much greater. Days can be scorching: Sun beats down on bare rock and soil, without shade to temper the heat. Thin mountain air does not filter out ultraviolet radiation as well as denser air at lower levels. The resultant ease of getting sunburned affects plants and animals, as well as mountain climbers and skiiers.

At night, sparsely vegetated deserts lose heat quickly to the clear sky. In mountains, chill spreads quickly through thin air and the small amount of land available to hold heat.

Desert and mountain also are subject to sudden storms and cold, even in midsummer. Oregon's high desert has seen snow in every month of the year. Mountain travelers must go prepared for the same.

These extremes, and climates large and small, make special demands on plants and animals. These demands, and how life copes with them, are discussed in the chapters that follow, dealing with water, mountain, desert, and alpine country.

## DOING IT YOURSELF

You can't do much about the weather. But you can get to know it better.

If you live in or visit an area with hills or large bodies of water, take a walk or drive to contrast the differences in temperature and fog between shore and inland, hilltops and valleys. Look for differences in vegetation. (Here, though, effects of weather may be masked by other factors, such as soils or past clearing and development.)

You usually can see differences in vegetation of shady north slopes and sunny south ones. Sometimes there is an east-west difference because the west gets the afternoon's long sun after it has warmed up. Can you see such a difference?

Can you see the Coriolis effect—the rightward twist of currents in the Northern Hemisphere—at work? Ask yourself this question as you look at a newspaper or television weather map.

Watch clouds for what they mean as well as to dream. Clouds show the movements of cooling or moisture-laden air. What is going on when you see a row of flat-bottomed clouds? When you see piled up thunderheads? How can the air be moving when the clouds are stationary?

The Northwest is not a particularly windy region, but you usually can see the way in which wind shapes plants on the seacoast or in mountains. Can you tell from such clues which direction winter storms come from? Where else can you "see" the wind? In clouds? Fog? Water?

When do the winds in your area usually change direction? Why? The differences may be daily or seasonal. What months are good sailing or kite-flying times? Why?

Analyze the microclimates in your own yard or in a nearby park. Where does paint begin to peel first, and why? Which parts are warmest, dryest, windiest, most stable? This sort of analysis has practical uses—most

**Figure 3-9.** Clouds seem to pour eastward only to
vanish again over Buck Creek Pass, in Washington's
Northeast Cascades. Moisture that condensed as air
rose to cross the mountains is evaporating as the air
grows drier and warmer on its descent.

homeowners and gardeners do it as a matter of course. You might enjoy
comparing your own barometer, thermometer, rain gauge, or wind vane to
official weather reports.

How does distant weather affect your area? A snowpack in mountains
probably supplies drinking as well as irrigation water. It may also cause
floods. In farming areas, someone else's good or bad weather may affect
prosperity.

# 4

# Forest Life

## THE EVERGREEN GIANTS

On some sunny days in spring, the dark evergreen forests of the Pacific Northwest wear a golden halo. The air is filled with puffs of pollen from red and yellow catkins, bright nubs amid the needles. Inevitably, some of this cloud bearing the male half of life settles on female cells, eggs naked on greenish or purplish scaly buds that will become cones. The fertilized egg becomes a seed. But this seed is not hidden in an ovary, as in flowering plants. (Conifers are members of the class Gymnospermae, which means "naked seed.") The seed is instead protected to maturity by scales of a woody cone, or of a fleshy, berry-like aril like those of junipers (*Juniperus* spp.) and Pacific yews (*Taxus brevifolia*).

This mode of producing new life is much older than that of the angiosperms—our familiar flowering trees, shrubs, flowers, and grasses. Their showy flowers are often specialized to attract pollinating insects. Although many flowering plants also use the wind to mate, the cone-bearers' absolute need for wind for sexual reproduction marks their kind as predating most of the insects that younger flowering plants depend on.

Thus, despite its geologic youth, the Pacific Northwest is in many ways a refuge for very old kinds of plants. This odd reversal happened during the

**Figure 4-1.** A ponderosa pine tree's pollen-bearing catkins and young cones: Needled evergreen trees reproduce by a method much older than that of flowering plants.

long march from the mild Mesozoic toward the Ice Age. As the world's weather cooled, Northwest summers dried, and the Rockies and Cascades rose, an exuberant flowering forest, of a variety unknown today, dwindled or retreated south and east. In contrast to the deciduous hardwood forests of the Eastern United States, the Northwest was left with only one ash, Oregon ash (*Fraxinus latifolia*). By contrast, there are more than a dozen ashes elsewhere in the country. Similarly, the Northwest retained only one member of the immense elm family (Ulmaceae): the deserts' little netleaf hackberry (*Celtis reticulata*); and one member of the huge beech family (Fagaceae): golden chinkapin (*Castanopsis chrysophylla*).

The older, cone-bearing evergreens came to rule again. Their tough, resinous needles, pungent in the sun, conserve water through two yearly droughts—summer's, when little rain falls; and winter's, when the ground is frozen. Those same evergreen needles are ready to produce food and growth as soon as mild days arrive in spring and late into Indian summer—times when trees that lose their leaves are dormant.

In this way, the cone bearers dominate Pacific Northwest forests. Moisture and mildness, carried east on storm tracks from the ocean, give these forests more unity than those in other parts of the West. But it is a changing, complex unity: northwestern North America, from northern California to Alaska, has the most diverse conifer forests in the world. In addition, different forest trees and their associated plant communities flourish in different areas, encouraged or out-competed because of moisture, temperature, soil, slope, aspect, age, and historical accidents such as fire and insect attacks.

## LOWLAND WESTERN CONIFERS

Because of the Pacific's moisture-bearing westerly winds and the north-south mountain walls that block them, differences in vegetation are most striking as you travel inland from the ocean, west to east.

From Alaska to just north of the California-Oregon border, Sitka spruce *(Picea sitchensis)* rules a narrow band of coastal lowlands, where fog drip adds to already heavy precipitation. Fast-growing and tall (ranking just below sequoia, that replaces it to the south, and Douglas fir), with prickly, stalked needles and scaly, purplish bark, Sitka spruce joins western redcedar (*Thuja plicata*) and western hemlock (*Tsuga heterophylla*) to create the Northwest's "rain forest." These are not really a distinct ecological type, like tropical rain forests. The Northwest's "rain forests," best known in Olympic National Park, are exceptionally damp, lush woods given a magical quality by their shadows and their ferns and mosses, which cover the ground and seem to drip from the trees. Even the light filtering through the needles seems greenish and watery. Like much of the Northwest's woods, the rain forests often are eerily silent. Deer and most other forest mammals prefer brushy woods broken by clearings. The few birds are more than 150 feet above— perhaps a flock of golden-crowned kinglets at the sunlit top of the canopy. An occasional winter wren, singing from the ferns, almost whispers his complex piping.

From the narrow Sitka spruce zone to the western slopes of the Cascade Mountains, the so-called "climax" dominant is Western hemlock, a retiring tree with delicate, irregular needles and drooping tip, growing slowly in the shade. Barring unpredictable interruptions such as insect plagues, logging, or fire, the forbearing hemlocks would become the most common trees in this huge region. A typical Coast Range or Western Cascade clearing, for example, might first sprout fireweed (*Epilobium angustifolium*), magenta-flowering herbs whose cottony seeds travel quickly on the wind. Next would come thickets of bracken fern (*Pteridium aquilinum*) and thimbleberry (*Rubus parviflorus*), topped by a deciduous forest of red alder (*Alnus rubra*) in less than a human generation. Bacteria in the alder roots would fix nitrogen, helping the trees grow quickly and enriching the soil. But alders live scarcely longer than a man—a short life, in tree terms. Within 100 years or so, the slim gray alders would be dying of old age or shaded out by Douglas firs (*Pseudotsuga taxifolia*) that sprouted with them.

**Figure 4-2.** Douglas fir is easily recognized by the little trident bracts on its cones.

The Douglas firs (which are not true firs—the Latin name means "the false hemlock with leaves like a yew"), largest of Pacific northwest conifers, could live another 500 to 1,000 years. But their seedlings do not thrive in shade. When at last they fell, western hemlocks that had sprouted and grown under their protection would take over. Since their offspring grow well in shade, the western hemlocks theoretically would rule forever.

The idea of climaxes helps us understand processes. But it often does little to describe the forests we see. The reason for this is that sudden and unpredictable events, ruled out in theorizing about climax forests, are very much a part of nature. In the Northwest, for example, even if lumbering did not interrupt succession, fire and insect plagues might keep most climaxes from ever occurring. In fact, few old-growth timber stands in the Northwest—those never logged or otherwise disturbed by man—fit the description of the theoretical climax.

Not only is the succession toward a climax forest often interrupted, the kinds of trees that flourish on a specific site also are influenced by such factors as soil, drainage, and whether a slope faces north, south, east, or west.

West of the Cascades, for example, dry sites are likely to bear Douglas fir, king of today's lumber industry. Douglas firs predominate in areas that have been logged, partly because clear-cutting, the usual practice, leaves a sunny forest floor; and partly because foresters generally seed or plant this high-value timber tree.

River bottoms and swampy areas often are dominated by bigleaf maples (*Acer macrophylla*) or western redcedars—graceful trees with fluted trunks, shreddy reddish bark, and scaly sprays rather than needles. The redcedars are not true cedars, but are members of the cypress family. The same is true of the other northwestern "cedars," with their scale-like leaves: yellow cedar (*Chamaecyparis nootkatensis*) of middle and high altitudes; and Port Orford cedar (*Chamaecyparis lawsoniana*) and incense cedar (*Calocedrus decurrens*) of southern Oregon.

Redcedars, still much valued for shakes and shingles, were the single most important tree to Indians west of the Cascades. They were a basic source of raw materials. Their wood, easily split into flat plates, provided shakes for houses. Rot resistant, it became dugout canoes, boxes, and supporting poles for houses. The bark, peeling off in sheets, became clothing, dishes, towels, torches, even diapers. The fine roots, more abundant at shallow levels than those of other conifers, were dug out to make baskets, fishnet, and twine.

Natural forests west of the Cascades also are likely to include scattered other cone-bearers: lodgepole pine (*Pinus contorta*) on poor soils; various

**Figure 4-3.** Shreddy-barked Western redcedars were a basic raw material for Pacific Northwest Indians.

other pines and true firs, some more common east of the mountains, others extending up from California into southern Oregon; and Pacific yew—a small, dark-needled tree twisting upward in the shade of others.

The evergreen forest of mild, wet lowlands from the Pacific to the Cascades is the most productive conifer forest in the world. It carries up to 1,000 tons of plant matter per hectare, and sometimes more. Its evergreen trees are runners-up for being the world's longest-lived and largest. In fact, needled trees are so successful here that they seem to crowd out other plants: Communities west of the Cascades are rather poor in other species.

## MOUNTAIN FORESTS

As the Cascades climb above about 1,800 to 3,200 feet, Pacific silver fir (*Abies amabilis*) replaces western hemlock as climax dominant. This fir's common name comes from the silvery undersides of its needles. Like other true firs, Pacific silver fir is distinguished by the cones held upright on its upper branches. Even though the scales of the stout cones soon fall off, the candle-like spikes usually remain to help you identify the trees.

As you move higher in the mountains, the Douglas fir, western hemlock, and western redcedar growing with Pacific silver fir gradually give way to noble and then subalpine fir (*Abies procera* and *lasiocarpa*), mountain hemlock (*Tsuga mertensiana*), and yellow cedar. At subalpine heights—roughly 4,000 to 5,500 feet on the west side of the Cascades—mountain hemlock becomes the climax dominant. In drier alpine and subalpine forests east of the Cascade crest, as far as Wyoming and Montana, the common climax is subalpine fir. It may be heavily mixed with Engelmann spruce (*Picea engelmannii*), whitebark and limber pine (*Pinus albicaulis* and *flexilis*), and, on the highest sites, subalpine larch (*Larix lyallii*). Because they usually are broken by clearings, with which their lives are intertwined, the subalpine forests are discussed in the next chapter, on broken woods, clearings. and high mountains.

## FROM THE CASCADES EASTWARD

The familiar Douglas firs, western hemlocks, and western redcedars reappear as one descends the east side of the Cascades. But the forests are thinner, and increasingly mixed with trees less common in the maritime west. Pacific silver fir all but disappears. Instead, one finds grand fir (*Abies grandis*), western white pine (*Pinus monticola*) and western larch (*Larix occidentalis*). Larch stands usually can be spotted from afar: The clustered needles are pale green, turning bright yellow in autumn before they fall. Like its relative, subalpine larch, this cone bearer is not evergreen.

Lodgepole pine (*Pinus contorta latifolia*), whose twisted close relative, shore pine (*Pinus contorta contorta*), forms salt-sculpted groves facing coastal gales, here grows slim and straight. Farther east, in Idaho, Montana, and Wyoming, it dominates entire forests. Walking in them, it is easy to imagine the Indians who traveled from the Great Plains, seeking these trees for tipi and travois poles.

Most common of all, from the lower forests of the Eastern Cascades, eastward, red-trunked ponderosa pines (*Pinus ponderosa*) spread their branches wide above park-like grassy glades.

As wildflower lovers will notice, the undergrowth in dry interior forests often is more varied than that in the damp country west of the Cascades. Sunny openings between trees leave room for more species, and for plants of different heights.

Wildflowers are brighter, too. They must attract color-sensitive pollinators like bees and butterflies. Many common flowers of the open woods have shapes and colors particularly attractive to their pollinators: for example, red and yellow columbines (*Aquilegia* spp.) with their long tubes, attractive to butterflies and hummingbirds; and penstemon *(Penstemon* spp.) with its lipped "bee platform." Dark lines, some visible to us and some visible only in ultraviolet light, which bees can see, point to the nectar chambers of many bee-pollinated flowers.

**Figure 4-4.** The lower lips of penstemon flowers serve as "landing platforms" for bees.

By contrast, many of the flowers of shady forests are white, with widespread petals and short stamens. They often depend on beetles and ants for propagation. Western trillium (*Trillium ovatum*) even has a small, oil-rich projection that attracts ants to carry its seed away, perhaps to a new and fertile home.

Instead of ferns and mosses, branches and rocks in dry woods are likely to be decorated with gray or yellow lichens. Mosses and ferns, ancient land plants, retain an affinity with their ancestors: At some stage, they depend on water to unite egg and sperm. This is one reason why mosses and ferns flourish so well in moist areas—although some of them are outstandingly adapted to dryness.

Woods east of the Cascades are are noisier as well as brighter. More levels and a greater variety of plants—medium-sized trees, brush, and clearings, as well as towering cone-bearers—provide homes and feeding sites for a greater variety of birds and mammals. Wildlife often is easier to spot in these open forests, and the animals, even members of the same or similar species, are often lighter in color. Animal species as different as Townsend chipmunks (*Eutamias townsendi*) and panthers (*Felis concolor*), for example, tend to be rusty brown and darker in the shady forests west of the Cascade Crest. They are lighter and more yellow-brown or grayish in the more open country eastward. The difference may help with camouflage or heat regulation: Lighter colored animals, for example, would reflect more heat and stay cooler in hot summers.

In the hottest, driest forests of the Northwest, the only trees are stubby, shrubby junipers. In Oregon, southeast Washington, and the dry San Juan Islands, these are mostly Western juniper (*Juniperus occidentalis*), in Idaho and farther eastward, they are mostly Rocky Mountain juniper (*J. scopulorum*) or Utah juniper (*J. osteospermum*). All have pungent, scale-like leaves pressed close to the twigs, and blueish "berries" actually composed of tiny, closely pressed scales.

A striking exception to this general west-to-east description is southwest Oregon. This mountainous region, a botanist's paradise, has its own rich and distinctive forest communities. A quarter of Oregon's rare and endangered plants are found in this Klamath-Siskyou area (14 percent of them in the valley of the Illinois River, an official Wild and Scenic River that is tributary to the Rogue). One of these rarities, *Kalmiopsis leachiana,* a small shrub with beautiful pink flowers in spring, even has a wilderness area named for it.

One reason for the unusual plant life of Southwest Oregon is that Northwest and California climates and plant communities meet and mingle here. The terrain provides a striking variety of conditions for the two groups—from coastal fog belt to parched interior slopes and valleys, scrubby with manzanita. (The Coast Range is broader and higher here than farther north, increasing the rain-shadow effect.)

**Figure 4-5.** The Illinois River and nearby Klamath
Mountains. Many of Oregon's rare and endangered
plants are found in this area, with its varied terrain and
unusual soils.

Coast redwoods (*Sequoia sempervirens*), the giants that replace Sitka
spruce in California's coastal fogbelt, reach about nine miles into Oregon.
Other characteristic California trees reach their northern limits farther
inland: incense cedar, Shasta red fir (*Abies magnifica shastensis*), white fir
(*Abies concolor*), Jeffrey pine (*Pinus jeffreyi*), and sugar pine (*P.
lambertiana*)—the largest of all pines, with 16-inch cones to match.

Southwestern Oregon also has distinctive plants because of its unusual
conditions—in particular, the largest outcropping of serpentine rock in the
nation. The Klamath-Siskyou Mountain area is the only home of two
"weeping" evergreens, Port Orford cedar and the rare Brewer spruce (*Picea
breweriana*). Once widespread, they seem to be confined to the serpentine
soils here by their inability to compete with other trees where conditions are
better. More than a dozen wildflowers also grow only on the area's serpentine

soils, relics of the deep ocean. Among them are a distinctive wild iris (*Iris bracteata*) and a rare and endangered furry-throated mariposa lily (*Calochortus howelli*).

## THE NORTHWEST'S BROAD-LEAVED TREES

In the Pacific Northwest, trees with leaves rather than needles generally fill specialized niches among the evergreen giants.

Several are trees of the "understory," growing in the shade of larger evergreens. One of these is cascara (*Rhamnus purshiana*), a small tree of shady, moist areas west of the Cascades, still sought for its laxative bark. Another is Pacific dogwood, whose "blooms"—actually four to six creamy bracts surrounding the tiny green flowers—shine in spring shade. In fall, some evergreen forests get their few touches of scarlet from dogwoods and two other "understory" trees—drooping, shrubby vine maple (*Acer circinatum*) west of the Cascades and the similar, small Douglas maple (*Acer glabrum*) that largely replaces it farther east.

Bigleaf maple and Oregon ash are mainly trees of swamps and river floodplains. They are among the few big, spreading shade trees native to the region. Most trees of the Northwest grow up rather than out, as if reaching for a bit of sunlight between columnar evergreens. (Sugar maples, *Acer saccharum*, barely cross the continental divide into Idaho. The sap of the less hardy bigleafs also can be boiled to produce sugar, but few people take the trouble.)

The Northwest's wild fruit trees also are mainly trees of damps. Bottomland thickets of Pacific crabapple (*Pyrus fusca*) are thorny, but delicate with pale apple blossoms in early spring. In fall they are bright with scarlet leaves and red and yellow fruit.

Many streamsides are snowy in spring—in southern Oregon with wild plums (*Prunus subcordata*), and in dry country with hawthorns (*Crataegus douglasii* and *columbiana*), serviceberry (*Amelanchier* spp.), bitter cherry (*Prunus emarginata*), and choke cherry (*Prunus virginiana*). Joined by two other white-flowering plants, mock orange (*Philadelphus lewisii*) and clambering wild clematis (*Clematis lingusticifolia*), these shrubs and small trees follow rocky stream canyons out of the pine woods and into grass and sage.

Another waterside group is made up of quick-growing but short-lived pioneer trees: black cottonwood (*Populus trichocarpa*), trembling aspen (*Populus tremuloides*); paper, brown, and water birches (*Betula papyrifera, occidentalis*, and *fontinalis*); red alder west of the Cascades; white and

**Figure 4-6.** Maples and other flowering trees give northwestern streamsides a snowy look in spring (Scatter Creek, Washington).

mountain alders (*Alnus rhombifolia* and *tenuifolia*) in the interior; and the many species of Northwest willows (*Salix* spp.). These trees' only "permanent" homes seem to be shifting stream banks and bars. Not surprisingly, they are all favored foods of beavers.

Like the cone-bearing trees they grow with, the alders, cottonwoods, aspens, birches, and willows are largely pollinated by the wind. Their catkin blossoms—for example, furry pussy willows and the red-plush tassels of cottonwood—are attractive. But other attributes of these trees are more striking. In winter you notice their bark: bright red and yellow willow twigs; white aspen trunks with black "horseshoe prints"; creamy or bronze red-twigged birches. The sticky balsam in cottonwoods' resinous buds sweetens spring and summer air. Used as a salve, it must have been Indians' and settlers' best-smelling medicine—no wonder pioneers called the tree "balm."

These trees' leaves, too, are striking: cottonwoods' dark and shining, silvery underneath, old gold in fall; aspens' pale, turning bright clear yellow in autumn, and always shaking because the petioles ("stems" of the leaves) hold them perpendicular to the wind.

Dryness as well as dampness provides niches for broadleaved trees. Dry or very well-drained areas on both sides of the Cascades have fingers of the chaparral community typical of California. The name is from a Spanish word for "brush" that also gave rise to "chaps," tough leather leggings that cowboys wore to get through the all-but-impassible tangles.

These trees and shrubs, with their tough, usually evergreen leaves and twisted trunks and branches, are best represented in the dry interior slopes of southwestern Oregon. Here, predominantly California scrub oaks (*Quercus kelloggii* and *chrysolepsis*) and tan oaks (*Lithocarpus densiflora*) mingle with ceanothus (*Ceanothus* spp.) and manzanitas (*Arcostaphylos* spp.) found on dry slopes throughout the Northwest. Pale barked, gnarled Garry or Oregon white oaks (*Quercus garryana*) also grow farther north. On dry, well-drained soil on both sides of the southern and central Cascades, their acorns support colonies of big, fluffy-tailed Western gray squirrels (*Sciurus griseus*). Unfortunately they also are often accompanied by poison oak (*Toxicodendron diversiloba*).

In near-desert conditions, curlleaf mountain mahogany (*Cercocarpus ledifolius*) becomes a dark, twisted little tree, fluffy from the little corkscrew plumes attached to its seeds.

Two of the loveliest broad-leaved evergreen trees seem to have been widespread until the hot, dry interval after the Ice Age. Then they became refugees, surviving only in the clement coastal strip of the Pacific Northwest.

Oregon myrtle is called California laurel, or bay across the state line. Indeed, it seems to live a double life in its confined home, from Southern Oregon through Northern California. In Oregon, the beautifully grained wood is carved, turned, and polished to support a thriving tourist industry. In California, attention goes to the tree's dense, fragrant foliage, a stronger substitute for the bay sold in spice jars.

**Figure 4-7.** A madrona tree clings to bluffs overlooking Puget Sound, Washington. The glossy-leaved evergreen trees with bright orange bark grow only in the Northwest.

More beautiful still is madrona. Its big, glossy leaves and bright orange bark, peeling in sheets to expose new, yellow-green skin in spring, decorate coastal bluffs and other well drained spots from British Columbia southward.

# MUTUAL AID

Like other plant communities, Pacific Northwest forests help build their own environment. For example, the trees and their epiphytes—ferns and mosses—trap moisture that helps keep the air around them moist and mild.

The trees' own evergreen needles are an important influence on the forests. A steady rain of resinous, slow-decaying needles builds a thick duff that is quickly kindled. This encourages the fires that are so much a part of natural forests.

Most cone-bearers grow best in acid soil. When evergreen needles do decay, they supply acids that promote leaching, helping to keep the soil acid. Needles also favor the mosses, liverworts, clubmosses, and lichens that grow so lavishly beneath the Northwest's trees: In deciduous forests, autumn's heavy leaf fall could smother these delicate evergreens.

Mighty as the needle-leaved trees are, they are surprisingly weak in some ways. Now and then you come across a mighty, fallen trunk, rocks still grasped in its surprisingly small claw of roots. Although some, like ponderosa pine, have deep tap roots, most Pacific Northwest conifers have shallow root systems, adapted to the thin soils covering mountain rocks. Such trees depend on each other for protection from the wind. Thinned out, they are endangered even by the few windstorms of the Northwest.

The giant evergreens also are surprisingly dependent on tiny plants that seem to huddle at their feet—the mushrooms. Weak as they seem, these morsels sought by mushroom hunters when autumn rain breaks summer's drought are among the most powerful forces in the forest. Their hygroscopic pressure can break asphalt. They can go months without moisture. They carry on their own wars—such common types as bright *Russula* spp., *Sullius*, and honey mushrooms (*Armillarea mellea*) have chemicals that inhibit other mushrooms' growth.

The often bright-colored, earthily fragrant mushrooms we see are only the short-lived "fruits," that release spores and wither or turn to slime in a few days. The hyphae, tiny tubes that are the real plant, worm through rotting wood, turning trapped nutrients back into concentrated food for new plants. This is a chief reason why young trees often flourish best on "nurse logs," the softened, powdery remains of their ancestors. You can see such nurselings in rows of small trees on fallen logs, or with roots arched over a hollow where the decayed tree once lay.

**Figure 4-8.** This hemlock was "nursed" by a decaying old Douglas fir log.

Mushrooms' work for the forest does not stop there. Fungal tubes called *mycorrhizae* encase and sometimes enter roots of other plants, helping them take up nutrients and moisture, and protecting them against harmful fungi. Forest trees would not grow as well without mycorrhizae. This aid, however, is not limited to trees. Members of the heath family, including the many huckleberries and blueberries of Northwest mountains, tend to be heavily mycorrhizal. Among plants that cannot synthesize enough food to survive without help from the proper fungi are orchids, including the delicate and fragrant calypso and lady's slipper orchids of the Northwest (*Cytherea bulbosa* and *Cypripedium montanum*). Also dependent on fungi are the strange sapprobes that live on dead matter and never become green: ghostly looking Indian pipe, coral root, and pine drops (*Monotropa uniflora*, *Corallorhiza* spp., and *Pterospora andromedea*).

**Figure 4-9.** Puffballs (above)—common edible mushrooms—and Indian pipe (left), one of the ghostly plants nourished by fungi and forest decay.

# READING
# THE UNDERGROWTH

Once you know the common Pacific Northwest trees and their usual habitats, undergrowth can tell you still more about local conditions.

Tough-leaved sword fern and evergreen shrubs like Oregon grape (*Mahonia* or *Berberis* spp.), salal (*Gaultheria shallon*), and evergreen huckleberry (*Vaccinium ovatum*) for example, usually indicate dryer, more rugged conditions than do lady fern (*Athyrium felix-femina*), mosses, or red huckleberry (*Vaccinium parvifolium*), all of which have pale, delicate leaves. Tough leaves can conserve moisture. And since evergreen leaves need not be "rebuilt" each year, they demand less nutrients from the earth.

Some shrubs are characteristic of damp places. Among them are hardhack (*Spirea douglasii*), its pink plumes of spring changing to seed husks the rest of the year; and salmonberry (*Rubus spectabilis*), with yellowish bark in winter, early magenta flowers that attract hummingbirds, and salmon-colored, rather insipid raspberry-like fruits. East of the Cascades, red-osier dogwood (*Cornus stolonifera*), with red bark and white berries; and shreddy-stemmed ninebark (*Physocarpus capitatus*) are among the common shrubs of creeksides and other damp spots.

Among shrubs typical of dryer woods are the very common snowberry (*Symphoricarpos* spp.), with waxy white berries; pink flowered wild Nootka rose (*Rosa nutkana*), and ocean spray (*Holodiscus discolor*), with showy white plumes of flowers. In fall, the most noticeable shrub of dry slopes is sumac (*Rhus glabra*), with bright red plumes of divided leaves and spires of red berries. (Some use the spires to make a tart "Indian lemonade.") Several evergreens characteristic of dry spots are northern extensions of the California chapparal community: Low, sprawling kinnikinnick (*Arcostaphylos uva-ursi*), its small, tough leaves an ingredient of Indian smoking mixtures; white-flowered snowbrush (*Ceanothus velutinus*), also used in smoking; and the related deer brush (*Ceanothus integerrimus*), whose small clusters of fragrant blue flowers give it the name of mountain lilac.

Other bushes are typical of higher elevations—above about 3,000 feet. Somewhat similar to sumac is mountain ash (*Sorbus sitchensis* or *occidentalis*), whose showy clusters of red berries stay on the branch tips long after the leaflets are gone. (These berries are barely usable for jelly making.) Hikers are likely to be confused as well as frustrated by tangles of white rhododendron (*Rhododendron albiflorum*), false azalea (*Menziesia ferruginea*), which looks like rhododendron but has a small copper-colored flower; and copper bush (*Cladothamnus pyrolaeflorus*), which in turn looks like false azalea. Another thing these shrubs have in common is limber limbs that bend rather than break under the high mountains' heavy snow. They share this characteristic with Sitka alder (*Alnus sinuata*), a shrubby tree typical of the same altitudes.

# IN THE SHADE

Two characteristics of Northwest forests—shade and fire—have demanded striking adaptations of native plants.

If you added up the total surface area of all the leaves and needles in a shady, damp Western hemlock forest, you would find it had about four times the total area of leaves as, say, a sunny, dry juniper grove. Reduced leaf area is plants' chief means of conserving water: Plants with less leaf area will lose less water through evaporation and gas exchange as they "breathe" through their leaves.

Where water is plentiful, plants can spread their leaves wide. In shade, there is extra advantage in doing so: Plants with broad leaves will catch the available sunlight, perhaps keeping it from competitors beneath them. So in shady forests you find plants with broad leaves spread flat: small ones like queen's cup (*Clintonia uniflora*), bunchberry (*Cornus canadensis*), western trillium (*Trillium ovatum*), and Oregon oxalis (*Oxalis oregana*); and large ones like devil's club (*Oplopanax horridum*), thorny enemy of those who would travel cross-country in damp Northwest woods.

**Figure 4-10.** In shady forests, the broad leaves of devil's club hide stems bristling with thorns.

# FIRE IN FORESTS

Fire has always been a part of Northwest forests. Particularly in the dry country east of the Cascades, summer lightning storms light the dry tinder on the forest floor. Indians set fires to make hunting easier and keep trees from taking over berry fields. Tree rings and old scars show that fires rolled through many dry forests about every 10 to 25 years.

Many of these fires, though, burned slowly through the undergrowth. They seldom turned big trees to torches, or disturbed cool, moist duff protecting roots and seeds. Animals could walk away from such fires, pass through them in the many unburned gaps, or hide in burrows until the flames had gone. Far from being disasters, such fires consumed the litter that would otherwise eventually kindle a holocaust. They opened clearings and burned back shrubs to browse height, helping animals eat. Forests almost everywhere east of the Cascade Crest adapted to life with fire.

Among the conifers, for example, the four trees that pioneer best on cleared land all are adapted to propagate themselves after fire. Old Douglas firs, western larches, and ponderosa pines have thick, deeply furrowed plates of bark. They insulate the cambium—the spongy growing tissue beneath them—against all but the worst conflagrations. Young, thin-barked trees perish, but a few matriarchs survive to reseed a new generation.

Lodgepole pine, the hardy pioneer that first braved much of the Northwest after the Ice Age, has thin bark at any age. Thus, single trees cannot survive fires. But if you look at the branches, you will see that they carry tightly closed cones in any year and all seasons. Some of these lodgepole cones are serotinous—that is, they open, release their seed, and germinate offspring only after being exposed to extreme heat, such as that from fire or from dark, bare earth absorbing intense sunshine. The tree killed by fire thus gets a better chance that its offspring will survive.

Some other characteristic plants of the dry forests also have serotinous seed—among them, several kinds of *Ceanothus*, or mountain lilacs. As the shrubs also have nitrogen-fixing bacteria on their roots, they are well prepared for the life they often choose in wasted places.

Similarly, fire stimulates flowering in pine grass (*Calamagrostis rubescens*), the common carpet in flowery ponderosa-pine "parklands."

Many familiar plants share an ability to resprout from special buds on roots or rhizomes. These phoenixes include the pioneering hardwoods—willows, birches, cottonwoods, and aspens. They also include many of the common shrubs of dry, open forests and stream canyons: snowberry with its white berries, white spirea (*Spirea betulifolia*), fragrant *Amelanchier*; and, unfortunately, poison oak. Other root-sprouters include chaparral shrubs—including-several species of manzanita and ceanothus—and some plants of deeper woods, including Rocky Mountain maple, the familiar pioneers bracken fern and thimbleberry, and two common huckleberries that all but carpet inland forests (*Vaccinium globulare* and *membranaceum*).

The coming of civilization doubly upset the balance between fire and life. For about 100 years, from the coming of the trappers on, fires set carelessly or deliberately wrought vast destruction. Fires were set to clear land, drive game, burn logging waste, or simply for cooking or warmth. Many got out of control, destroying millions of acres. Sparks from railroad steam engines kindled conflagrations along the tracks. Such fires contributed to avalanches like the Wellington Station disaster: the 1910 avalanche that killed 96 people near Stevens Pass, Washington, hurtled down slopes that had been burned bare of trees that might have held the snow.

That same year saw a dry summer. Thousands of small fires set by lightning and loggers smoldered in moss and undergrowth. On the night of August 20, a gale and the flames' own heat whipped these scattered hotspots into a hurricane of flame. It roared across the Idaho panhandle, into Eastern Washington and Montana. At least 85 people died, and more than three million acres burned.

The 1910 fires, disastrous in the Midwest as well, shocked the nation into action. Fire control improved steadily from then on. Although fire continues to needlessly destroy millions of dollars worth of timber, Northwest forests now suffer from a new set of problems—the result of suppressing the natural, slow fires once so common.

Part of the beauty of mountains near the continental divide—in places like Jackson Hole, Wyoming—is the forests of aspens, with their pale bark and trembling leaves. Few visitors see the slim, graceful trees for what they are—hardy but short-lived pioneers that sprang up after the great fires of the late 19th century. The trees are now in their dotage. As the aspens reach the age when their cones no longer sprout vigorously—about 80 to 100 years—they are fast being replaced by evergreens. The landscape we think of as "natural" may be very different within our own generation.

With fire suppression, savannahs of juniper have spread far into country that once was grass and sage. Junipers mean homes and food for many animals, from deer to deer mice. Even coyotes eat their blue "berries" in hungry times. Ranchers in parts of Idaho and Oregon, though, are unhappy. The evergreen trees can shade out grazing plants or steal precious moisture before grass can sprout in spring.

With fire suppressed, shrubs and trees are taking over many of the mountain berry fields where Indians for centuries held their summer gatherings.

Aging lodgepole-pine forests are becoming vulnerable to destructive insect plagues. Ponderosa pines, instead of growing scattered in grassy, park-like clearings, sprout so thickly that they stalemate one another's growth.

**Figure 4-11.** In parts of the Northwest, forests of white-barked aspens like these are growing "senile."

Most seriously, unburned litter piles up on the dry forest floor, turning forests into tinderboxes. When a fire does start, it is likely not to smolder through the brush, but to blaze to the treetops and cause disaster.

As a result, fire is being brought back to the forest. Never exiled from some Indian and range lands, it is being tried as a way to restore berry fields and wildlife browse. In the early 1970s, most of the Northwest's national parks and wilderness areas began letting lightning fires burn in remote areas where they did not threaten lives or property. Today's visitors to wilderness thus may again experience what early trappers and explorers described—smoky air, a gray pall hiding the mountains; an angry red glow on the horizon at night. If it happens to you, remember—it may spoil the view, but it is part of nature.

## ANIMALS AND
## THE LIFE CYCLE OF A TREE

Deep forests are not the best places for animal watching. Species are more varied in more varied habitats. Birds are hidden in high treetops. Carnivores hunt by night and sleep hidden in dens by day. You can see the cycle of forest life, though, if you understand the way animals use the forest.

Most animals in Pacific Northwest forests depend on the evergreen trees around them. Birds, mammals, and cold-blooded creatures use the trees from the beginning of their lives until long after their deaths.

The seeds in cones are a rich, and storable, source of fat and protein. In some forests more than 95 percent of these seeds are eaten—most by animals whose lives depend on them. Forest populations of deer mice (*Peromyscus maniculatus*), for example, soar after good cone years and plunge after bad ones. The bright colored red and rarer white crossbills, characteristic birds of dense evergreen forests, have been literally shaped by the cones. Their scissor-like bills, the top half crossed over the lower half, are adapted for prying woody cone scales apart. In addition, these birds have no fixed breeding season. They mate the raise young when and where cones are abundant.

Another bird physically adapted to use evergreen seeds is the Clark's nutcracker of subalpine forests. These noisy, crow-sized gray birds have a special pouch beneath their tongues. They use it to carry cone seeds, which they cache in tree hollows and other crevices. The stores, shared among their flocks, let Clark's nutcrackers come back to the high mountains earlier in spring than other birds.

**Figure 4-12.** Clark's nutcracker can return to high mountains early because of the cone seeds it cached the previous fall.

In fall, the usually quiet deep evergreen woods become noisy, as chipmunks and the small native tree squirrels scold, trill, and chase one another. They are competing for the seeds that mean survival.

The chipmunks usually are dark-colored Townsend's chipmunks, *Eutamias townsendii*, west of the Cascades: *Eutamias amoenus*, lighter yellow-pine chipmunks, in drier interior forests; or again darker red-tailed chipmunks, *Eutamias rificaudis*, in moist forests of the Idaho panhandle and Montana. They harvest near and on the ground, scold bird-like from bushes, and hide their stores in underground burrows. There they doze through cold periods, but do not truly hibernate.

The tree squirrels usually are dark brown, cinnamon-bellied Douglas' squirrels, *Tamiasciurus douglasi*, in the Cascades: and white-bellied red squirrels, *Tamiasciurus hudsonicus*, in the Rockies. They scold, trill, and chase one another in the tall evergreens, defending territories of the cone-bearing trees they depend on. Their sharp teeth nip off cones that come crashing 150 feet through branches. Many of these are cached for winter in small holes and hollows, along with dried mushrooms and other finds. Often, you can spot their favorite feeding trees by little heaps of cone spines and torn-off scales. Look up, and you may see the squirrel, turning and nibbling a cone rather as if it were an ear of corn.

Despite all this predation, seeds survive to sprout. Sometimes they sprout because an animal stored and forgot them in some moist, rich, protected, or sunny place. Thus, the animals that eat seed farm them as well.

The seedling and the young tree, for as long as a human generation or two, are morsels to more animals. Pocket gophers eat roots and shoots. Deer, elk, grouse, and snowshoe hares nibble its leaves and branches, particularly in winter when they cannot find tenderer fare. Deer mice, porcupines, and bears strip and girdle its tender bark to get the sweet sap and cambium within. Black bears can be quite particular: they seem to prefer young silver and Douglas firs west of the Cascades, young lodgepole pines east of them, and young alpine firs in the high mountains.

Bark also carries other animal signs: Elk wear bark from trees by rubbing their antlers against trunks. From the size of tooth marks on branches, you sometimes can guess whether feeding was done by very small animals such as voles; somewhat larger ones such as squirrels, snowshoe hares (*Lepus americanus*), or porcupines (*Erithizon dorsatum*); by beavers; or by bears.

Such treatment takes a toll on young forests. But some thinning is beneficial. And parents that normally live 400 years or more do not need many offspring to replace themselves. As surviving conifers reach young adulthood, they begin to supply the forest and its animals with nourishing seeds and their own seedlings. As their green crowns rise higher, above long, straight trunks, they take another part in animals' lives. They become homes and feeding perches.

**Figure 4-13.** Porcupines are among the animals that relish the sap and cambium beneath tough bark.

Many birds specialize in specific levels as well as specific types of trees. Hammond's flycatcher, for example, loops out from high evergreen branches to catch insects. The dusky flycatcher, which looks and sounds almost the same, prefers deciduous low trees and brush. Similarly, Townsend's and hermit warblers forage and nest in evergreen treetops. Orange-crowned warblers are most common in brush under deciduous trees. Yellow warblers may hunt high up in those same trees. By specializing, the different species avoid too much competition for the same limited resource.

**Figure 4-14.** The Steller's jay is a familiar, noisy scolder in evergreen forests.

Among the characteristic birds that roost and nest in trees of damp evergreen forests are deep-voiced, cooing band-tailed pigeons; dark-blue, scolding Steller's jays; and varied thrushes, whose orange wing bars provide better camouflage than the red breast of their cousins, the robins. This thrush's long, single plaintive notes are among the loveliest of bird songs.

In more open pine forests, you are more likely to find the flycatching western wood pewee, gray jays (aptly called camp robbers), and the handsome, yellow and black pine grosbeak.

The squirrels that eat cone seeds also nest in the conifers. Branches become their highways, lookouts, resting and feeding places. Porcupines, lumbering rodents that eat bark, catkins, and leaves mostly by night, apparently do not fully trust their protecting quills. They usually spend their days high in trees or hidden in rocky dens.

Even more specialized is the red tree mouse (*Phenacomys longicaudis*) of western Oregon. Generations of these little mice may never leave a single tree, usually a Douglas fir. They build a large nest of needles and twigs in branches, and eat needles and tender bark.

Hunters have become adapted to the conifers. The northern flying squirrel (*Glaucomys sabrinus*) dens in hollow trees by day and glides after insects at night. Martens and fishers, long-bodied, short-legged, pointy-nosed members of the weasel family, make dens in hollow trees and range easily from limb to limb. Their long, bushy tails, like those of the squirrels they hunt, help them balance when they leap. (Martens, *Martes americana*, are a little more than two feet long, and are brownish with an orange throat patch. Fishers, *Martes pennanti*, are about three feet long, almost black, with white throats. Fishers are rare, and neither species is often seen, as they hunt mostly in dim light or darkness.)

Bark, limbs, and twigs are home to dozens of species of insects—leaf nibblers, sap suckers, a few borers in bark and wood. These are food to a guild of bird species whose members mostly specialize in one or two types of feeding. In fall, for example, when birds have abandoned their nesting territories and are joined in loose flocks, you may see a brown creeper working its way in spirals up a trunk. In the same tree, a nuthatch calls nasally as it hangs, sometimes upside-down, on limbs. Meanwhile, groups of bushtits, kinglets, and chickadees forage in the crown. These flocks of mixed species may help each other by startling insects, which are caught when they move. Or flock members may simply follow birds that find food, getting in on the goodies.

As a tree becomes old or weak, its role in animal life changes again. Often, the insects that lived more or less harmlessly on its sap, wood, and needles depart. New and predatory species bore deep into the wood, starting its reconversion to soil while the tree still lives. Others shred the sap-carrying tissue, bore powdery holes in the wood, and loosen the plates of bark. Even when drought, mistletoe, or some other factor causes the tree's "illness," the insects that attack it when it is weakened often cause its death.

The remaining snag can be as essential to the forest as when it was alive. After all, forests by definition have plenty of trees. But snags can be scarce, particularly in the young forests planted or grown up after clear-cut logging, with trees all sprouted at about the same time. In terms of animal life, such monotonous forests are the most sterile in the Northwest.

Dead and dying snags are homes to a succession of animals that often starts when one of the Northwest's many woodpeckers hammers through still-tough bark to the tree's rotting interior. Like other birds, woodpecker species specialize in specific habitats. In an old-growth forest, the hole may be drilled by a pileated woodpecker—the big, loud-drumming, crested "Woody woodpecker." In pine forests the excavator might be a white-headed woodpecker. Instead of a crest, this bird with its rattling cry has a skull-like white head contrasting with its black plumage. In higher mountains you are more likely to see one of the two three-toed woodpeckers (black-backed or northern), with yellow crowns and sides barred black and white.

The cavity that first is home to a woodpecker often is used later by an amazing variety of animals. Larger holes, for example, may be taken over by tree squirrels or flying squirrels. These holes also serve tree-nesting ducks such as mergansers, wood ducks, and goldeneyes; hawks such as the American kestrel; and owls including screech owls and saw-whet, pygmy, and northern spotted owls. Smaller holes become nests for chickadees, nuthatches, brown creepers, hairy and downy woodpeckers, and western bluebirds.

**Figure 4-15.** A white-headed woodpecker—one of the excavators whose holes are recycled by other animals.

**Figure 4-16.** Wood ducks (the showy male is below) are among the unexpected hole-nesting birds of Northwest forests. (Photo taken at Northwest Trek, Eatonville, Washington).

Vaux' swifts nest in hollow, burned-out tree trunks (and in abandoned chimneys). Bats roost under loosened plates of bark, coming out at dusk to flutter and glide after insects that they locate by echos. Hawks, including eagles, often rest their stick platforms on the bare branches of the highest snags.

Hollow limbs are favorite dens of raccoons. Among the larger animals using rotted-out hollows are martens and fishers, as already mentioned; foxes (*Vulpes vulpes*), bobcats and lynx (*Lynx rufus* and *L. canadensis*), and black bears seeking winter dens, where they sleep and give birth to young. (All these animals also den in caves and crevices.)

Even long after it finally crashes to earth, the rotting snag remains vital to forest life. Fallen trees are lookouts and highways for small animals, such as chipmunks and flying squirrels. They are platforms for rituals, like the strutting and "drumming" of male spruce and ruffed grouse in spring.

Such logs, softened and powdery inside, are homes for small hunters like weasels (*Mustela erminea* and *frenata*) and shrews (*Sorex* spp.). Both need protection: Weasels, whose long bodies are specialized to hunt burrowing animals, cannot curl themselves into a tight ball to conserve heat. Shrews' small bodies lose heat quickly; they are fierce partly because they must eat so often to survive.

Damp, rotten wood protects the permeable skins of amphibious frogs and salamanders from drying. Among those that hide beneath logs are the common Pacific tree frog (*Hyla regilla*), which actually spends much of its time on the ground; and the Pacific giant salamander (*Dicamptodon ensatus*), at up to 13 1/2 inches the largest living land salamander in the world.

The fall of a forest giant may open a small clearing. There, sunlight, the nutrients stored in the wood, and nitrogen fixed by bacteria that cause decay help new and varied plants to sprout and grow. These in turn are food and homes for animals. Such are the fallen tree's last gifts to the cycle of forest life.

## DOING IT YOURSELF

Visit distinctive forest communities. National parks and many national forests have short nature trails with clear explanatory signs, as well as long wilderness hikes. Most famous are the rain forests of Olympic National Park in Washington.

Many state parks also have interesting and educational nature trails. For example, Federation Forest State Park, on the White River and Highway 410 near Washington's Mount Rainier, has a small museum explaining western Washington ecology and well-marked short walks. On one, you can see ruts made by pioneer wagons coming across the Cascades.

Use a field guide to get to know the native trees of your area and their preferred habitats. It's hard to memorize the length and number of needles of all the pines in the Pacific Northwest, for example. But learning the descriptions of pines in any one area is easy.

**Figure 4-17.** The silky tails of its seeds, carried on the wind, help fireweed pioneer quickly in a clearing.

Try to figure out how plants function even when you don't know their names. Do the leaves indicate that the plant could survive drought? Does the shape of the flower tell you anything about how the plant is pollinated? Is this plant likely to do better in bright sunshine or in shade? How are its seeds likely to be spread—on the wind? In animals' fur, feathers, stomachs? Maple seeds, for example, have wings that catch the wind and whirl them like helicopters. Mistletoe seeds shoot out of pressurized capsules with a "pop"—a common sound in late-summer woods. They also have a sticky coating that will cling to animals, birds, or branches.

Notice which plants commonly grow together in your area. Recognizing such groupings makes you feel at home in new places: You have seen these old friends before, and know what they tell you about conditions around you.

Crush a leaf or a bit of bark to get to know interesting smells. Among surprises are pungent wild currants and gooseberries (*Ribes* spp.); Indian plum; wild ginger (*Asarum caudatum*); mints (*Monardella, Agastache, Mentha spp.*); wild onions (*Allium* spp.); vanilla leaf (*Achlys triphylla*); yarrow (*Achillea* spp.), balsamroots (*Balsamorhiza* spp.), sages (*Artemesia* spp.), Oregon myrtle, cottonwood buds, and of course evergreen needles. (Don't try this unless you can recognize stinging nettle and poison oak.)

Look at the woods (or any wild area) as Indians would have, searching for food, medicinal plants, and useful raw materials. Here are some they used:

Alder and bigleaf maple—wood used for bowls, clubs, and small implements. Alder bark used as dye; maple leaves used as wrapping.

Berries—huckleberries (*Vaccinium* spp.), cranberries (*Vaccinium oxycoccus*), salmonberry (*Rubus spectabilis*), raspberry (*Rubus idaeus*), blackcaps (*Rubus leucodermis*), thimbleberry, salal, *Amelanchier*, wild strawberry (*Frageria* spp.), and wild currants and gooseberries were among those eaten fresh or dried. Blackberry and salmonberry shoots were used as relish; huckleberry leaves made a kind of tea.

Bitter cherry (*Prunus emarginata*)—bark used in baskets and twine.

Bracken fern and wood fern (*Dryopteris dilatata*)—roots roasted as food (Bracken also has delicious young shoots, but mature leaves can be poisonous).

Fireweed—seed down mixed with duck down to make blankets. Inner stems and young leaves are edible.

Ginger, wild—fleshy roots and stems used as seasoning.

Hazel (*Corylus cornuta*)—nuts gathered and eaten raw; flexible limbs used as rope and to make snowshoes.

Horsetails (*Equisetum* spp.)—roots used in baskets: young stems eaten raw; used for scouring, as stems contain silica.

Kinnikinnick—ingredient in Indian smoking mixture: berries used in pemmican.

**Figure 4-18.** Red alders along the Snoqualmie River, Washington, in winter. Indians used the wood to make bowls, spoons, and similar small implements.

Nettle, stinging (*Urtica lyalli*)—bark spun in blankets and used to make twine. (Nettle greens are edible after being cooked—pick them with rubber gloves, however.)

Oaks (chiefly *Quercus garryana*)—acorns eaten after being cooked and soaked (not a treat for modern palates).

Oregon grape—yellow bark used as tonic and dye.

Rattlesnake plantain (*Goodyera oblongifolia*)—variegated leaves used as a love potion.

Skunk cabbage—leaves used to wrap food for steaming (Caution— these leaves contain an irritating, burning oil).

Western redcedar—wood used for houses, canoes, boxes; bark used for clothing, wrapping, diapers; roots used for twine, baskets; many other uses.

Willow: bark chewed for toothache (it contains salicylic acid, the active ingredient of aspirin). Bark and limber twigs used to make baskets and twine.

Yew and ocean spray (*Holodiscus discolor*)—used for arrows. Yew also made knife handles, wedges, and combs.

Note: If you want to eat wild foods, identify them carefully. Gather and try only a small amount the first time, for your own sake as well as the plants'. Use good judgement. There's no harm in eating common wild berries, or common, widespread edible greens such as miner's lettuce (*Montia* spp.). But don't dig or pick if the plant is at all scarce (it can be scarce even if you have found a large stand of it), or if you will spoil beauty for others. Be careful with water plants, such as cattails and watercress. They can be unsafe if grown in polluted water.

Look at snags and fallen logs, trying to imagine how animals may use them. (If you sit quietly you may see the inhabitants.) Look for burrows and dens—entrances may be hidden under logs or rocks. Don't poke around inside, though: One animal that uses burrows and holes under rocks is the skunk.

Look for tracks and other signs of forest animals, including scats (feces). Heaps of cone spines and scales and mushrooms left to dry on limbs usually mean squirrels. Clawed or gnawed bark can mean anything from deer mice to black bears—try to guess by the size of tooth or claw marks. Tracks are easiest to follow in snow. Look, too, for tunnels and signs of animals "swimming" through soft snow. Many use it for insulation and protection in winter.

Some curious animals, including winter wrens and chipmunks, come closer if you stay still and make "tsk" sounds.

Get to know bird songs and calls (records are a good way to do this) and the distinctive flight of certain groups of birds, such as woodpeckers. You then can be aware of much that is going on around you without having to stop, sit still, and watch.

# 5

# Meadows, Clearings, and Broken Country

## CLEARINGS IN LOWLANDS AND MIDDLE ALTITUDES

Brush and clearings break the Northwest's forests at all altitudes.

Many are old burned or logged spots or silted-in lakes on their way back to becoming forests again. You often can trace the ancestry of such clearings in cut or charred stumps, or by flowers typical of moist places, such as cheerful little yellow monkeyflowers (*Mimulus* spp.), waist-high clumps of blue-belled lungwort (*Mertensia* spp.), spikes of greenish ladies-tresses orchids (*Spiranthes romanzoffiana*), or poisonous hellebores (*Veratrum* spp.), which have paddle-like leaves and are tall as a man.

A tangle of bracken fern and thimbleberry probably is on its way back to forest. Other clearings, though, are more or less permanent. Such spots are too dry, too wet, or too unstable for trees.

Early explorers and settlers west of the Cascades, for example, found grassy clearings amid the maples and ashes of river floodplains. Drier prairies, golden in summer, interrupted oak and madrona groves on well-drained or rain-shadowed spots, such as the Oregon's Willamette Valley, the glacial gravels south of Puget Sound, and the San Juan Islands. (One cannot say that such clearings were entirely "natural." Indians burned many to improve hunting and gathering.)

**Figure 5-1.** The cheerful flowers of yellow mimulus brighten damp, sunny spots throughout the Northwest.

Because of development, these lowland clearings are among the "endangered habitats" of the Northwest. For example, only isolated bits of natural Willamette Valley grasslands remain, some harboring wildflowers found nowhere else.

Some of the Northwest's loveliest wild lillies grow in the dry west-side meadows: wild onions and brodeias (*Allium* and *Brodeia* spp.); pink and white fawn lillies (*Erythronium revolutum* and *oregonum*); chocolate-colored rice-root lily (*Fritillaria lanceolata*); and orange, brown-spotted wild tiger lily (*Lilium columbianum*). As is true of other plants, most of the wildflowers of these meadows also grow, or have very near relatives, east of the Cascades. But in that drier country they frequent relatively moist areas.

More easterly mountain ranges also have flood plains and other open spots along rivers. Probably the most interesting of these break not forest, but desert. The canyons of the Columbia and Snake Rivers, the two largest rivers of the Northwest, are homes to grasses and wildflowers found nowhere else, or found elsewhere only on mountaintops. Some alpine species took refuge in the Columbia Gorge during the Ice Age, and survived on shady cliffs near waterfalls. Other plants, long isolated in the moist canyons amid badlands, have had time to develop distinctive characteristics.

In the dry interior mountains, much of the lower slopes get too little moisture for continuous forests. Trees become scattered, wind along streams, or gather in copses separated by wildflower-rich parklands. Low peaks, too, are often grassy and bald. Sun and wind dry them too fast for trees to flourish.

**Figure 5-2.** Plumes of bear grass are common in dry, rocky slopes.

These areas of transition between forest and desert are among the brightest wild gardens of the Northwest. Among their common flowers are blue lupine and larkspur (*Lupinus* and *Delphinium* spp.); pink shooting star (*Dodecathon* spp.) and wild geranium (*Geranium viscosissimum*); and yellow arnica (*Arnica* spp.), and wild parsley (*Lomatium* spp.). Some of the most striking flowers are partial parasites, drawing some of their nourishment by tapping the roots of others. These are red Indian paintbrush (*Castilleja* spp.), the closely related owl's clover (*Orthocarpus* spp.), and spires of purplish, beaked elephant head (*Pedicularis groenlandica*).

Throughout the Northwest, very steep areas often are treeless either because their soil drains too quickly or because trees cannot gain toeholds in bare or loose rock. The most striking flower of steep, dry slopes is bear grass (*Xerophyllum tenax*), raising a foot-long plume of creamy flowers above a clump of narrow, tough leaves that Indians used in baskets.

Crevices in dry rocks may support pioneering little tufts of stonecrop (*Sedum* spp.), with yellow flowers above a low clump of fleshy, cactus-like leaves. Other pioneers in rocks, saxifrages (*Saxifraga* spp.) and wild buckwheats (*Eriogonum* spp.), also bear small flowers above basal clumps of tough leaves. Low clumps of leaves, as well as tough coatings and hairs, help protect the plants from drying. Most also have tough tap roots to help them cling.

Unexpectedly, several small ferns and their "allies," the spike mosses, are typical of dry crevices. Among them are parsley fern (*Cryptogramma crispa*)—some of its leaves parsley-like and others rolled lengthwise around spores; the similar pod fern (*Aspidotis densa* or *Cheilanthes siliquosa*); and the spike moss *Selaginella wallacei*. Its needle-like leaves turn grayish when they are dry, and the plant all but ceases to function. Supply them with water, though, and they promptly turn deep green and begin to photosynthesize again.

Members of the chaparral community, described in the chapter on forests, cover many dry, well-drained slopes. Snowbrush and kinnikinnick are the most widespread of these evergreens, with their tough leaves and twisting, reddish, limbs. Other slopes have scatterings of serviceberry, mock orange (*Philadelphus lewisii*), or mallow ninebark (*Physocarpus malvaceus*), all white-flowering and deciduous.

## CLEARINGS THAT MADE HISTORY

Openings in the forest were important to native tribes. They gathered there at wild harvest times—which became times of trade and celebration as well. Tribes still retain their rights to the huckleberries of Indian Heaven, a chain of clearings in the gentle volcanic country between Mt. Adams and Mt. St. Helens. The race track worn by ponies' hooves there is still visible.

**Figure 5-3.** The Indian race track, gathering place of tribes for centuries, with pre-eruption Mt. St. Helens in the background.

In the days of the fur trade, grassy valleys became the sites of the annual "Rendezvous," where trappers and tribes met to trade for furs, baubles, guns, and sometimes wives. Most of these big, riotous meetings were held in the drainages of the Missouri or the Colorado—most often in Wyoming's Green River Valley. Some, though, were in the Columbia drainage. The 1832 Rendezvous, for example, was at Pierre's Hole, the valley at the western foot of the Tetons, opposite Jackson's Hole (both were named for fur traders).

Maps of the Northwest record many "Camaslands" and "Camas Prairies." The star-like blue flowers mark sweetly starchy little bulbs. They were an Indian staple as important to many tribes as salmon. Stays at these moist interior meadows in spring, while the women dug, dried, roasted, and pounded camas, were a vital part of the annual cycle that took tribes to various summer camps. White settlers' encroachment on one of these flats, in southern Idaho, led to the Pacific Northwest's last major Indian uprising— the Bannock Indian war of 1878. It ranged into Oregon and Wyoming before the tribe's inevitable defeat.

## THE UPPER LIMIT OF FORESTS

At subalpine heights, snow and the long frozen winter begin to govern life. One of the most obvious signs of this, even in mid-summer, is the species of trees that grow at high altitudes. Some have a slim, elegant steeple shape that easily sheds snow—examples are subalpine fir and Engelmann spruce. Others look tough but ragged—their long, supple, irregular limbs bend but do not break under snow and ice. Three such trees are whitebark pine, Sitka alder, and, toughest of all, subalpine larch. Its pale green needles on furry young twigs turn bright yellow and drop off, leaving the tree bare in winter.

At the upper limits of their range, trees must struggle and seek one another's aid to survive. Many, perhaps most, picturesque subalpine meadows are the result of old burns. (Pioneer travelers sometimes set the resinous trees afire just to watch the show.) Trees near the upper limits of their range can require human generations, even centuries, to recover.

Other alpine tree clumps survive amid meadows because one tree shelters later seedlings from wind, or because the warmth absorbed by its trunk and branches helps melt the snow a few days earlier in spring. Soil deep and rich enough for trees also becomes scarce in the steep, rocky mountain heights. Thus, for several reasons, much subalpine forest is not continuous, but broken by rockfields and meadows.

As one goes higher, the harsh mountain winters prune more and more. Steady winds may trim a steeply slanted evergreen hedge, thick and smooth.

**Figure 5-4.** Near timberline, storms bend and twist trees, often pruning them close to the height of winter snow.

Or they may nip the "backsides" of trees and bushes bare. Buffeting storms and burdens of ice twist and break limbs, leaving irregular "candelabras," or "flagpoles"—trees whose thick base of spreading lower limbs, protected by each winter's snow, is topped by a spindly pole and a few tufts of needles.

By definition, alpine means above where trees can grow. Subalpine means the often broken forest below, with many species not found at lower altitudes. Neither word refers to a fixed height, however. The upper limit of forest growth depends on partly local conditions such as slope, soil, and exposure. Trees may grow highest on the south side of the mountain, for example, because the snow there melts earliest. Upper limits also are influenced by the size of the mountain. Big volcanos like Mt. Rainier have higher timberlines than small mountains, for example. Latitude is important: As you would expect, the North Cascades have lower timberlines than Southern Oregon. Finally, timberlines are higher in the dry interior than in the more coastal ranges. Thus the Rockies have higher timberlines than the Cascades.

Timberlines also move as climate changes and soil develops. Before the recent eruptions, Mt. St. Helens' timberline was marching up into the raw pumice fields on the volcano's slopes. Timberlines on Hurricane Ridge in the Olympics shifted upward in the warm years that led to the Dust Bowl, early in this century.

Near timberline, trees become misshapen, twisted dwarfs. Then they disappear altogether. Lush meadows and shrubby heathlands often flourish to much greater altitudes. Mosses and small plants that look like tough gray pincushions find toeholds in crevices higher still. They add their organic matter to the slowly crumbling mountain, building soil. Finally, just below perennial ice and snow, only lichens cling to the rocks. These papery gray partnerships between a fungus and an algae survive because the rock face catches what little warmth is available—and because, when even that is lacking, lichens can remain in suspended animation almost indefinitely.

## IN AND ABOVE SUBALPINE AND ALPINE MEADOWS

One reason high-mountain scenery is so interesting is that over a given area in alpine and subalpine country, plant communities are likely to differ much more sharply than in the same-sized area at lower altitudes. On the rugged heights, differences in direction of exposure, moisture, soil, slope, drainage, and stability are extreme. These differences are magnified still more by a general lack of cover. On mountaintops, wind and sun beat directly on the surface. Instead of the filtering, moderating effects of forest, mountaintops have sunscorched bare earth and whistling winds in one spot, while rocks create deep shadows and still air a few feet away.

As in other areas, you can read local conditions by studying which alpine and subalpine plants live where. Grasses and the similar sedges, for example, often do well in the coolest, wettest sites, where snow melts late. Moist but slightly warmer sites may bear more succulent mountain flowers. Western anemones (*Anemone occidentalis*) and avalanche lilies (*Erythronium montanum*) bloom with snow still at their feet. Summer replaces them with fragrant white mountain valerian (*Valeriana sitchensis*).

Where snow melts late and the ground then becomes dry, you may find heathlands of dwarf shrubs—crowberry (*Empetrum nigrum*), red and white mountain heathers (*Phyllodoce* spp. and *Cassiope mertensiana*), and the delicious alpine huckleberries (*Vaccinium* spp.), scarlet in the early mountain fall. Steep and rocky places, where soil is unstable and quickly parched, are left to tough mats and pincushion plants, like the saxifrages and wild buckwheats familiar from rocky slopes at lower altitudes.

**Figure 5-5.** Avalanche lilies are ready to bloom with snow still at their feet. As snow melts, they cover subalpine meadows like these at Spray Park, Mt. Rainier National Park, Washington.

**Figure 5-6.** The delicious blue fruits of huckleberries invite picking in high-mountain meadows.

# HIGH-MOUNTAIN ADAPTATIONS

The plants that live at subalpine and alpine heights commonly are different species from those living below them. Some, especially in the Rocky Mountains, are immigrants from the north, whose nearest kin are in regions surrounding the Arctic. Most Pacific Northwest high-mountain plants, though, seem to have developed from ancestors already within the region. They probably adapted to tough new conditions as mountains rose and the world's climate cooled toward the Ice Age. Thus lowlands and heights have different species of monkey flowers, cinquefoils (*Potentilla* spp.), and other common and widespread wildflowers. Some, like Piper's harebell (*Campanula piperi*) of Washington's Olympic Mountains, are confined to a single range and hence are rare or even endangered. These "endemics" are most common on isolated ranges—the Olympics, the Blue and Wallowa Mountains of Washington and Oregon, even Oregon's small Steens range, standing alone in the desert.

One of plants' most common high-mountain adaptations is that their roots may have five to ten times more volume than do stems and leaves above ground. The abundant roots help plants cling to the earth, of course. But more important, large roots, bulbs, or rhizomes store nutrients so that growth can start at once in spring. Thus large roots help alpine plants use all of a short growing season.

Most high-altitude plants are perennials. These long-lived plants can use nutrients stored underground, and start the year with shoots and flower buds formed the season before. Another disadvantage of annuals in high mountains is that the seed on which they depend has slim chances of finding welcoming soil. Even alpine and subalpine perennials, in fact, commonly have alternatives to spreading by seed. Many can reproduce from roots or other tissues.

High-mountain plants' roots often take in moisture and nutrients at lower temperatures than do those of other plants. Leaves, too, commonly synthesize food down to several degrees below freezing. You may see patches of grass-like sedge (such as *Carex nigricans*) green and growing under still-unmelted snow.

The adaptations, though, are to more than cold. Skiiers and mountain climbers know the painful sunburns of high altitudes—plants, too, must cope with extremes of solar radiation. Some mountain plants continue to photosynthesize (that is, to produce food) in unusually strong light.

In thin, high-altitude air, swept by strong winds, plants rapidly lose moisture through their leaves. Bare rock can heat up quickly. Warmth is lost quickly at night, however, with little land area, vegetation, or atmospheric clouds and dust to hold it. When the mountain soil is frozen, plants cannot take in water through their roots. When it is not, moisture often drains quickly from the thin soils and steep slopes.

**Figure 5-7.** In the highest alpine gardens, cushions of moss campion hug frost-shattered rocks.

Mountain plants thus often face conditions much like those of desert plants, even when the average temperatures they encounter are not extreme. Thus, it is no surprise that some high altitude plants have the same adaptations as desert ones. Among these are small overall size; small leaves; thick "skins" or leaf cuticles; and light-reflecting, moisture-trapping hairs. Such plants tend to have thin, grass-like leaves, or they hug the ground like mats, pincushions, or rosettes.

Wildflower lovers can easily remember high-mountain plants with these characteristics: sandworts (*Arenaria* spp.) with perky pinwheel flowers above mats of tough leaves; wooly pussytoes (*Antennaria* spp.) and *Dryas* spp.; cushions of phlox or moss campion (*Silene acaulis*); and American bistort (*Polygonum bistortoides*), waving tough, grass-like leaves and bottle-brush flowers.

Thus, lovely as they are, alpine and subalpine meadows reflect a bitter struggle for survival. Plants hug the ground to make use of the warmth where sun meets soil—the level at which soil and the plant's own tissues will most often be above freezing. Almost nothing survives that projects above winter's protective blanket of snow, which insulates plants and keeps them from drying.

It is a quiet, slow struggle. A setback can have long-lasting consequences. Even snow that has been packed and turned to ice by cross-country skiers can be fatal to alpine plants. Much more serious is soil trampled, blown away, or charred by hikers, cyclists, and campers. Thus, as

114

more people come to enjoy alpine wilderness, they require more and more regulation—permits, closures, bans on fires and requirements that people stay on trails. Otherwise, we destroy the things we love.

## EXPLORING FOR ANIMALS IN CLEARINGS AND BROKEN COUNTRY

Meadows or breaks in woods of any sort, even old rock slides, are good places to find animals, or, more often, their signs.

Openings in woods are good places to look for animals because, in effect, they more than triple your chances of encountering wildlife. This is true of almost any place where two or more kinds of habitat meet—Ecologists call it the "edge effect."

The creatures near a glade, for example, may include (1) forest dwellers like the Douglas and pine squirrels, (2) animals that like brush, such as snowshoe hares or Townsend's chipmunks, (3) those that need grassy openings, such as coast moles or Washington ground squirrels, and (4) creatures that like a mixture of habitats and vegetation for cover and feeding—for example, elk and deer. If the clearing includes a stream or lake, so much the better—you may see signs of muskrat, beaver, otter, even mink.

**Figure 5-8.** Elk (here at Jewell Meadows Wildlife Area, Oregon) do well in country that offers clearings and brush for food, and woods for cover.

An open, broken, varied forest thus will contain more animals than a stand of dense evergreens. Fires or logging that break the forest may lessen numbers of deep-woods species such as fishers, martens, and small native squirrels. The resulting increase in clearings, brush, and deciduous trees, however, is likely to increase numbers of black bears, beavers, snowshoe hares, coyotes, cougers, deer, and elk.

This same rule applies to birds—the more varied the habitat, the more numerous the species. Probably the most numerous and colorful songbird community in northwestern summers is in deciduous streamside woods— aspens, cottonwoods, and the like. They include the bright blue lazuli buntings, yellow-flashing warblers and goldfinches, red and yellow western tanagers, and orange and black Bullock's orioles, as well as less colorful house wrens, western wood peewees, and others. It is close to a birdwatcher's paradise to see these in the same general area as woodland birds and others of grass, brush, and reeds—American goldfinches skipping from weed to weed; white crowned sparrows in brush near water; bluebirds in clearings among pines; Oregon juncos on brush-shaded ground, and many others.

When you explore meadows and clearings, look for diggings and burrow openings. Craters with centered, plugged openings, like small volcanos, are likely to be the work of moles (*Scapanus* spp.), which are most common in moist soils west of the Cascades. Those with off-center plugs probably were made by pocket gophers (*Thomomys* spp.), more common east of the Cascades.

Chipmunk burrows usually have entrances two to four inches in diameter, well hidden under rocks or logs. Another group of burrows have open mouths about four to eight inches in diameter. Such burrows, well hidden in moist fern and brush west of the Cascades, probably are homes of mountain beavers. Look carefully and you may find small mounds of nipped-off, drying greens nearby. Mountain beavers are not beavers, but primitive rodents found only in the coastal Northwest. Like moles and pocket gophers, they live solitary lives except during a short breeding season. Almost blind, they venture out mostly at night to nip greens. Indians sought their soft fur as clothing—the animals were "discovered" by science when Lewis and Clark traded for a mountain-beaver robe. Now these quiet vegetarians live largely ignored—except when they take an unwelcome interest in someone's garden.

Burrows of this size in low meadows, generally east of the Cascades, are likely to be those of ground squirrels. These are burrowing squirrels with tails less bushy than those of tree squirrels. They may be speckled, solid colored, or striped on the side—but they lack the eye stripes of chipmunks.

The fact that animals of this shape and having these habits are related to squirrels seems to be more or less a North American coincidence. Almost every continent has similar-looking burrowing, vegetarian animals—but they come from many quite unrelated families. This is an example of what

**Figure 5-9.** A Columbian ground squirrel at his burrow entrance.

biologists call "parallel evolution"—the animals' tendency to develop similar adaptations in response to similar condition.

If you find one ground squirrel burrow entrance, you probably will find several. Ground squirrel tunnels often are six feet or more long, with several exits. Wait quietly at a distance, and the animals probably will emerge.

Unlike moles, pocket gophers, and mountain beavers, most ground squirrels are community dwellers. They also live their active lives in daytime, and above ground. Thus, their feeding and social interactions are easy to watch. Such a colony is a good introduction to animal behavior. Sitting quietly at a distance, the patient observer can note how the animals become more or less active at different hours and temperatures. One can see the way animals investigate unfamiliar things, eat, give alarms, groom themselves, and interact socially: Like nearly all group-living animals, ground squirrels have an order of dominance; subordinate animals usually give way to dominant ones. But the order is maintained and occasionally changed by aggressive gestures, postures, and some actual fighting.

Ground squirrels also are interesting because the Northwest has so many species. Idaho alone has two species found nowhere else: the Idaho ground squirrel (*Spermophilus brunneus*), of dry, rocky flats in west-central Idaho; and the elegant ground squirrel (*Spermophilus elegan*s), of grassy clearings in highlands.

Most larger mammals can wander and interbreed widely. To survive, they usually must adapt to a rather wide variety of conditions. Thus, you can count on the fingers of one hand the North American species of beaver, elk, wild cats, wolves and coyotes, and other large animals. Smaller animals are more easily isolated. They also can adapt to and survive within a set of narrow and specialized foods, climate conditions, and other requirements. Thus, a genus or family may develop many closely related, but specialized and isolated, species. The golden-mantled ground squirrel (*Calospermophilus lateralis*), for example, is a solitary dweller in high-altitude open pine woods and subalpine meadows (more of him later). The colonial Columbian ground squirrel (*Citellus columbianus*) is fond of grassy meadows and wheat fields at lower altitudes, in eastern Washington, northeastern Oregon, and western Idaho. The California ground squirrel (*Otospermophilus beecheyi*), common in Oregon, crossed the Columbia River into Washington in this century. Fond of oak groves and acorns, it is out-competing the native western gray squirrel in some of its specialized habitats on both sides of the southern Cascades. There are many others, including specialists in desert habitats, discussed in the chapter on arid parts of the Pacific Northwest.

If you get down on your knees in a grassy meadow, you are likely to find tunnels in the matted dead grass. These are protected routes used in the nighttime feeding of Western harvest mice *(Reithrodontomys megalotis megalotis)*, or one of the many species of meadow mice (*Microtus* spp.). In high northern mountains, the runways could be made by northern bog voles, (*Synaptomys borealis*). Sometimes you can follow such trails to cup-like nests.

Check brush and grass for nipped-off shoots. Missing seed heads may indicate seed-storing rodents, such as chipmunks. If leaves and succulent stems have been bitten off instead, the meadow may be favored by voles or meadow mice.

(The Northwest has even more species of mice than of ground squirrels. Some can only be identified by experts in anatomy and in the animals' specialized habitats. In general, mice fall into four broad groups. Pocket mice, *Perognathus* spp., have tails at least as as long as their bodies, small ears, and fur-lined cheek pouches, used to transport seed. Kangaroo mice and rats, *Microdipodops* and *Dipodomys* spp., also have these characteristics, but their hind feet, on which they hop, are much larger. Both of these groups live mainly in arid lands. Crecitine mice, which include the common deer mice and harvest mice, *Peromyscus* and *Reithrodontomys* spp.; as well as the larger wood or pack rats, *Neotoma* spp., have large ears, no external cheek pouches, and tails about 3/4 the length of the rest of the body. Microtine mice, including meadow mice, voles, and tree mice, *Microtus* spp., *Phenacomys* spp., and others, mostly have stout bodies, small ears all but covered with fur, and tails less than half the length of their bodies. Old world rats and mice, our domestic pests—*Rattus rattus*, *Rattus norvegicus*, and *Mus musculus* are most easily distinguished by their hairless tails.)

As in forests. you can find animal signs on leaves, bark, and needles in clearings and around their edges.

Your best chance of seeing animals themselves, aside from ground squirrels, is at dusk and dawn. At these hours, rabbits come out of their "forms," depressions hidden in brush, to nibble in clearings. Those with rather short ears and very large hind feet are snowshoe hares (*Lepus americanus*). As is true of many species, they tend to be reddish brown west of the Cascades and more grayish in the drier areas to the east. They are further camouflaged by turning white in winter in areas of deep snow.

Rabbits with longer ears and "powder puff" white tails probably are one of three species of cottontail. Native Nuttall's cottontail (*Sylvilagus nuttalli*) favors dry country. Brush rabbits (*Sylvilagus bachmani*) are restricted to western Oregon. Eastern cottontails (*Sylvilagus floridanus*) descended from escaped pets, are found in western Washington. Yet another escapee, the European rabbit (*Oryctolagus cuniculus*) has all but overrun San Juan Island. Despite the damage done on the island, it's an ill wind that blows no good: the rabbits are a large part of the diet of local bald eagles. The eagles' spectacular comeback makes the island the best place in the Northwest to see our national bird when it is nesting.

Another animal you may meet in dusky clearings—although you may not want to—is a shambling skunk, peacefully grubbing for insects, confident that he can drive you off merely by raising his fluffy tail. If he further does a comic "hand stand," better run—you are about to be sprayed. This posture is the skunk equivalent of baring the teeth. That is, the skunk is following the common pattern of threatening by displaying his weapons.

**Figure 5-10.** Snowshoe hares, brown in summer but camouflaged white in winter, nip brush and juicy greens.

The Northwest has two skunk species: the familiar striped skunk (*Mephitis mephitis*), with a broad white band along each side, is a generally more northern animal. The spotted skunk (*Spilogale putorius*), with spotted face and broken stripes on his sides, is a more southerly animal that reaches the northern limits of his range in the Pacific Northwest. Both are fond of stream valleys and farming country dotted with woods.

# HUNTERS IN THE SNOW

In winter, snow preserves tracks and tunnels. Many small creatures become near-burrowers in the white blanket. Snow gives them a hiding place and insulation: Temperature beneath its surface will stay near freezing even when the air temperature above is much colder.

Traces in snow can tell stories. You can see how creatures were startled; how they fled or were attacked. You can see regular highways used by some animals, such as deer. As their narrow hooves break through the crust, deer must keep paths stamped down to survive. If snow is too deep or prolonged, these paths can become deadly traps, as the animals are unable to leave them to find new food supplies.

Snow tracks are often the easiest way to detect predators, from tiny insect-hunting shrews (*Sorex* spp.) to weasels (*Mustela frenata* and *erminea*) and foxes on the long, solitary hunting circuits they patrol over and over. With the exception of coyotes (*Canis latrans*), which are common, large, and often hunt by day, meat eaters are seldom seen. Predators must have many potential prey to survive, and so are generally scarcer than plant-eating animals.

Unfortunately, tracks of larger meat eaters, such as bobcats (*Lynx rufus*), lynxes (*Lynx lynx*), or the rare wolverine (*Gulo luscus*), are not only scarce but can be difficult to identify. This is partly because of the thick pads of fur on these animals' paws in winter. The fur serves both to insulate and as a supporting "snowshoe." (The snowshoe hare, the lynx's chief prey, has a similar adaptation in his large hind feet.)

Many of the carnivores have an unusual adaptation to harsh winter conditions. Breeding, which is time consuming; and pregnancy and nursing, which make heavy demands on nutrition and energy, are both best accomplished in summer. Most members of the weasel family—wolverines, badgers, martens, fishers, and otters, among others—have delayed fertilization. After the animals mate, the sperm stays in "suspended animation" for from five to ten months. Only then does a fertilized embryo implant itself in the uterus and begin to develop. Black bears also follow this pattern, although their young are born in winter. (Other animals with delayed implantation include sea lions and seals.)

**Figure 5-11.** Stories in the snow. Left: A snowshoe hare peacefully crossed an open spot. A mouse, though, was swept up by an owl, which left wing marks in the snow (below).

The meat-eating animals do not defend territories. Rather, they follow fairly well-established paths on a range that they, like dogs, commonly mark with the scent of feces and urine. In most species, females have smaller ranges than males, probably because they must return to dens to care for young. A male long-tailed weasel (*Mustela frenata*), for example, may spend a week or more on his circuit. A nursing female could not be absent long.

Exceptions to the rule of male carnivores leaving the mother to care for young are the members of the dog family—coyotes, foxes, and the few gray wolves (*Canis lupus*) perhaps remaining in remote northern mountains.

Bears, too, have home ranges rather than territories, although they are omnivores, eating fruits and greens as readily as meat. (Actually, nearly all carnivores occasionally seek out insects, fruits, and berries—as the Aesop fable of the fox jumping for grapes indicates.) Male black bears thus usually spend all their adult lives in an area of about two square miles. Females may never venture out of about a single square mile—a range that usually overlaps that of a male or two. About every third year, the female also is accompanied by cubs. Her one to two young, born blind and helpless while she is still in her winter den, stay with her through their first summer and commonly den up with her the following winter. (Their winter sleep, however, is not considered hibernation because bears' metabolism is not markedly slowed.) Cubs' long "childhood" is almost the only thing that makes black bears dangerous. They normally will flee from people, especially noisy ones. But a hiker can be in trouble if he accidentally gets between mother and her young.

**Figure 5-12.** Although black bear cubs quickly learn skills like tree climbing, they stick close to their mothers through their first year of life.

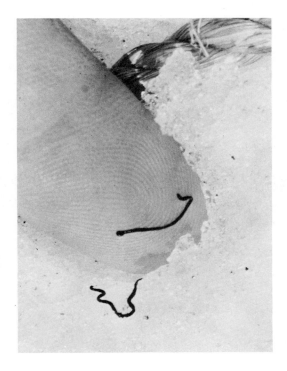

**Figure 5-13.** Ice worms are among the tiny creatures of the Northwest's highest-altitude community.

## ANIMALS OF THE HEIGHTS

The highest-altitude community in the Northwest is a rather lowly one. On year-round snowfields—occasionally stained pink by algae—beetles, spring-tails, crickets, spiders, and ice worms forage for pollen and frozen fellow insects, swept there by the upslope daytime winds.

Despite frigid temperatures, many of these small creatures lead their active lives at night. In daytime, though, you may spot them by a gray-crowned rosy finch, come to hunt them and their prey. These pink-tinged, sparrow-sized birds are among the few that regularly make the upward pilgrimage to nest in rocky mountaintops. Another, the little brownish water pipit, stakes out a territory on lakesides. There he walks and bobs his tail, searching for insects.

The white-tailed ptarmigan, smallest of the Northwest's many grouse, is the bird that comes closest to being a year-round resident of the heights. Ptarmigan winter in the highest timber, often half burying themselves in snow for warmth and protection. As the snow melts, they make the short flight back to high meadows, change white winter plumage for mottled cinnamon, and break their softly clucking flocks into pairs for the alpine mating season.

**Figure 5-14.** The white-tailed ptarmigan, well camouflaged summer and winter, sticks close to the heights.

Lower on the mountains, in country with at least occasional trees, life becomes more diverse. A varied bird community includes perhaps the Northwest's most virtuoso singer, the hermit thrush. This and other relatives of the familiar robin are examples of specialization by habitat: Robins like broken country, including city lawns. Varied thrushes, with camouflaging black on their orange throats, are birds of deep evergreen woods. Swainson's thrushes prefer deciduous woods and watersides. Hermit thrushes make their summer homes in subalpine meadows, caroling their long, elaborate songs from the tops of scattered evergreens.

Somewhat similarly, the big weasel family (Mustelidae), with members specialized for almost every habitat, has a member that leads a high-mountain life in the Pacific Northwest. This is the wolverine, a rare and clever hunter in high mountains. Like lynx, caribou (*Rangifer tarandus*), and moose (*Alces alces*), wolverines are basically animals of the far north. They are part of the circumpolar community that extends fingers south along high mountain ranges. None of these big animals of the north is really common in the Pacific Northwest. A few woodland caribou, for example, wander from Canada into northeastern Washington and the Idaho panhandle. The only one easily seen in the wild is the largest—moose are a common sight in protected Yellowstone National Park.

The grizzly bear (*Ursus arctos* or *horribilis*) is a largely subalpine animal today largely because he has been exterminated in other parts of the Northwest. The bear was a legend in his time. The Lewis and Clark party, the first whites to report seeing a grizzly, were chased by the bear after he had been shot six times at close range. Today, almost the only sizable populations of grizzlies remaining are protected ones, in Glacier and Yellowstone National Parks. There, visitors must be educated about the potential problems of coexisting with fearless, half-ton carnivores. Nevertheless, grizzly attacks occasionally occur.

Incidentally, color does not tell you what kind of bear you are seeing. Grizzlies and black bears can be light brown to almost black. Grizzlies are larger than black bears, their claws are longer, and they have distinctly humped backs.

Fortunately for the entertainment of hikers, meadows and rockfields below snowline do have year-round residents that are harmless, noisy, busy, and easily seen.

These are ground-dwelling animals: pikas (*Ochotona princeps*), golden-mantled ground squirrels (*Spermophilus lateralis*), yellow-pine chipmunks, and marmots. (Most marmots in high mountains are hoary marmots, *Marmota caligata*. But drier mountains may have alpine populations of yellow-bellied marmots, *Marmota flaviventris*. The Olympic range has a species found nowhere else: the golden Olympic marmot, *Marmota olympus*.)

All these creatures are among the easiest animals to watch. Watching also easily gives you an idea of their lives.

**Figure 5-15.** Near the timberline, pikas fiercely defend their bit of rockpile and meadow.

For example, you generally hear the nasal "enk, enk" of pikas before you see these fluffy, nearly tailless little inhabitants of rockslides, with their big round ears. Watching, you will see a lone pika call, venture out to nip the grasses near his home, and dash back to a burrow whose entrance is hidden under rocks. Although many pikas live in a single field of stones, they seem to have little time for sunning or play. Perhaps this is because pikas, despite living in the same piles of mountain rock, are rugged individualists. They defend territories from other members of their kind.

From those territories, they must literally make hay. Pikas harvest greens. They then dry them in small haystacks under rocks near the centers of their territories. Finally, they store them in their rocky tunnel systems as food to last the winter, for pikas do not hibernate.

Marmots, on the other hand, seem much more easy going. They are larger, and they waddle rather than scurry. Although they live in "harems," the dominant male seems to accept rather than conquer females that choose to make their homes in his boulder pile. And with individual exceptions, the females seem to get along rather well, most making their homes in the same rockpiles as their mothers.

The whistle you hear from their bouldery home may come from a marmot sunning himself on a rock. Others heed the warning and dive for cover. Soon, though, they are out again, the youngsters play-fighting, elders munching a convenient lupine.

**Figure 5-16.** This hoary marmot's lookout boulder has a view of Pinnacle Peak, near Mt. Rainier, Washington.

Despite their relaxed habits, marmots are in their way exceptionally efficient. Instead of storing food, they spend more than half the year in deep hibernation, their heartbeats and all other bodily processes slowed drastically. This enables them to put a very high percentage of their energy into growth and reproduction—many times that devoted by most other warm-blooded animals.

Yellow-pine chipmunks and golden-mantled ground squirrels are often confused with one another. Both have fluffy tails, both have dark and light stripes along their sides, and both readily learn to beg or steal from campers. The easiest way to tell the difference is to know that in the chipmunks, but not the ground squirrels, a dark stripe seems to extend through the eye. Just what function these stripes have, if any, is uncertain. Speculations range from siting lines to camouflage—helping conceal the glittering eye from predators.

Both yellow-pine chipmunks and golden-mantled ground squirrels range widely, from subalpine meadows to foothills. While pikas and marmots generally protect themselves from coyotes, bears, badgers and other enemies by denning under rock, the burrows of these chipmunks and ground squirrels are as likely to have entrances half-hidden under an old log, as befits animals that like open, broken forest. Both eat nuts and seeds. But the chipmunk climbs more readily for his food and stores it for winter, while the golden-mantled ground squirrel forages mostly on the ground and eats what he finds to gain weight for a long hibernation.

**Figure 5-17.** A mountain goat dam and kid in Olympic National Park, Washington. Introduced to the Olympics by man, the thriving herds are damaging some high-mountain meadows.

The mountain goat (*Oreamnos americanus*) is not quite a year-round resident of alpine country. Their small herds, led by experienced nannies, move just to the upper limit of shelter in winter, returning to the crags in spring. (As with other hoofed grazers, males fight and court their way to leadership only during mating season. Young unmated males, like teenaged boys, form their own groups apart from others.)

Mountain goats are native to the North Cascades and the mountains of Idaho and Montana. Indians sought their long, white wool for blankets—in some tribes, only prominent families could wear such garb. Goats can still be found in the Washington Cascades as far south as Mt. Rainier and in Idaho in high mountains almost to the Snake River Valley. Although the animals are shy, you may know they are nearby by long strands of white wool and dusty bedding spots.

Introduced into Oregon, mountain goats are still struggling there. The place where they are thriving best, though, is not their native home. Goats transplanted to Olympic National Park are remarkably tame. Some all but pose for visitors with cameras. Their herds have grown so numerous that they are being trapped and transported to keep them from destroying high-mountain vegetation.

In one of the many misnomers of the wild, mountain goats are not goats, but members of the antelope family. Their ancestors reached North America by way of the Bering land bridge. Pronghorn "antelopes" (*Antilocapra americana*) are not antelopes and thus no relation—they evolved in North America.

# MOUNTAIN MIGRANTS

Like other residents of popular resort areas, the citizens of mountain heights must tolerate the hordes of animal visitors to their homelands in summer. The Pacific Northwest's mountains see seven major migrations each year. Each one radically changes the wild world.

The first two—the north and south movements of birds—are well known. Most migrants leaving the Pacific Northwest winter in the Southwestern United States, Mexico, and Central America. A few, mainly shorebirds, travel as far as southern South America. Fall's departure and spring's return bring visitors not seen at other times. The milder parts of the Northwest itself are a winter refuge to a few birds that nest in the far north—among them, snow buntings and Lapland longspurs, both birds of open places.

Less well-known are the east-west migrations of gulls, shorebirds, and herons. Many of these birds winter in the mild coastal country, but cross the

Cascades in spring to nest on remote lakes and potholes in the dry Great Basin country.

Just as important as these movements are the pilgrimages of birds and mammals up to moist, lush high-altitude brush and meadows in summer, and down to sheltering woods and valleys in winter.

Most of the animals that make the mountain-to-lowland migration are birds—for example, blue grouse, whose drumbeat calls add mystery to broken woods as high as subalpine meadows. The birds are talented ventriloquists: the male's deep hoots seem to come from a tree far from his real location. You wonder how mates find each other.

Big grazing animals also make annual up-and-down treks—those of mountain goats have already been mentioned. The migrations of elk and deer have had considerable impact on local Western politics.

In summer, elk or wapiti (*Cervus elaphus*) follow grass and young brush, often as high as subalpine meadows. The groups you see may be several females—not-yet-mated yearlings, and older females with spotted fawns born in spring. Young males, two and three years old, commonly band together

**Figure 5-18.** The throbbing courtship sounds that male blue grouse make by inflating air sacs on their throats are part of spring on Northwest mountain slopes.

until the time comes to compete for mates. Older bucks may be solitary. With the fall rut, bucks trumpet and joust for harems—their whistles, ending in a sort of grunt, travel far under the full moon. Up close, the bucks could appear absurd, pawing the ground, urinating on themselves, and butting their antlers against trees. Up close to a bull elk at mating season, however, is not a very safe place to be.

When snow grips the mountains, the elk stream down to the lowlands. Harems join into herds that can number in the hundreds.

Unfortunately, the elks' winter ranges generally were the same grassy valleys where Western ranchers most wanted to build fences and run cattle. Into the 1920s, hunting and exclusion from winter food threatened to wipe out the animals. By purchase and cooperative agreement, often amid much controversy, states and the federal government have gradually reestablished winter food supplies. Elk also have been captured and transplanted to replace local herds that had become extinct. (Most elk west of the Cascades, for example, are transplanted Rocky Mountain elk, rather than the native, darker Olympic subspecies.) The most famous of these protected winter ranges probably is Jackson Hole, in Wyoming. There, most of the valley east of the Tetons has been added to Grand Teton National Park or otherwise made available to wild things as well as cattle.

The life history and migratory patterns of mule deer (*Odocoileus hemionus*) are similar to those of elk. (The subspecies west of the Cascades, *O. h. columbianus*, is commonly called black-tailed deer for its dark tail.)

This common deer of the west was discovered by Lewis and Clark. It has a bounding gait (Clark wrote that it "jumps like a goat"), large ears (hence the name), and antler tines branching symmetrically. (Elk have short antler tines projecting over the brow, a longish mane on neck and throat; and a light, buff to orange rump patch. They also are much larger and more heavily built than deer—an elk can weigh up to 1,000 pounds.)

Mule deer were never as endangered as elk. They too, however, are sustained by valley refuges and winter feeding stations. These state and federal reserves are among the best places to see the animals.

The native white-tailed deer (*Odocoileus virginianus*) are recognizable by their "rocking horse" run; by their big white tails, held up like a flag when they are alarmed; and by their antlers, which project singly from a main beam.

They are less migratory than elk or mule deer—and have suffered for it. This is the common species of the East Coast, once found across the continent, mostly in damp brush and deciduous woods. (They tend to hide, rather than flee as do mule deer.) In the Northwest, white-tails were always outnumbered by mule deer. They have lost even more ground as farming and ranching took over lowlands where they once flourished, although they still are numerous in suitable dense cover as far west as northeastern Washington. The west coast subspecies, *O.v. leucurus* or Columbian white-tailed deer, actually came close to extinction. It survives on the Umpqua River in

**Figure 5-19.** Columbian white-tailed deer came close to extinction as settlers took over their brushy lowland homes.

Southwest Oregon, and in and near a federal refuge in lowlands near the mouth of the Columbia River.

Animals have a seventh great migration, one seldom seen. This is the yearly dispersion of adolescent and just-grown animals. This movement takes place mostly in late summer—a time of year that is often exciting for birdwatchers, as a few of the wanderers show up in unexpected places.

This scattering and exploration takes place even in species whose members usually settle and stay in a territory, range, or hunting circuit once they find one—for example, black bears, raccoons, and beaver. Sometimes the young are driven from their homes by adults. This is the case with most rodents.

On the whole, young males on these journeys wander farther than females. The adolescents and young adults perish in great numbers in their first winter on their own. They are inexperienced. Many do not find suitable homes and food supplies, or must settle for second-rate territory outside the boundaries already held by others. Without the dispersion, though, the animals might exhaust their food supplies. The wandering animals also find and populate new areas. Thus, they extend the range of their species, and in the long run increase its numbers.

## DOING IT YOURSELF

Get to know wildflowers, with the aid of a guidebook. Beginners will find it less frustrating to start with one covering only a small area. With plants, drawings often are more useful than photographs. As with any field guide, it helps to read over the book so that you are familiar with its layout and with descriptions of species you have not seen.

Almost any high meadows will have gardens of wildflowers. Probably the most beautiful and accessible alpine meadows are at Paradise, in Mt. Rainier National Park.

Imagine how Indians and early settlers would have used the plants in clearings and brushy spots. Here are some examples:

Bear grass—leaves used in baskets and hats, roots boiled as a substitute for soap.

Bedstraw (*Galium triflorum*)—Indian women used it as perfume; settlers stuffed mattresses with the sweet-smelling dried stems.

Blue curls (*Trichostema*)—thrown into summer ponds to intoxicate fish, which floated to the surface and were easily caught.

Boisduvalia *(Boisduvalia)*—Indians ate seeds.

**Figure 5-20.** Fritillary, or yellow bells (*Fritillaria pudica*), one of the bright flowers that makes spring a joy in grassy clearings from the Cascades eastward.

California tea (*Psoralea physodes*)—Settlers' substitute for tea.

Gum plant (*Grindelia*)—sticky buds used as cough medicine.

Hellebore *(Veratrum* spp.)—Indians used green hellebore (*V. viride*) as a charm; whites used white hellebore (*V. californicum*) as insecticide.

Milkweed (*Asclepias speciosa*)—young seed pods and shoots eaten as a vegetable; fiber used to make cords.

Mock orange—Indians used wood for arrows, leaves as soap.

Sand verbena (*Abronia latifolia*)—Indians ate roots.

Soapolallie (*Shepherdia canadensis*)—berries rubbed to make frothy soap.

Water hemlock (*Cicuta douglasii*)—sap used to make poisoned arrows.

Wild sunflower (*Balsamorhiza* spp.)—Indians ate the dried, pounded seeds and used the roots as medicine.

Yellow waterlily (*Nuphar polysepalum*)—Seeds ground to make flour.

Wyethia (*Wyethia* spp.)—seeds eaten; roots used as medicine.

Sample abundant wild foods, but with caution. Camas, for example, usually grows with deadly poisonous death camas.

Try to analyze why clearings you see exist, how old they are, and whether they are likely to be covered for forest. In alpine and subalpine meadows, try to determine from vegetation whether snow melts early or late; whether soil dries quickly or not at all; and how conditions differ from those on other parts of the mountain.

Spring and early summer are the best time to see wildflowers, and to watch most birds and mammals. (Birds are easy to see then because they are courting and singing. This tends to keep them in one place.) Early fall, however, can be just as good a time to get to know wildlife in high mountains. Young are out of their dens or nests. Bird populations are at their peaks, with the year's hatchlings on their own, and winter's high death toll not yet taken. The birds also are joining flocks and preparing for their journey south or to the lowlands. Chipmunks and other rodents are busy at the harvest, gobbling or storing the bounty to survive the winter in their own ways. Elk bugle on moonlit nights, beginning another mating season. As an added bonus to fall travel, huckleberries are ripe, and snowmelt doesn't get your feet wet.

If you are a beginning birdwatcher, try a clearing where you can also see tall trees (evergreen and deciduous), brush, and water. In short, find the greatest possible variety of heights and types of habitat. You don't need a fancy telescope—binoculars are fine. Settle yourself comfortably at the edge of the clearing. Sit still for awhile. Birds will soon all but ignore you, and move about normally again. Listen as much as you look. You will locate many birds first by songs or calls. Don't just settle for identifying birds by species. Watch the different ways they eat, fly, show alarm, court, care for young, and interact with other animals.

Explore clearings and brushy areas, looking for signs of mammal life. Get down on your knees and peer up into branches. Try to guess what lives there. If you can, visit the clearing at different hours—including night, with a flashlight covered in red plastic or cellophane. Mammals are shyer than birds (they can't fly away). Thus, you need a more inconspicuous vantage point, and more patience.

Get to know national wildlife refuges and state wildlife areas. Both usually allow hunting at some seasons, and at other times may close large areas to protect breeding animals. Thus, you need to find out where as well as when to go.

The best elk-watching areas are Jackson Hole in Wyoming, Jewell Meadows Wildlife Area in northwestern Oregon (a wintering area planted in grass for elk), and Oak Creek and L.T. Murray Wildlife Recreation Areas west of Yakima, Washington, two other big winter feeding areas.

Deer are a fairly common sight throughout the Northwest (except during hunting season). They spend most of the day bedded down, moving and feeding between dusk and dawn. In winter, however, they are active during daylight hours. Large groups are easily spotted on wildlife refuges and many state game areas. To see the rare Columbian white-tailed deer (along with many other animals), visit the Columbian White-Tailed Deer National Wildlife Refuge, which has headquarters and a mainland unit at Skamakowa, Washington. (With a boat, you also can reach nearby refuge islands in the Columbia River.)

**Figure 5-21.** For winter survival, elk herds depend on valleys like this—Jackson Hole, Wyoming, at the foot of the Grand Tetons.

# 6

# Dry Country

When we think of the Northwest, we envision snowy mountains and evergreen forests. In fact, more of the area is desert or semiarid. Irrigation has veiled the natural face of much of this land with orchards and green fields. But the natural cover east of the Cascades, except in highlands and stream canyons, is bunchgrass and gray desert shrubs.

The Northwest's true desert ends north of southeastern Oregon and southern Idaho. This is the end of the geological Basin and Range province, which includes most of the American deserts farther south. It also is the northernmost home of some typical desert animals, such as kit foxes (*Vulpes macrotis*), ringtails (*Bassariscus astutus*), and kangaroo mice (*Microdipodops megacephalus*).

The ordinary visitor, though, is not likely to see much difference among the Northwest's rain-shadowed plateaus and valleys. Precipitation in all of them ranges from about five to 20 inches a year—about a seventh of that west of the Cascades. All have dry summers and frozen though somewhat wetter winters. All have buttes, cliff-walled stream canyons, and rare stretches of sand dunes. They also have similar plant and animal communities, with similar adaptations to the rigors of drought and cold. For these reasons, this book treats Washington's Columbia Plateau, Oregon's High Lava Plains and Basin and Range Area, and Idaho's Snake River Valley as one region, calling it the Pacific Northwest's desert.

**Figure 6-1.** Irrigation has greened much of the arid Northwest, but the desert shows its true face where the artificial watering ends—as it does here at the rimrock of Moses Coulee, Washington.

If you see this land almost any time except in the spring, it is likely to strike you as it did the pioneers—as rugged, dreary, and monotonous. True, there are dramatic high points. You catch your breath at the red, yellow, and green "painted desert" of Oregon's John Day country. The immense dry waterfalls and coulees of Washington's Channeled Scablands have the grandeur of noble ruins. Fresh lava flows, like those at Craters of the Moon, breathe otherworldliness. The Snake River's 7,900-foot-deep canyon is deeper than Grand Canyon. Many of the other river canyons, from the Columbia to the Owyhee, are magnificent or mysterious, highlighted with rare plants, ancient rock shelters, and occasional Indian pictographs.

But between the "oohs" and "aahs," parched gray sage and clumps of dry grass seem to stretch as far as the eye can see. A vulture, soaring on slightly uptilted wings, seems to be the only thing that moves.

You are seeing a land in suspended animation. Facing extremes of dryness, heat, and cold, plants and animals here have developed adaptations that keep them dormant for as much as three-quarters of the year. You are seeing a land whose real life is lived underground, or under the cover of darkness. To understand this desert, you must learn to read the signs of its' hidden life. Then, even better, visit it in spring, when the intensity of its blooming, birth, crowded life, and sudden death are almost overwhelming.

**136**

**Figure 6-2.** Hells Canyon on the Snake River: The deepest canyon in North America is one of the spectacular parts of the dry Northwest.

## LAND OF EXTREMES

In the Pacific Northwest desert, things don't happen in moderation. One aspect of this is steepness. The dry plateaus are broken by cliff-like canyons and, in some areas, table-like mesas. Part of the reason for the nearly vertical faces is the underlying geology: The Basin and Range mountains started out as cliff-like mountains edging basins. In addition, flat layers of lava sometimes formed hard, erosion-resistant caps on softer sedimentary rock. The softer rock then wore away, except beneath the cap. The result is flat-topped mesas with steep sides.

Desert processes also work to make a land with a tough crust and steep sides. Many factors combine to harden desert floors. Salts, for example, can cement the soil. Winds can blow away fine particles, leaving a rocky pavement. With a hardpan floor and few plants, the desert absorbs little water. Rainfall and melted snow rush quickly to gullies and down hillsides. The quickly-dried hilltops are subject to relatively little erosion, while the wetter base is weakened and worn by chemical reactions. These differing rates of erosion sharpen cliffs.

Again because of the lack of vegetation, desert water (as well as wind and frost) erodes forcefully. A raindrop falls at about 20 miles per hour. Rain brings tons of these little projectiles crashing down on the land. Pried-off bits of rock are washed out onto broad, low fans, leaving cliff-like scarps and arroyo walls behind them.

Wind and water sort desert soils into extreme types. They leave bare rimrock on high places. They carry fine particles of dust and sand far out into basins. The Ice Age, too, left Northwest deserts with extreme soils: Gravels and scoured rock from the floods of Lake Missoula; fine sediments that floored Great Basin lakes. Where only sparse desert shrubbery holds the old lake bottoms, winds easily whip up dust storms and build shifting dunes—as pioneers found, to their sorrow.

Strong sunshine evaporates rainwater, snowmelt, and even part of the rivers of subterranean groundwater flowing under the dry land. (These aquifers are the source of much of the irrigation water that has transformed a large part of the desert into pastures and wheatfields.) As this water evaporates, the minerals it carried are deposited near the surface of the soil. Where there is not enough water to wash these minerals into deeper layers of soil and away, they build up as salts.

The type of salts, and hence the type of soil, is due partly to the chemical makeup of nearby rock and partly to the relative amounts of water flowing through the soil or evaporating. Where evaporation is not extreme, only minerals that are not very soluble, such as carbonates, build up. Soil and water become alkaline, as settlers and explorers, forced to drink the laxative water, found. In the pioneer song, "Sweet Betsy from Pike," having "Crossed the big mountains with her lover Ike," sings:

"Don't dance me too hard, do you want to know why?
Doggone you; I'm chock full of strong alkali!"

More evaporation deposits even the readily dissolved salts, such as sodium chloride, sulphate, and nitrate. In extreme cases, such evaporation builds gleaming salt flats and borax deposits—around the turn of the century, borax in southeastern Oregon's Alvord Desert was mined by Chinese laborers and hauled by 20-mule teams to the railroad in Nevada.

Desert temperatures are as extreme as the topography and soil. Forests or grassy fields absorb the sun's radiation. Moisture evaporating from soil and plants acts as a cooler. These moderating influences hardly operate in the desert, however. There, sparse, pale vegetation absorbs little heat. There is little water to be evaporated. Thus, equal amounts of sunshine will make a desert day hotter than one in a forest or meadow.

Desert nights, though, are likely to be colder. The desert stores little of the day's intense heat, for three main reasons: (1) Dry soils, with air spaces between the particles, absorb little heat. (2) Light-colored desert soil reflects about twice as much radiation as dark soil or forest. (3) The desert has little

**Figure 6-3.** The edge of a hot-spring-fed pool in Oregon's Alvord Desert, where Chinese miners once mined borax. Saltbrush or greasewood, common where evaporation has made soils alkaline, is dark green rather than the prevailing gray.

vegetation to absorb heat. When night comes, what little heat the desert has stored vanishes quickly through the cloudless skies. Winds, sweeping along with little vegetation to baffle them, speed the chilling.

The extremes are daily and seasonal: Northwest deserts, unlike those nearer the equator, have hot summers but cold winters.

## READING THE DRY LANDS

Desert extremes interact in complex ways. In one area, plants may be thickest in a depression because it collects rain runoff. In another, a slope may bear more flowers than a sink, because the slope faces shady north, and so retains moisture.

As you spend more time in the dry country, though, you begin to read its signs. The gray shrubs and brownish clumps of grass seem less monotonous as you learn their names and specializations. You recognize evidence of animals, the habitats they prefer, and learn the hours and places where you can see the animals themselves. You come to understand life's many ways of dealing with cold and drought.

Before settlers grazed, plowed, burned, and irrigated the dry Pacific Northwest, the area was covered by various mixtures of three broad communities. Grasses tended to dominate the moister areas—those not quite wet enough to support forests. Scattered shrubs, especially big-leaved sagebrush (*Artemesia tridentata*) dominated a much larger, drier area. The relatively small areas of salty soils—mostly old lake basins in Oregon and Idaho—were dominated by saltbush and greasewood (*Atriplex confertifolia* and *Sarcobatus vermiculatus*). These three communities still rule the dry plateaus, although their outlines have been somewhat changed by man.

## GRASSLANDS

The grasses of the arid Pacific Northwest can be pictured as occupying moisture conditions between sagebrush and pine or juniper forest. To some extent, such a geographic belt actually exists—for example, in extreme eastern Washington, as the land begins to rise on the way to the Rockies. Just as often, though, local soil conditions, microclimates, or a history of fires or overgrazing create a complex interfingering of trees, grass, and desert shrubs. Sage, for example, often grows well up mountain slopes, under pines.

Grasses, unpretentious but remarkable plants that spread, along with hoofed animals, as the continent cooled and dried from the Mesozoic era onwards, have amazing resilience. They are a near perfect example of co-evolution—potential "enemies" changing so as to help one another. Grass leaves, or blades, grow from their bases rather than their tips. Thus they continue to grow even when nipped by animals. The saliva of some grazing animals even contains substances that make grass leaves grow faster.

Wildfires, common in dry areas, are another potential foe. Grass buds usually are at or beneath ground level, so they can sprout unharmed after fire races over them. In fact, moderate grazing and occasional fires seem to help many grasses, by removing dead matter and converting minerals back into forms plants can use.

Northwest range grasses were never the continuous waving carpet of the Great Plains. Summer drought gave the Northwest a community of perennial grasses that grow in scattered clumps—bunchgrasses. Most common were tall bluebunch wheatgrass (*Agropyron spicatum*) and Idaho fescue (*Festuca idahoensis*), and the smaller Sandberg's bluegrass (*Poa sandbergii*). These bunchgrasses sprout in the fall rains, grow in small spurts on mild winter days, and then shoot up and bloom in spring's warmth and moisture. In late summer, they become brown and dormant, evading drought.

The bunchgrass community, though so well adjusted to the Pacific Northwest, could not survive changes brought by settlers.

Pioneers on the Oregon Trail in the 1840s, coming out of the long trek through desert along the Snake River, gratefully noticed the grass and its year-round supply of nourishment for cattle. Cattlemen and sheepherders began moving into the range in numbers about 1858, when the Northwest's first Indian Wars were settled. They drove long-horned cattle and tough merino sheep up from California. Wheat growers followed in less than a decade. The three groups battled each other off and on for almost 50 years, burning, and shooting cattle, sheep, and occasionally each other. The conflict was largely over the parts of the range where soil was deepest and moisture most plentiful—that is, the bunchgrass lands. These lands were the first casualties.

Overgrazed by sheep and cattle, the grasses exhausted their stores of nutrients in trying to regrow. Fires, accidental and deliberately set, burned during the spring flush of growth as well as in the dry summer. Annual "weed" grasses traveled with the stockmen. They sprouted before the native perennials and used up precious moisture. Farmers plowed up the mat of grass roots to plant their crops. Even where farming finally failed, or overgrazing left the land abandoned, soil often was so badly eroded that former grassland was reinvaded by sage.

**Figure 6-4.** Cattle near Boise, Idaho. Conflicts over the Northwest's grasslands sometimes were disastrous to both range and ranchers.

Today you find the native bunchgrasses mostly scattered among desert shrubs, or heavily mixed with nonnatives like cheatgrass, whose sharp seeds can kill cattle by puncturing their intestines. Some of the Northwest's loveliest wild lillies, including species of wild iris and *Calochortus*, the furry-throated mariposa lily, have grown scarce along with bunchgrass range.

## SAGE AND ITS COMPANIONS

Almost everywhere you look in the arid Northwest you see scattered bushes, seldom more than shoulder height, with small, tough leaves. Mostly evergreen or evergray; most with tiny, nearly hidden flowers, they give the cold desert a drab monotony until you look closely.

Big-leaf sagebrush, ruler of this gray land, is easily distinguished by its twisted, loose-barked limbs and "trident" leaves, with three little lobes on their otherwise blunt ends.

If bunchgrass brought war to the dry Pacific Northwest, sagebrush brought heartbreak. The story was saddest on the lava plains of eastern Oregon. Land-swindlers' promises or the dream of a last piece of the frontier brought thousands of would-be farmers here in one of the nation's last land rushes, from about 1905 to 1915. The sage land they plowed dried up and blew away, taking their dreams with it. Today it is hard to believe that desolate crossroads, with little more than a name and a gas station, were thriving settlements in those few hopeful years.

Like coyotes and jackrabbits, the other symbols of this dry land, sage has been the focus of hatred. Because cattle cannot digest sage well, thousands of acres have been burned, sprayed, plowed, and dragged to eradicate it. Sagebrush, however, shows no signs of disappearing. If it did, man and the desert might be worse off. Sage's dead leaves and twigs enrich the desert's poor soils. Its branches shade seedlings of grass, flowers, and other shrubs, as well as small animals, such as rabbits and lizards, that could not otherwise survive the strong summer sun. The leaves cattle scorn are vital foods for other animals, from pronghorn to pygmy rabbits. Little sagebrush voles and big sage grouse depend on these leaves almost entirely.

The gray leaves of sage and other plants reflect light and so keep the plant cooler in desert heat. (The color comes from waxes and fine hairs, not pigments.) The waxes and pungent oils that you smell in a crushed leaf lessen loss of water through the leaf's cuticle. The hairs trap a thin layer of still air around the leaf, further reducing evaporation.

Small leaves are less likely to overheat than large ones. In addition, a plant with a large root system can fairly easily supply a few small leaves with enough water to keep them from wilting. Like a number of desert plants, sage grows larger leaves in spring. These help it capture more light and synthesize

**Figure 6-5.** Sagebrush, king of Northwest deserts, in Christmas Valley, Oregon.

more food while water is plentiful and temperatures mild. Sage drops these large leaves in summer's drought—but not before it has transferred the water and nutrients in them to other parts of the plant.

Sage's companions have many of the same adaptations. But they have their own stories. Antelope bush (*Purshia tridentata*) has three-lobed leaves like sagebrush. But they are dark green. Unlike sage, whose relatives are on the steppes of Asia, antelope brush has tropical forebearers. It moved north as mountain walls dried the interior of the continent. Antelope brush and others of southern ancestry, such as thorny hop sage (*Grayia spinosa*), also grow in the great southwestern deserts, where sagebrush is replaced by creosote bush (*Larrea tridentata*).

Rabbit brush (*Chrysothamnus nauseosus*) is an exception to the rule that desert shrubs have dull flowers. In parched late summer and early fall, its masses of bright yellow flowers make dry desert roadsides look landscaped. Rabbit brush thrives in disturbed soils, and in slightly wetter areas than does sagebrush. Sandy, gravelly road shoulders are among these, not only because they get extra runoff from the concrete. Almost paradoxically, sandy and somewhat rocky soils tend to be the desert's wettest areas. Water can soak in deep and stay there. Where soil is a clay crust, rain may wet only the top layers and then evaporate quickly as sun heats the upper soil.

143

**Figure 6-6.** The bright yellow flowers of rabbitbrush (here in Christmas Valley, Oregon) bring unexpected color to the gray late summer in Northwest deserts.

Winterfat *(Ceratoides* or *Eurotia lanata)* is a small shrub almost white with fine hairs and fuzzy flowers. It gets its name because, unlike sagebrush, it is very nourishing to cattle. Stockmen cherish it in cold months.

Greasewood and saltbrush or shadscale can face still greater extremes than sage. Along with winterfat, these two shrubs manage to thrive in the desert's white-crusted alkaline and salty soils. They have even turned the salt that poisons other plants to their advantage: Plants draw water from soil by osmosis—that is, for water to move into the plant, it must contain solutions that are more concentrated than those in the soil. Salt gives saltbrush the highly concentrated solutions it needs to draw water from nearly dry earth. When its leaves die and wood decays, saltbrush makes the top layer of soil still more salty: Minerals that the plant's roots have drawn up from deeper layers are re-deposited on the surface, discouraging other plants.

Saltbrush also has special glands—tiny bladders—that excrete salts it does not need. Desert mice strip off these glands before munching on the stems—which, since they are green, let the plant photosynthesize with a minimum of water loss through leaves.

Greasewood and saltbrush share an adaptation common in southwestern deserts, but unusual in the cold deserts of the Northwest. They have a different chemical pathway for photosynthesis—that is, for converting carbon dioxide in the air to food, using the sun as energy. The $C_4$ pathway, used by saltbrush and greasewood, seems to make photosynthesis more efficient in strong light and great heat.

Prickly pears (*Opuntia* spp.) are among the Northwest's few representatives of the cactus family, so common in deserts of the Southwest. Cacti, with their fleshy lobes, vicious spines, and delicate, tissue-like flowers, use an entirely different repertoire of defenses against drought. Desert shrubs have deep, widely branching networks of roots, armored against water loss at all but their absorbent tips. Cactus root systems, by contrast, are shallow but widespread. They gather water when it is plentiful, and store it in the plant's succulent tissues.

**Figure 6-7.** Prickly pears are among the Northwest's few true cacti.

More common in the Pacific Northwest are plants that cope with arid lands by not really living in a desert at all. The dry Northwest's stream canyons, for example, sparkle with the shiny leaves of cottonwood and aspen. Like willows, they send deep roots down to the underground water table, and draw water year-round.

Many other plants survive hard times in various states of suspended animation. The surprising ferns of dry rimrock curl their fronds and wait for water. Mosses stop respiration and photosynthesis—until seconds after rain begins to fall. Then the hard brown tufts on rocks unfold their soft green tissues, take in water, and begin to live again.

Spring's wildflowers, which so suddenly splash color on the drab gray land, escape the true desert by leading almost ephemeral lives. That is, they grow and bloom in the short periods when moistures makes the area not a desert at all. Then they wither and vanish.

Many wildflowers store nutrients in bulbs, rhizomes, or fleshy roots, readying themselves for a quick start in spring. These include wild onions; delicate lilies such as calochortus and brodeia; furry-leaved, yellow-flowered balsamroots or sunflowers; and dawn-flushed bitterroots or *Lewisia* (named for Meriwether Lewis of the Lewis and Clark expedition). Such starchy desert roots and insects were staple foods for Indians who eked out a living in Northwest deserts, desperately poorer than tribes blessed with salmon, seafood, deer and elk, or buffalo.

**Figure 6-8.** "Sunflower," or balsamroot: Its oily seeds and thick roots were Indian staples.

**Figure 6-9.** Bitterroot's leaves and delicate flowers wither in spring; the plant survives the dry season as tuber, fleshy with stored energy.

Desert flowers that wither and spend the hot, dry months as seed include vivid scarlet gilia (*Gilia aggregata*), salmon pink collomia (*Collomia grandiflora*), and clarkia (*Clarkia pulchella*) with its strange lobed and pinched petals. (It was named for Captain William Clark, the other leader of the Lewis and Clark Expedition.)

One difference between the Northwest's two big wildflower shows—alpine and desert—is that the desert has more annuals. Most in the dry Northwest are winter annuals: like bunchgrass, they sprout in fall and grow on mild winter days, even at temperatures slightly below freezing. These flowering plants are spindly. The leaves are sparse and narrow, the roots short and few. It is as if all their energy went into the beautiful flowers, to draw insects that will fertilize what becomes the seed.

## THE PYRAMID OF DESERT LIFE

The arid Northwest's animals are rather like its plants. Most are gray. Many—the rodents for example—seem much alike at first glance. Like plants, these animals survive drought by either tolerating or evading it. Many go underground, or are active only in the short times when the desert is moist and mild. And like plants, animals cope with extremes with a fascinating variety of mechanisms.

If you could see a cross-section of a typical tract of bunchgrass and gray shrubs, you would see how much the arid Northwest is an underground world. In dry weight, only about 15 percent of the organic material is above ground—and more than half of that is dead. Most of the underground material is roots, filling the wide spaces between desert plants, gathering every available drop of moisture, and storing food for hard times or quick spring growth.

An even larger proportion of desert animals live underground. Burrowing is small desert animals' most important protection against heat and drought. By total mass, though, the dominant animals in the desert are tiny creatures such as below-ground insects, soil mites, and nematodes. Nematodes, for example, probably digest and recycle more organic matter than any other animal in arid lands. Strangely, although these tiny worms thrive in dry areas, they can function only in a thin film of water surrounding roots and particles of soil. When ground is dry, the nematodes curl up, dry out, and remain in a state of suspended animation—for years if necessary—until water is available again.

**Figure 6-10.** Cores of earth, pushed into snow tunnels by pocket gophers and left behind in spring, are a sign of the desert's underground world.

Such tiny creatures, and all the other animals—pronghorn, meadow-larks, rattlesnakes, ground squirrels—are only about 1/1000 the dry weight of the vegetable matter they ultimately depend on. Those that eat plants directly are about 2/3 of this minuscule fraction. What little remains includes all the carnivores—animals that live by eating other animals. These range from insect-eating birds and lizards through coyotes. This is what biologists mean when they describe life as a pyramid. Each group of consumers depends on a much larger base of producers. The producers must be much more numerous or larger than the consumers because (1) they have to reproduce themselves, as well as feed whatever eats them and (2) at each level, energy is used in converting whatever is being eaten to tissue and energy.

Since vegetation is the base of this pyramid, it is not surprising that populations of small desert animals fluctuate with winter rainfall. Predator populations follow. Numbers of coyotes, for example, seem to follow those of jackrabbits, with a lag of a year or two.

## WHAT DESERT ANIMALS EAT

Many of the animals in the desert pyramid depend on seeds—an abundant, easily stored food supply. The seed-eaters include many of the little "desert rats," as well as harvester ants (*Pogonomyrmex* spp.), whose mounds you can spot by the surrounding circle of earth, clipped bare by workers. Dependence on seeds leads to some unexpected competition: rodents are rather uncommon near concentrations of ant beds, and vice versa. Specializing in seeds also leads to some unusual adaptations: Pocket mice, probably the most common mice in the arid Northwest, get their names not from their small size, but from cheek pouches they use to transport seeds.

Another group of animals depend on greens. Among them are colonial ground squirrels (several species) and yellow-bellied marmots, among the few desert animals active in daytime. Their colonies are a joy to watch—the youngsters tussling, adults scurrying after food, sitting up lookout-style, sunning, grooming, or popping in and out of their holes.

These animals crowd their sociability into a short period. They come out of their burrows to sun themselves and munch around March or April, and disappear underground about July or August. The rest of the year—about 2/3 of their lives—they sleep. Active only when the countryside is moist and warm, they do not really live in a desert at all. (Perhaps they can lead sociable, communal lives because they need not face hard times or competition for sparse food or dwindling stores.)

The desert's tough shrubs support animals, too. Pronghorn antelope and bighorn sheep browse on them, although they need softer, more succulent plants as well for adequate nutrition. Sage grouse, the big birds whose spring courtship "struts," held on long-established mating grounds, are part of the excitement of desert spring, eat mostly those unappetizing looking gray leaves for which they were named. Sagebrush voles and pygmy rabbits burrow under the bushes that are their main food supply. Jackrabbits—both black-tailed (*Lepus californicus*) and the larger, less common white-tailed species (*Lepus townsendii*)—eat mostly twigs and leaves. (Incidentally, if you can't see the tail, you often can tell which kind of jackrabbit you are seeing by its hop. Black-tailed jackrabbits zig-zag more, while white-tails take higher leaps. White-tails also are concentrated in slightly higher, moister areas.)

Carnivores of one kind or another are a fascinating part of desert life. The most common desert birds—liquid-voiced, yellow-breasted western meadowlarks, dry-voiced sage sparrows, and brown, ground-hugging horned larks—eat many insects, although seeds also are important in their diets. Sagebrush is the home of the loggerhead shrike, a small gray bird whose hooked, heavy bill shows he is a hunter of small mammals, birds, and insects. (Victims sometimes are impaled on barbed wire.) As discussed below, dry lands are the best places in the Northwest for watching hawks.

Desert lizards and toads also hunt spiders, ants, various insects, and occasionally other lizards.

Other meat eaters are owls, badgers (*Taxidea taxus*), bobcats, coyotes, and foxes (kit foxes in the extreme south; and gray foxes, *Urocyon cinereoargenteus*, in Oregon's east Cascades and dry southwestern valleys).

**Figure 6-11.** Male sage grouse, strutting and inflating their yellow throat sacs, are one of the spectacles of the arid Northwest.

**Figure 6-12.** Western meadowlark, above, and rough-legged hawk—two "hunters" of dry country.

# HOMES IN THE DESERT:
# ANIMALS OF SAND

The desert's extremes of soil and slope provide homes for different predators and prey. In sandy areas, for example, you can expect to find low mounds built by the excavations of kangaroo mice and rats (*Microdipodops megacephalus*; *Dipodomys ordii* and *microps*). In daytime they sleep, the entrances of their burrows plugged with sand to conserve moisture. At night they gather seeds. Their broad feet and long hind legs let them move easily even on shifting dunes, and escape predators with quick, zig-zag hops.

**151**

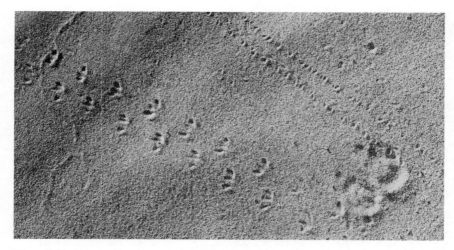

**Figure 6-13.** Animals of sandy deserts lead their active lives at night. By day, you see little more than tracks, like these near Wallula Gap, Washington.

Hopping is not the only protection these mice share with rabbits—they also have sensitive, enlarged ears, although it is the inner ears of kangaroo mice and rats that are oversized.

Another sand animal is the little yellow kit fox, which ranges from more southern deserts into Oregon and Idaho. He spends days in a sandy burrow (partly for protection from coyotes) and hunts rodents at night.

Different soils cut down competition among desert rodents that eat similar foods. Least chipmunks (*Eutamias minimus*), for example, seem to be able to dig through clay soils, while pocket mice need looser soil.

## RIMROCK ANIMALS

The rimrock—cliffs and canyon rims, with boulders, ledges, caves, and piles of loose fallen rock called *talus*—is home for many other desert animals. These include the yellow-bellied marmot, Idaho ground squirrel (*Spermophilus brunneus*), and the aptly named canyon mouse (*Peromyscus crinatus*) and canyon wren.

The collared lizard (*Crotaphytus collaris*) frequents rocky areas, using boulders as lookouts and jumping easily from rock to rock as it makes a quick rush after prey. By contrast, the related leopard lizard (*Crotaphytus wislizenii*) is at home in bunchgrass and scattered brush, where it lurks waiting for unwary prey.

The ringtail, a desert relative of the raccoon, ranges into southern Oregon and Idaho, denning in caves and crevices in cliffs. Bobcats sleep in the rimrock, emerging by night to hunt ranges of about six square miles.

Pronghorn antelope are North America's fastest-running animals—they can reach speeds of up to 40 miles an hour. They graze in the open sagebrush, where they can spot enemies at a distance, and depend on speed for escape. By contrast, the desert's other big native grazer, bighorn sheep (*Ovis canadensis*), pick steep, rugged rimrock. There, these deer-sized sheep with the curly horns have little competition for food, and few enemies can threaten them.

This habitat did not protect them, though, from human hunters and scabies, a parasitic disease brought by flocks of domestic sheep. The last of the Northwest's native desert bighorns (*O. c. californianus*) died off shortly after the turn of the century. Those found today in their original habitats—such as Idaho's Owyhee Mountains, Oregon's Steens Mountains and Hart Mountain National Antelope Range, and Washington's Sinlahekin Wildlife Recreation Area—have been reintroduced from other areas.

**Figure 6-14.** Bighorn sheep like steep, rocky areas where they can climb to escape enemies.

The hunting hawks that soar over the desert also need the cliffs for nesting. You may see a golden eagle's big stick platform. Streaks of white excrement down the rocks may indicate a peregrine or prairie falcon's "scrape"—little more than a hollow on a ledge. Red-tailed and ferruginous hawks nest in high and low cliffs, respectively, as well as in trees. Desert scavengers—vultures and ravens—also nest on rock ledges.

Explore such nests only with binoculars. Some hawks will abandon a nest if they are disturbed. Exposure to desert sun, even for a few minutes, can kill eggs or young. And when youngsters are not ready to fly, your presence could frighten them into plunging to their deaths.

Not surprisingly, the limited supply of shaded caves and ledges leads to "recycling" and even competition. Falcons, though they do not build stick nests, sometimes rear young on abandoned eagle platforms. Swainsons, ferruginous, and red tailed hawks, as well as great horned owls, use nests in rotation or drive one another away from the coveted spot.

## COPING WITH DROUGHT AND COLD

Large animals like pronghorn antelope and bighorn sheep (and the wild horses of southeastern Oregon) can survive days in hot sun mostly because of their size. Any large object can absorb more heat than a small one without raising its temperature significantly. In addition, large animals can drink large amounts of water and cool themselves the way we humans do, by sweating.

Pronghorn show this close dependence on water: Every herd's range includes a seep, stream, or pool that it visits daily. In summer, animals may have to drink more than a gallon of water a day to survive. Most pronghorns—large winter herds and smaller summer harems—live within five to ten miles of these waterholes. With the best areas preempted in this way, however, a few groups have been forced to make daily trips of up to 50 miles. Another indication of pronghorns' dependence on water is that game managers have been able to greatly increase the animals' numbers by providing them with artificial waterholes. (Thanks to refuges and other aid, these fleet animals have increased from only around 20,000 survivors in the 1920s to about a half million today.)

Small desert animals, by contrast, could not survive a day in the pitiless sun. A kangaroo rat would have to lose 13 percent of its body weight per hour to cool itself by sweating—and the desert offers no such water supply.

Animals' most obvious way to cope with this problem is to sleep in moist, cool burrows in the daytime, living their active lives at night.

If you spent a night in the arid Pacific Northwest, watching life with a dim red light (such as a cellophane-covered flashlight) that nocturnal animals

**Figure 6-15.** Pronghorns, North America's fastest mammals, prefer open country with low brush, where they can spot predators at a distance and run without meeting obstacles.

hardly see, you would find a different and not entirely friendly world. Scorpions come out to immobilize and eat even mice, larger than themselves. Western rattlers (*Crotalus viridus*) emerge from burrows, hunting in darkness by using the heat sensing pits between their eyes and nostrils. Most desert snakes, as well as amphibians like salamanders and toads, are nocturnal. Even common king snakes (*Lampropeltis getulus*) and gopher snakes (*Pituophis melanoleucus*), which hunt by day elsewhere, are active at night in the desert.

**Figure 6-16.** Western rattlesnakes hunt by night, sensing prey by their heat.

The desert's fascinating variety of small mammals comes fully alive at night. Kangaroo mice and rats hop like their namesakes. Bushy-tailed woodrats (*Neotoma cinerea* and *lepida*) better known as packrats, pound the ground with feet and tails, fiercely defending their hoards of debris. Shy burrowing pygmy rabbits (*Sylvilagus idahoensis*) nibble at sage leaves: In America, these desert-dwellers are the only rabbits that live in burrows— another sign of the value of a moist, cool hole in the ground.

Like rimrock ledges, the tunnel systems of desert animals are valuable property, often recycled. Solitary antelope ground squirrels (*Ammosper-mophilus leucurus*) use burrows dug by kangaroo rats. Coyotes and badgers, in turn, sometimes inhabit the enlarged hole of unfortunate ground squirrels. Badgers, flattened yellow animals with big claws, use such burrows year-round. The coyotes you hear yelping on desert nights, though, generally use such dens only while their pups are young. The rest of the year, families wander their home ranges, sleeping in protected places on the ground.

The misnamed burrowing owl, which eats mostly insects, does not dig its own burrow. It, too, uses those of ground squirrels. Salamanders lurk in mammals' burrows to avoid fatal dehydration—because they are amphibians, salamanders absorb water through their skins, but can lose it just as easily. A number of snakes also inhabit rodent burrows. Some harmlessly escape the heat there. Others, like king and gopher snakes, ungratefully hunt the rodents that built their homes.

One kind of rodent common in arid country, the pocket gopher, has moved almost entirely underground. Solitary except during breeding season, pocket gophers move through a network of tunnels, munching juicy tubers, bulbs, and the like. Pocket gophers are the source of small mounds with off-center plugs, and of most of the hard cores of earth you find on the ground after snowmelt. Digging pocket gophers throw dirt behind them, then turn around and push out the waste, bulldozer fashion. The cores you find are this excavated dirt, pushed into winter tunnels in the snow.

Small animals active during the day use a number of tricks to cope with heat. Desert ground squirrels retreat to their burrows between outings, exchanging heat with the cool earth walls.

The half-dozen kinds of lizards that hunt in the arid Northwest are of course cold-blooded, with little control over their body temperatures. On chilly mornings, they warm themselves by sprawling on warm rocks, broadside to the sun. Later in the day, they keep cool with such tricks as climbing high into the breezier parts of sagebrush; standing "on tiptoe" so that their bodies don't touch hot soil, or orienting themselves tail to the sun.

It takes some patience to learn to distinguish the roughly half-dozen kinds of lizards in the region. Body color is not a reliable indicator, as it varies widely, often matching nearby soil. Two species, though, are easily identified. The collared lizard (*Crotaphytus collaris*) has a striking black and white collar. The "horned toad," or desert horned lizard (*Phrynosoma platyrhinos*)

**Figure 6-17.** Uinta ground squirrel (left), burrowing owl (above), and badger (below)— three animals that may use the same burrow, in succession. (Badger photographed at Northwest Trek, Eatonville, Washington).

has prominent spines projecting from his head and smaller ones from his stout body.

Besides specialized behavior, many desert animals have physical adaptations that help them cope with extremes of heat and cold, and lack of water.

The most obvious of these is color: Like desert shrubs and soil, desert animals are nearly all buff to gray. The sagebrush vole, for example, is lighter than voles of meadows, mountains, and marshes. The desert-dwelling least chipmunk is pale gray, while his relatives in pine or spruce forests are red-brown to yellow-brown. Color works to camouflage as well as cool animals, though, and it's hard to say which is more important. Mice and ground squirrels living on beds of fresh dark lava, for example, sometimes are dark, while their kin on other rocks are pale.

Desert lizards are light-colored, but a black membrane lines their abdominal cavities. Its dark pigment, melanin, may protect the lizards' internal organs from damage by ultraviolet radiation from the strong desert sun.

Two real "desert rats," kangaroo mice and pocket mice, can survive the desert without ever taking a drink: Their bodies metabolize all the water they need from a diet of dry seeds.

Such rodents' narrow nasal passages even serve as water savers: Warm air leaving their lungs is cooled by incoming air to below body temperature. Moisture condenses before the animal exhales the air. This liquid is re-absorbed into the animal's body.

Another built-in heat exchanger, almost a symbol of the desert, is the jackrabbit's huge ears. In hot weather, blood vessels in those ears dilate. Blood pumped through the thin flesh loses heat and helps cool the animal. In cold weather, the blood vessels contract. Little blood flows through the ears, and the rabbit stays warmer.

Many desert animals also are extraordinarily flexible about their body temperatures. Most human beings know that something is wrong if their temperature gets more than a degree away from normal. Ground squirrels, and jackrabbits that crouch through daylight hours in the sparse shade of desert shrubs, tolerate body temperatures several degrees above their normal: They simply wait to cool down at night, cutting their need for costly cooling.

Pocket, canyon, deer, kangaroo and other desert mice can fall into a deep daily torpor. Their metabolism slows down. Their body temperatures plunge to nearly those of the air around them. As a result, they lose less water through evaporation and save energy for the hours when they can replenish it by eating. A few birds, including desert swifts and poor-wills, also have such bouts of torpor.

Daily torpor is echoed by a longer cycle in animals for whom estivation, a rather light, often broken summer torpor, can merge into hibernation, the deeper sleep of winter. In addition to mammals such as colonial ground squirrels and marmots, the Great Basin spadefoot toad (*Scaphiopus intermontanus*) sleeps through dry and cold in a burrow dug with the horny black "spades" on his hind feet. In warm wet weather, the toads emerge, eat, and breed. Since even their breeding ponds may dry up after rains, the young are transformed with extraordinary speed—metamorphosing from new egg to tadpole to frog in three weeks. (Spadefoot toads may be distinguished from the two true toads of the Northwest, the western toad, *Bufo boreas*, and Woodhouse's toad, *B. woodhousei*, by nearly smooth skin, lack of a distinct stripe down the back, and a tough black "spade" projecting from each hind foot.)

## DOING IT YOURSELF

The best time to visit Northwest deserts is in the spring—roughly April through June. Mammals are active. Wildflowers are at their peaks. Bright songbirds flash in woody stream canyons. Lakes and reservoirs are busy with blackbirds, geese, ducks, and shorebirds. Arid spots, seemingly empty, contrast sharply with the intense activity around even the smallest body of water.

**Figure 6-18.** Shooting star, one of the flowers that brighten spring in arid country.

Enjoy the pungent smells of desert vegetation by crushing a few leaves. Look down for inconspicuous wonders like the little sagebrush violet (*Viola trinervata*), with a fragile, deep purple flower above tough gray leaves. Look up at cliffs and canyon walls to see mourning doves flying from rim to rim, or red-tailed hawks screaming as they circle and dive.

Among the most interesting places are:

—Idaho's Craters of the Moon National Park and other lava beds

—Central Washington's Crab Creek Wildlife Recreation Area; Potholes, Winchester, Desert, Lava, and Goose Lake W.R.A.s; and the nearby Columbia National Wildlife Refuge

—Oregon's John Day Country (including John Day Fossil Beds National Monument and Murderers Creek Wildlife Area), Malheur National Wildlife Refuge, and Hart Mountain National Antelope Range.

The Hart Mountain and John Day areas probably are the best places for antelope watching. Antelope may simply appear, outracing your car, as you drive on desert roads in Oregon and Southeastern Idaho. Bighorn sheep are elusive, but you may see them near Hart Mountain, or Washington's Sinlahekin or W.T. Wooten W.R.A.s.

Hawk enthusiasts will enjoy the Bureau of Land Management's Birds of Prey Area, near Swan Falls in the Snake River Valley desert of Southwestern Oregon. Contact the Bureau's Boise office, 3948 Development Street, Boise, Idaho 83705, for information.

For many, the highlight of desert bird watching is seeing sage grouse "struts" in spring. The males inflate their yellow throat sacs and posture to maintain small desirable patches of a traditional courting ground. Females are attracted to central positions, not specific males. Thus, whichever male holds the best area gets to mate with the most females. For information on when and where to go, contact local Audubon Society chapters or state game departments.

Probably the easiest mammals to watch are yellow-bellied marmots and ground squirrels. If you spot a group of holes with fresh earth at their mouths, or if you spot a bit of movement, find a comfortable place at a distance and wait. Before long, the animals will be out again, the youngsters tussling, the adults nipping at greens, seeds, or flowers.

To see desert night life, wear tough, snakeproof boots and warm clothing. Cover a flashlight with translucent red plastic, or go by the full moon and watch for animals' eyes shining.

# 7

# At the Edge of Salt Water

## SEA VS. CONTINENT

The Pacific Ocean meets the Northwest in continual warfare. This is obvious where surf pounds at rocky headlands directly facing the Pacific. Wind and waves continually grind sand and gravel against such cliffs. Air, compressed into crevices by waves, blasts away bits of rock. Thus the sea hammers and chisels pinnacles, natural arches, and sea caves.

The gains and losses can be more sudden, however, on what seem like quieter shores. An example is Willapa Bay, a haven in rainy Southwest Washington, its waters stilled by a long spit dotted with cranberry bogs. Small clouds of shorebirds, wheeling above oyster beds, seem livelier than the waves. Yet on the bay's north shore, the relentless twice-daily ebb and flood of tidal currents have eaten away homes, roads, and miles of land.

The land fights the sea with its very substance—rivers carry dust of the eroded continent into bays or far out to sea. The result is less a continual nibbling away of the continent than a shifting equilibrium. While waves pound Oregon's rocky coast, many of its protected bays are gradually silting in.

Particles carried away from one shore are deposited somewhere else. The prevailing winds, from the south in winter, and from the north in summer, drive along-shore currents. Like rivers, they carry and drop tons of sand along the shore each day.

The finger-like spits and bars at so many Northwest bay mouths show these currents' flow. They grow north where prevailing currents run that way, south when they run south. Cut off the flow of sand—say, with a jetty that changes currents—and the fragile spits are quickly broken and eaten away. Thus, a jetty built at the mouth of Tillamook Bay caused the destruction of a nearby spit that once was the resort community of Bayocean; some former beach was left a half mile offshore. On the other hand, settling sand has extended some Washington ocean beaches hundreds of feet, provoking a bitter legal battle over whether the new shore was owned by the state or by landowners whose houses were now well back from the waterfront.

Rocky shores thus can be seen as those stripped of their defenses by waves or currents, or robbed of their sand supply by some obstruction that turns sediment-bearing currents away from land.

A muddy shore is a sign of calm water—fast-moving, roiled water would keep fine particles, which make mud, in suspension. Mud also signals a river mouth or some other place where deposition from the land dominates.

**Figure 7-1.** Waves at Toleak Point, Olympic National Park, Washington: The Pacific batters the Northwest's open coast.

**Figure 7-2.** This spit at the mouth of Oregon's Salmon River, like many in the Northwest, was built by the along-shore currents that continually pick up and drop sand along the coast.

Sand or gravel beaches represent a middle ground. Their waves or currents are too strong to let the finest particles settle, but the sea continually picks up, drops, and rearranges their loose fragments. Thus summer's gentle waves carry sand to shore and build a wide, gently sloping beach. Winter's steeper, more frequent waves steepen the beach and carry sand to deeper water (where it is stored as submerged bars until the next summer). Sandy beaches also become more rough and gravelly in winter, when stronger waves and currents carry away the finer grains.

## BEACHES AS A BASE FOR LIFE

One of the first problems faced by living things on and near the shore is the variety of kinds of beaches—rock, sand, gravel, and mud; wave-beaten or sheltered. Different plants and animals favor each kind of beach. Exposed, wave-battered shores in the Northwest, for example, bear the California mussel (*Mytilus californianus*), which has a thicker shell and stronger anchoring threads than the smaller "edible mussel" (*Mytilus edulis*) of sheltered bays. (Actually, both are delicious, though they may harbor the poisonous "red tide" dinoflagellate in summer months.)

Another powerful influence on shore life is the plant or animal's position in relation to the fluctuating height of tides.

The pull of the moon on one side of the earth, and a corresponding bulge due to centrifugal force on the opposite side, are the basic reason for the twice-daily rise and fall of tides. The weaker pull of the sun, joined to that of the moon or acting against it (depending on whether sun and moon are on the same or opposite sides of the earth) accounts for the regular variations between "neap" and "spring" tides. When the sun counteracts the moon's influence, there is little difference between high and low tides. When the two act together, the differences are much greater.

Land that blocks, channels, or slows the bulge of water chasing the moon usually accentuates the differences between low and high tides. Thus the effects of tides on life are most easily seen in deep, narrow bays like Puget Sound, where differences between high and low tides commonly exceed eight feet.

Which animals thrive at which tidal heights also can be seen on manmade vertical "shores," such as pilings. Only a few tough-shelled barnacles (*Balanus* spp. and others) and stout little periwinkle snails

**Figure 7-3.** Barnacles and mussels are among the few creatures that can cling to exposed rocks on the wave-battered shores of Olympic National Park.

(*Littorina* spp.) cling to the upper part of such surfaces. Meanwhile, the seldom-bared base a few feet below supports a miniature forest of delicate sea anemones, hydroids, feather-duster worms, and crust-like sponges. Although they look like plants, these creatures all are animals. The feather-duster worms and anemones wait for prey to drift through their colorful tentacles, withdrawing them if startled. Anemones, though they spend most of their lives attached to a firm base waiting for prey, can move—they even attack other anemones. Moss-like hydroids, though they are fixed to one spot as adults, spend part of their lives as floating jellyfish. Sponges are colonial animals which, like corals, build a tenement of their stiff external skeletons. When a single animal dies, its skeleton remains.

Plants or animals that live between high and low tide levels obviously must lead at least two lives. They will be drenched at times and dry at others. They must withstand not only the rather constant chill of the North Pacific, but also extremes of summer heat and winter cold. Exposure, though, is not the only stress that determines where animals live in relation to the water level. Competition, predation, light levels, slope, and temperature are among the other influences. Scuba divers can see this—animal and plant species vary with depth well below the level of lowest tide.

## ESTUARIES

A third influence on sea life, less obvious than tidal levels and type of shore, is salinity—mainly influenced by fresh water flowing from the land. Most Pacific Northwest bays are estuaries—meeting places of river and sea, with heavy inflows from streams, especially in winter and spring.

The estuaries' variable dilution discourages many sea animals, but it benefits others. Oysters, for example, seem to thrive best in somewhat dilute sea water. Small processing plants and piles of white shells along the shore of many Northwest bays are the most visible evidence of the many oyster farms beneath the surface. The farmers supply larvae, called "spat," and the hard surface they need to settle on—commonly strings of oyster shells hung from rafts.

Very few grow the small native Olympia oysters (*Ostrea lurida*). They were common in pioneer days, but were all but wiped out by pulp-mill pollution in the 1920s. Japanese oysters (*Crassostrea gigas*), introduced by Japanese growers shortly after the turn of the century, have proved tougher. They have spread from cultivation to the wild, thriving in sheltered waters that grow warm in summer, such as Washington's Hood Canal. For the oysters to be safe eating, though, the bays where they grow must be pollution free. Oysters filter immense quantities of water through their gills, and concentrate pollutants in their bodies.

**Figure 7-4.** John's River Estuary, Washington—a place where fresh and salt water meet.

Rocks, seaweed, and sunshine filtering through shallow waters make most coastal areas nurseries for sea life. These inshore areas are richer in light, nutrients, and protection than the deep open ocean. Pacific Northwest estuaries, with their rich supply of nutrients from runoff and their shallow and often protected waters, are particularly valuable in this way—young salmon and flounder are among the many fish they nurture. Estuaries also make well-stocked, sheltered homes or resting places for shore birds and waterfowl.

Unfortunately, shallow, swampy river mouths are among the areas man is most likely to change, dredging or filling them for harbors or building. In the Northwest, well over half of this kind of habitat and related salt marshes have been destroyed.

## ROCKY SHORES

Rocky beaches, the most dramatic and picturesque of shores, also are the most crowded with visible life. Some of this life is noisily obvious. The island rocks that jut up from the waves off Washington and Oregon are sanctuaries for crowded colonies of sea birds—cormorants and murres nesting on bare ledges; auklets, guillemots, and puffins laying their eggs in burrows and crannies.

**Figure 7-5.** Common murres nesting on Right Island, Oregon Islands National Wildlife Refuge. Such seabirds need the rocky islets for protection because they move awkwardly on land, and could not protect themselves from predators.

These sea birds look rather odd-shaped and awkward above the waves. Cormorants swim so low they seem about to sink. When they come ashore, they even spread their wings as if to dry them. Stout little puffins, scarcely able to waddle, must launch themselves from cliffs or splash along the water to take off. They are able divers and swimmers, however, paddling with wings as well as webbed feet to come up with a silvery, still wriggling fish.

**Figure 7-6.** Harbor seals are also called leopard seals because of their spots.

The Northwest's rocky waters and crescents of beach are feeding and resting places for marine mammals, mostly spotted harbor seals (*Phoca vitulina*) and Northern or Steller sea lions (*Eumetopias jubata*). These sea lions are recognizable by the yellowish mane on the males, which are three to four times the size of females. Casual visitors to these coasts also include the much larger northern elephant seals (*Mirounga angustirostris*), whose males have trunk-like snouts; and small, solid-colored California sea lions (*Zalophus californianus*), whose males lack trunk or mane but have a sort of crest on their heads. Sea otters (*Enhydra lutris*) once lived well on the fish and shellfish of kelp beds off rocky Northwest coasts. All but trapped into extinction, they have been reintroduced, but are still struggling to make a comeback.

At low tide, exposed rocks are draped with algae. Rocks provide secure footing for these seaweeds' holdfasts—small discs or protuberances resembling short roots. Such sea-gardens are colorful without flowers, as the plants themselves are red and yellow-brown as well as green—Reddish and brownish algae do a better job than green at absorbing the blue-green light that filters through water.

Algae forests have lacy fronds, trailing blades, and gas-filled bladders to keep the deeper-water species afloat. They have no trunks, roots, or leaves

**Figure 7-7.** Northern, or Steller, sea lions inhabit Oregon's rocky coasts.

like those of forests on land. Sea plants need flexibility, not support (though algae of wave-beaten shores have tough stems that resist abrasion). In addition, since nutrients and water are all around them, algae do not need specialized leaves to synthesize food and stems to conduct food and water elsewhere.

Despite the color and sound on some coasts, most life on rocky shores is not outgoing. It can be seen, though, by taking a slow and careful walk when the tide is out.

On wave-battered coasts, sand may scrub boulders clean of everything except the toughest and most firmly attached plants and animals. Even these—yellowish sea-palm algae (*Postelsia palmaeformis*), barnacles, and purple-black mussels—cluster together, thus lessening the impact of water.

Turn even bare rocks over, however, and you find bustling cities. The crevices beneath and between rocks provide moisture, shade, and shelter. You find scuttling crabs, bug-like isopods or "sea lice," soft-bodied worms, tough chitons, bristling purple sea urchins, orange sea stars, crusts of grainy sponges, and gelatine-like compound ascidians—not to mention bright-colored eel-like fish and a wide variety of eggs. (If you turn over beach rocks, do it carefully, and replace them just as you found them. Exposure to sun, air, and predators can quickly destroy these fascinating colonies.)

Even below the lowest tidal levels, crevices are vital protection. Some animals dig their own—piddock clams (*Penitella penita*) and the purple sea urchins (*Strongylocentrotus purpuratus*) of wave-battered coasts can burrow in soft rock. These and other caves or depressions are eagerly colonized by other animals: worms, soft-bellied crabs (*Oedignathus inermis*), sea cucumbers, even (in larger openings) octopuses.

Tide pools, trapping the sea even at low tide, are natural aquariums. There you can watch marine life when it is relaxed and natural. Colorful feeding tentacles of sea anemones and tube worms float expanded like flowers, waiting for unwary prey. The varied snails of the sea, whose whorled shells fascinate us when they wash up on the beach, creep about. Despite their soft bodies, they live by means of a hard rasping organ on their snouts. Some use it to peacefully scrape algae from the rocks. Others hunt oysters, mussels, and barnacles, piercing their shells with a fatal hole.

In tide pools, look too for tide-pool sculpins (*Oligocottus maclosus*) lurking on the bottom. These toadlike fish change color to match the substrate. You can see other defenses: Hermit crabs (*Pagurus* and *Orthopagurus* spp.) hide inside abandoned snail shells. Decorator crabs (*Oregonia gracilis*) camouflage themselves with bits of seaweed stuck to their shells.

With luck, at the lowest tidal levels, you may even see an octopus scooting into his hole, or a sea slug or nudibranch grazing on a crust of sponge. These are colorful snails without shells, with ruffly gills, usually white to orange.

# SAND AND MUD BEACHES

By contrast with rocky shores, sandy beaches may seem almost barren below their berms of washed-up decaying seaweed, and flea-like beach hoppers (*Orchestoidea* and *Orchestia* spp.). This is especially true on sands exposed to waves. Bits of organic matter and other nutrients are easily washed out of the loose substrate. In addition, neither plants nor animals can find secure homes in loose grains of sand and gravel, continuously stirred by waves, eroded in winter storms, and redeposited in summer.

But there is life on such beaches. This is evident from flocks of shorebirds—sandpipers, dunlins, knots, and the like—probing the sand with their long, thin bills. (The black oyster catcher, which pries oysters and mussels from rocky shores, by contrast has a bill like a chisel.)

**Figure 7-8.** The pointed beaks of sandpipers (above), which probe soft beaches for food, contrast with the chisel-like bill that the oyster catcher (left) uses to pry shellfish from rocks.

Despite their appearance of fragility, the long-legged, long-billed shore birds are long-distance champions among migrants. The little wild strawberries of the beach are their gift. Native to the Pacific Northwest and coastal Ecuador and Chile, but not the lands between, their seeds must have been carried by these delicate but swift-flying birds. The beach strawberry's Latin name, *Fragaria chiloensis*, reflects this origin: Chiloe is an island off Southern Chile.

As the probing shore birds indicate, animals on sandy beaches must go underground to keep from being washed away. Fragile worms, small shrimps (*Crago* spp.) and shrimp-like animals such as mysids (*Archaeomysis* spp.) cling to the sand, burrowing into it again and again as waves displace them. Out near the low-tide line, where the bottom is seldom exposed, eager clam diggers find the fast-digging razor clam (*Siliqua patula*). Its speed in escaping the shovel is an adaptation for survival in places where waves can expose the animals at any moment. The clam's muscular "foot" stretches into the sand, expands to gain a hold, and pulls the shell toward it. In this way, a razor clam can dig down a foot or more faster than you can.

Sandy beaches protected from waves have a richer life, but one that is still mostly hidden. Plants still are scarce, at least down to the low-tide mark. Beneath the apparently barren sand, though, moon snails (*Polinices lewisii*) hunt clams. The egg cases of moon snails, fine sand cemented with mucus into a collar, are a familiar sight on such beaches in summer.

**Figure 7-9.** Razor clams are adapted to fast digging on sandy, wave-battered beaches, so diggers like these at Long Beach, Washington, must be, too.

Sand dollars (*Dendraster* spp.) plow along, half buried, filtering edible detritus from the water as they go. One atypical species of sea cucumber (*Leptosynapta clarki*) has adapted to a miner's life, and lives buried in sand.

As more mud is mixed with sand and gravel, a beach holds more organic matter. Decomposition of this rich supply is what gives so many mud flats their "rotten egg" smell. Besides supplying food, mud usually is stiff enough for animals to maintain permanent burrows. A beach of fine, easily stirred mud, however, can be deadly, silting in both tunnel homes and gills.

Small mounds in the muddy sand mark the lairs of ghost or mud shrimp (*Callianassa and Upogebia* spp.). Thin coils or sausages of mud are the feces of a variety of fragile, burrowing worms, some several inches long. Breathing holes larger than the pinholes made by these worms show that several species of clams are at home where sand is mixed with some mud. Among these species are the bent-nosed clam (*Macoma nasuta*), horse clam (*Tresus capax*), heart cockle (*Clinocardium nuttallii*), horse mussel (*Modiulus rectus*), and soft-shelled clam (*Mya arenaria*). More gravelly beaches are likely to have butter clams (*Saxidomus giganteus*) and littleneck clams (*Venerupis tenerrima*). (If you dig clams, refill the hole. Otherwise, the pile of sand, gravel, and mud you pushed aside may smother other beach creatures, including smaller clams.)

Life becomes more obvious below the low tide line of protected sandy and muddy beaches. Miniature forests of bright orange sea pens (*Ptilosarcus gurnyi*) flourish. Actually, these are colonial animals, like corals. The base of the rigid "quill" remains buried in the sand. The "plume" is dozens of little mouths that take in water and small animals and share them via an interconnected gut. A variety of colorful sea stars hunt clams and other prey in these miniature forests.

Still more interesting, and far more important ecologically, is the eel grass (*Zostera marina*) community of protected Northwest waters. Eel grass is one of the few flowering, seed-forming plants that live in salt water. Its roots weave thick mats in sand and mud, stabilizing them. The abundant grass blades, kept afloat by air pockets, shelter dozens of animals, including Dungeness crabs (*Cancer magister*), sea anemones, and sea slugs and other nudibranchs.

These in turn attract hunting animals such as harbor seals and diving birds. The grass and small animals on it are vital food for geese and ducks in protected waters like Dungeness Bay and the mouth of the Skagit River in northern Puget Sound (both in Washington State). Although only a small percentage of the water birds on the Pacific Flyway actually winter in the Pacific Northwest, a large proportion of those that do make heavy use of the eel-grass beds. They include black brant, dark, noisy little sea geese moving back and forth from the Arctic; and the wintering snow geese of Washington's Skagit Flats—a group that comes all the way from breeding grounds on

**Figure 7-10.** A black brant, one of the dark little sea geese that migrate along Northwest ocean shores; and a cloud of snow geese that also use coastal eel grass beds.

Wrangell Island, 90 miles north of Siberia. When the island has a late spring, the flock dwindles. In good years, though, 30,000 snow geese make a spectacular sight as they fly from flats to farmers' fields through the winter.

# THE SECRET LIFE OF THE SEA

The life you see on the beach, and even the much more varied communities explored by divers, give an oversimplified picture of life in the ocean. The saltwater food chain, for example, begins with tiny floating plants and animals called *plankton*. Too small to be spotted as individuals, these creatures nevertheless can be seen. They make the waters cloudier during their periodic "blooms," or they create irridescence that makes wavelets, boats, and fish glow palely in the night.

One kind of tiny floating plant, *Gonyaulax catanella*, can produce chains of cells in such numbers that it stains the sea yellowish to red—and makes it deadly poisonous. Fish can die outright. Shellfish with *Gonyaulax* poison concentrated in their tissues become deadly to man. Although the condition is rare, it is sufficiently deadly to warrant warnings against gathering shellfish from untested areas in summer.

Along with the plankton, the sea carries numberless spores of algae and tiny, free-swimming larvae of most of the animals seen along the Northwest's beaches. Strange-looking as they are, the bottom-dwelling, spineless creatures such as crabs, anemones, and shellfish have life histories that are still stranger.

Living beings can expend only a limited amount of energy in reproducing themselves. They allocate this energy in ways that range between two extreme strategies. In the first extreme, they produce few young, nurturing them carefully so that most survive. Examples of this are human beings, avocado trees with their big seeds and fleshy fruits, and the sea birds that nest on offshore rocks—most of them lay only one or two eggs a year. The other extreme is to produce many young, giving each one little care or energy, and letting many perish. Weeds such as thistles, with their many wind-born seeds, are examples of this strategy, which is also followed by most Pacific Northwest marine plants and animals. For example, a female oyster or sea star may produce 100,000 eggs a year.

Among most Pacific Northwest bottom-dwelling invertebrates, the almost numberless young are released from the parent as nearly helpless larvae, as embryos, or even as as unfertilized eggs and sperm, dependent on currents to find each other. These youngsters drift or swim. They feed on plankton once they reach larval stages. The larvae, tentacled, oared, or "winged," look like tiny monsters out of someone's nightmare. It requires one or two metamorphoses for them to take on adult form, settle to the bottom, and begin their growth as creatures we would recognize.

Similarly, marine algae release into the water vast numbers of spores containing half the plant's maximum number of chromosomes. The male or female plants that grow from these spores release male sperm and female eggs (collectively called *gametes*) which must find one another in the sea in order to form another plant with the full number of chromosomes. (Every plant goes through these stages, but in flowering plants, as in animals, the phase of sexual reproduction, and having half the full number of chromosomes, is short and largely sheltered within internal organs.)

Obviously, many spores, eggs, and larvae drifting in the sea never become adults. They are devoured, swept out to sea, or washed onto beaches. Some young, though, are likely to reach almost any new place suitable for colonization. This advantage balances the apparent "waste" of juveniles. Thus, tidal currents and the wind-driven along-shore currents also are rivers of life, moving cradles for the young of the shores.

**Figure 7-11.** Starfish and sea anemones, here in a tide pool in Olympic National Park, have life histories even stranger than their appearances.

# BEHIND THE BEACH

In contrast to the rich life in salt water, the nearby shore is often a near desert. Few plants can survive winds that whip them with grains of salt and sand; in shifting dunes; and in fast-draining, salt-laden soils with few nutrients. Those that do survive resemble the plants that grow under tough conditions elsewhere, in deserts and poor soils.

*Salicornia* or pickleweed, for example, is a yellowish, succulent plant of salt marshes that also grows on the edges of alkaline lakes in the desert. It shares with other desert plants the $C_4$ method of synthesizing food. (As its common name indicates, the juicy stems can make a good relish.) Succulent yellow or pink sand verbenas (*Abronia latifolia* and *umbellata*), bright ground-covers on many beaches, have a white-flowered desert relative (*Abronia mellifera*). The seashore lupines (*Lupinus littoralis*), beach peas (*Lathyrus japonicus* and others), and black knotweeds (*Polygonum paronychia*) also have similar dry-area relatives. Yarrow (*Achillea millefolium*), another flower of seashore meadows, grows in dry and poor soils almost everywhere.

The characteristic features of these plants, though, may serve different purposes on the seashore and in deserts. Thick, waxy skin, low growth, and dense hairs are thought to help desert plants by preventing water loss. While beach sands also drain quickly, the main function of these adaptations on seashores may be to keep salt out of the plants. Succulence, which helps desert plants store water, may help beach plants just as much by diluting the concentration of salts in their sap.

In dune areas, plants change as you move back from the still-shifting foredunes. Loose sand exposed directly to sea winds often is colonized by pioneering dune grasses, such as the native beach rye (*Elymus mollis*) and introduced Marram grass (*Ammophila arenaria*). Their fast-growing fibrous roots bind the dunes. Their underground shoots can spread even if the original plant is buried by blowing sand. Their blades catch sand, building the front dune higher and so sheltering the land behind it.

The sandy, partly stabilized areas in the lee of this foredune are soon invaded by salt-tolerant, hardy wildflowers, such as sand verbenas and beach peas. When the decay of these plants has enriched the soil, still other plants appear.

Older dunes still farther back from the shore support shrubs and trees not very different from those of poor soils elsewhere in the Northwest: kinnikinnick, salal, the coastal variety of lodgepole pine (*Pinus contorta contorta*). Salt prunes these plants on windier shores: Entering tiny wounds on leaves and stems, it accumulates and kills the shoot, shaping the plant. Some, though, seem to use the salts: Sitka spruce, the climax dominant of coastal forests, may actually draw nutrients from the salty sea fogs.

**Figure 7-12.** Sand verbena, with bright yellow or pink flowers, helps stabilize sand in the teeth of ocean winds.

The Northwest's natural seaside communities are among its most threatened. Salt marshes and shallow lagoons once were common where spits and bars were being gradually joined to land. Today more than three-quarters of such areas have been drained and filled for various kinds of development.

Dunes are easily damaged—either by disturbing their vegetation or by adding to it. If the roots that stabilize dunes are destroyed, sand can quickly blow inland, covering meadows and forests. Today, though, such "blowouts" or creeping sands are less a problem than shrinking dunes.

Introduced grasses have stabilized many foredunes, cutting off the supply of ocean sand to dunes farther inland. Such dunes "feed on themselves." The remaining sand gradually shifts inland, and vegetation takes over more and more. In a couple of human generations, some of Oregon's dune areas have lost half their former width.

## DOING IT YOURSELF

To get an idea of the complexity of tides, look at maps (preferably Coast Guard charts), tide tables, and charts of stages of the moon. (Tide tables and stages of the moon are listed in newspapers; charts are available at sporting goods stores.)

Looking at sand and rock, try to guess how wind, waves, and currents have shaped a coast. On sand dunes, see if you can determine from their shapes which way the prevailing winds blow.

Walking on a beach, try to guess from its base material and waves what might live there. Then see if you can find these organisms or their traces. A falling tide is the best time for finding treasures on a beach; very low tides are best for seeing sea life.

If you disturb rocks, replace them carefully. If you dig holes, fill them when you are done. There's no harm in collecting empty shells or pebbles, but don't take living specimens home.

Look for ways that salt and wind have shaped coastal vegetation. Behind the beach, and in lagoons and coastal marshes, notice how vegetation changes as you move away from the shore.

**Figure 7-13.** Sand marching on the wind killed this forest in the Oregon Dunes National Recreation Area.

The best birdwatching along the coast is fall through spring. (Waves often are most dramatic then, too.) Repeated visits give you an idea of when and how different species move, and which stay the winter.

In developed areas, look at life clinging to pilings of piers and floats at marinas. These artificial "shores" clearly show how sea life changes at deeper levels.

Visit one of the Northwest's aquariums to get a look at life in deeper waters. The Vancouver Aquarium, in Vancouver, British Columbia, is one of the largest in North America. The Seattle Marine Aquarium on the city's downtown waterfront stresses native life, including marine mammals. At Newport, Oregon, the Marine Science Center of Oregon State University and Oregon Undersea Gardens, Inc., let you see—and feel—sea life. Smaller aquariums are the Point Defiance Aquarium in Point Defiance Park, Tacoma, Washington; and aquariums at Westport, Washington; Seaside, Oregon; and Depoe Bay, Oregon.

Oregon's 400 miles of seacoast offer almost endless variations on a theme of beauty and relaxation. All but 23 miles of the coast belongs to the public.

You'll find wide sand beaches, dramatic cliffs and pinnacles, sea caves and "spouting horns," seals and sea lions, lighthouses, picturesque towns and fishing fleets.

Among the highlights (from north to south) are:

- Astoria's fishing fleet.
- Ecola State Park and other beaches near Seaside.
- Coves, headlands, and pinnacles from Tillamook Head south to Sea Lion Caves (the easiest place to see marine animals). The headlands are mostly remnants of old undersea volcanos. Flat terraces behind the beach are mostly old Ice Age beaches. "Spouting horns" near Depoe Bay and the Devil's Punch Bowl near Newport show the force of waves dramatically.
- The dunes from Honeyman State Park, south of Florence, to Coos Bay. (They are widest, about three miles, near Florence.)
- Cliffs, pinnacles, and rocky coves from Cape Blanco southward.

Highlights of Washington's open coast include:

- The coastal strip of the Olympic National Park; a unique opportunity to hike and camp on a spectacular coastal wilderness.
- Rocky islets offshore where sea birds nest. Most are in Olympic Park, but those near Kalaloch, Ruby Beach, La Push, Cape Flattery, and the Pt. Grenville Coast Guard Station require only short walks.
- Long Beach Peninsula guarding Willapa Bay. You pass cranberry farms and the pioner settlement of Oysterville on your way to Willapa

National Wildlife Refuge, an outstanding place to watch sea birds from fall to spring. The refuge also has units in the estuary, including Long Island, accessible by canoe.

Washington's inland waters, like Oregon's ocean coast, have more points of interest than can be named here. Among them, again from north to south are:

- The dry San Juan Islands, particularly the rocky shores of San Juan Island itself, with varied tide pools and nesting bald eagles. The ferry ride through the islands is worthwhile by itself.

- The wildlife areas near the mouth of the Skagit River: Skagit Wildlife Recreation Area, where whistling swans graze in fields and snowgeese gather on the mudflats. Nearby Barney, Clear, and Beaver Lakes are winter homes of rare trumpeter swans.

- Dungeness National Wildlife Refuge in the Strait of Juan de Fuca, where you can hike a 5 1/2 mile long sandspit, watching sea birds and seals in the sheltered eel-grass beds.

- Washington's many-fingered inland sea: Ferry rides on Puget Sound; drives along Hood Canal and Whidbey Island, with stops at the many state parks.

**Figure 7-14.** A ferry ride offers a look at the peaceful inland sea that is Puget Sound. Here, the Edmonds-Kingston Ferry crosses toward the Olympic Peninsula and Range.

# 8

# Fresh Waters

## THE SHAPES OF RUNNING WATER

If you climb to the foot of one of the Northwest's larger glaciers, you will find that the ice sheet ends in a rubble of rock and a roar. Streams white with fine-ground rock pour out of the glacier's snout. They knock boulders against one another so loudly you have to shout to talk.

The rock laden water rushes through a maze of channels. They join only to divide again. Many such rivers rearrange their braided beds each day. The reasons for these channels' shape and flexibility are (1) the heavy sediment load, (2) the loose "bedding material," and (3), the many changes in such rivers' volume. In daytime, for example, sunshine melts the ice quickly, creating a torrent of meltwater that cuts deep channels in the loose rock. At night melting slows; the stream drops and flows more slowly. Overloaded with rock, it drops pebbles into the deep channels where two strands join, creating a bar. When the river rises again, it may cut two new channels, on either side of the bar. (You'll find it easiest to cross such streams in the early morning, before the sun hurries melting again.)

All rivers have a shape that can be read in this way. Some are cutting their beds deeper, creating canyons; or wider, making broad valleys. Some are building their beds higher, dropping sediments in repeated floods that build a plain. Some stretches flow smoothly. More alternate riffles and pools.

**Figure 8-1.** A characteristic stream shape: meanders of the Napeequa River, snaking through a valley scooped out by ice in Glacier Peak Wilderness Area, Washington.

Most Pacific Northwest streams start in rain or snow that falls on high places. Water quickly gathers in a clear stream that chortles as it plunges over logs and boulders in a series of riffles and pools. Such steep rills flow nearly straight.

Where the stream reaches a meadow, though, it meanders across. Streams large and small cut these sinuous bends as they flow across relatively flat places. A small deflection in the water's course will direct the full force of the current against the outside bank. There, it will "bounce" back to the other side.

At the same time that water undercuts the outside banks on alternate sides of the channel, slacker water on the corresponding inside banks drops its sediments. Bars there gradually grow out into the stream.

Thus, a single deflection can set the current to cutting a series of increasingly wide bends in the river. The process normally continues until the bends are about seven to fifteen times the width of the stream. By this time the bends may be nearly complete loops. The river then often cuts through their narrow remaining necks, leaving a crescent-shaped lake called an oxbow.

These shapes influence life in the river.

# A SMALL WORLD

Where it first forms a rivulet, high in mountains, the Northwest's pure, fast-moving water contains few algae, water plants, or other nutrients. Most of the food that starts a chain of life in Northwest streams comes from outside—from leaves, soil, and insects washed into the stream. In the little rills that hurry down slopes, such accidental matter supports miniature communities: algae, fungi, bacteria, small insects, and insect larvae. Most of

**Figure 8-2.** In clear mountain creeks, like this one near Mt. Adams, Washington, much of the food for tiny animals comes from forest debris.

these larvae eventually crawl from the stream and metamorphose into the delicate hoverers familiar to fishermen: caddisflies (Trichoptera), damselflies (Odonata), mayflies (Ephemoptera), and others. (These large groups are orders, each containing many quite varied species. The order Odonata, for example, includes all dragonflies, as well as damselflies.)

Turn over rocks and bits of wood in streams and you will see small clinging creatures. These larvae (looking rather like small caterpillars or other insects), tiny worms, and crustaceans are specialized for life in fast water in a number of ways. They are small and often flattened. This minimizes the water's pull on them. It also lets them stay in a thin film of water that moves slowly because of friction against the stream's sides and bottom.

To hold themselves against the current, these creatures burrow, grow grappling hooks or suckers, build cases of sand grains or leaves, or secrete sticky substances.

These little stream animals are specialized feeders as well. Some, including small snails, scrape the thin coat of algae from rocks. Caddisfly larvae shred leaves and other vegetable matter that happens to fall into pools. Such "shredders," including many mayfly larvae, are likely to be concentrated in pockets of organic matter, such as a bundle of needles and leaves held by a fallen log. Downstream, other groups of larvae feed by filtering tiny bits of organic matter from the stream. The digested feces of the "shredders" are an important food for such filter feeders, which include the larvae of blackflies—whose adults are pests to campers, but popular with fishermen as favored foods of trout.

Larvae and the insects that hatch from them also feed other creatures. Carnivorous insects lurk in and near the water. Spiders string webs between fern fronds. On high, rocky mountain streams, little Pacific tailed frogs (*Ascaphus truei*) hide in the moss and monkeyflowers (*Mimulus guttatus*). Less than two inches long, these little frogs have two distinctive adaptations to swift waters: Males have a "tail" that lets them fertilize females internally, so the sperm will not be swept away. Tadpoles have sucking mouths that help them cling to rocks.

The small aquatic invertebrates at the base of streams' food chain thrive best in shallow riffle areas, in streams with firm bottoms where they can cling securely, and in streams with plenty of organic matter. Thus, a rocky stream running through woods, with plenty of riffles, is likely to support more life than a sandy one meandering through a sunny meadow.

## LIFE IN LARGER STREAMS

The larger the stream, the larger the animals it can feed and house. Larger streams provide more food and are less subject to seasonal freezing and drying. As several very small streams join, they become a creek big enough for small minnow-like fish such as dace (*Rhinicthys* spp.) and for juvenile fish such as salmon fry and young trout.

The reason trout and other fish, including salmon, journey to small streams to lay their eggs probably is that the young are safer there from larger predators. Small streams also have shallow, shaded riffles and gravel bars, where the eggs, buried in gravel, will stay cool and get the large amounts of oxygen they need.

As the creek swells still more, adult trout and other hunting fish stake out territories in its pools. A very small fish may defend a few square inches; a large trout usually defends several square yards. From a set "station" facing up current, the fish watches for drifting prey that are its main food, and for intruders. After an excursion, it will usually return to exactly this spot. The fish also has a set escape route and refuge, to which it will retire if frightened.

The trout's behavior in defending its territory is much like that of other animals. That is, it tries to make itself look as large as possible—as a dog does when its hair stands on end. The trout faces the intruder, stretches out its fins, flares its gill covers, and opens its mouth. Alternatively, it turns its side to the other fish, flares its fins, and arches its back downward. If the rival fish does swim away or show submission by dropping to the stream bottom, the territory holder is likely to charge and try to nip the other fish's tail.

With patience and polarizing sunglasses (to eliminate the water's glare) you can watch these interactions in a pool containing several fish.

The predators of larger bodies of water include other fish, such as the voracious northern squawfish (*Ptychocheilus oregonensis*), which favors warmer water and slower currents than trout.

They also include birds that are among the easiest and most interesting carnivores to watch. Diving ducks, such as goldeneyes and mergansers, frequent swift, cold rivers. They nest, surprisingly, in holes in trees. Blue kingfishers, with small bodies but large heads, rattle loudly as they fly, or plummet from branches to come up with a fish. For nests, they excavate holes in the nearby bank.

A nest in a tall snag near water may belong to ospreys—fishing hawks that whistle as they wheel, and then dive suddenly. Bald eagles build still larger platforms in snags, and also hunt along the waters. But they seem lazier than the ospreys, welcoming a dead fish as eagerly as a live one. Especially during salmon-spawning season, they sit quietly in trees, waiting for a chance carcass to drift by.

Otters (*Lutra canadensis*) are among the sizeable hunters that require fairly large streams or rivers. They prefer fairly slow waters, as these are frequented by slower-swimming fish species that are easier to catch. Otters are nimble swimmers and divers, however, and are seldom seen. You are more likely to notice them on land—they live in burrows and make fairly lengthy overland journeys. If you fish, canoe, raft, or kayak, you are likely to spot their slides—bare stripes down steep riverbanks.

**Figure 8-3.** Three river fisherman: The common, or American, merganser (top) swims and dives for fish. The kingfisher (above) plummets from a perch. The bald eagle (left) waits on shore for carcasses of spawned-out salmon.

Still less often seen is the mink (*Mustela vison*), another member of the weasel family. Minks, which split their time between land and water, are one more step removed from aquatic life than otters. They lack otters' webbed feet, and have bushy tails instead of otters' broad, tapering ones, useful for steering and swimming.

Larger streams also become homes to larger vegetarian mammals. Best known is the beaver (*Castor canadensis*). More than any other animal, these big rodents with scaly tails and webbed hind feet influenced Pacific Northwest history. In the 1820s and 1830s, trappers who were part of an international rush for beaver pelts became the Northwest's real explorers—although they seldom recorded what they found. They gave Northwest landmarks names with a cosmopolitan flavor. French-Canadians christened the Tetons (meaning "big breasts"), the Idaho's Boise River (meaning "wooded"—a welcome contrast to the desolate Snake), Oregon's Deschutes ("river of falls"), and many others. Owyhee is an old name for Hawaii; the river and mountains were named for Hawaiians who came with the Hudsons Bay trappers and died far from home.

Many names tell of such tragedies. Jenny Lake, at the foot of the Tetons, commemorates a trapper's Indian wife who died of smallpox. American Falls on the Snake was named for trappers who were swept over it to their deaths.

**Figure 8-4.** River-dwelling beavers are seldom seen, as they work mostly by night and rarely build dams or lodges. (Photographed at Northwest Trek, Eatonville, Washington.)

The adventurers came because of a whim of fashion—demand for stiff felt hats that could be made best from beaver fur. The prize was rich for a time—in good years, the Hudsons Bay company took 5,000 beaver pelts out of the Salmon River Country and nearby Idaho streams. But by the 1830s, streams were all but trapped out. Changing fashion was the death blow. Mountain men turned to guiding wagon trains across the old route of their caravans—the Oregon Trail.

We associate beavers with still water. That, however, is because they can dam small streams, and the dams make their presence obvious. In lakes or rivers that are naturally deep enough, all you are likely to see of beavers is an occasional pointed stump with toothmarks. Beavers living in rivers dig tunnels in the bank instead of building lodges.

Another reason beavers are seldom seen is that they carry on most of their activities between dusk and dawn. This shows their adaptability: Before the era of the fur trapper, beavers built and fed by day. They changed their habits as a result of man's harassment.

Fairly low altitude streams have another peaceful, mostly vegetarian rodent, the muskrat (*Ondatra zibethicus*). Muskrats are only about a tenth the size of beavers which commonly weigh 30 pounds or more. Muskrats' hairless, scaly tails are flattened sideways rather than horizontally, like those of beavers. In still waters they often build domed lodges of rushes. But like beavers, they generally burrow in the bank when they live in moving water. Occasionally you will see them nibbling roots on the bank. More often they are spotted as a silver "V" wake behind their heads as they swim, the tail making sinuous ripples behind them.

## THE ADVENTUROUS LIVES OF FISH

You can see minute water creatures by turning over rocks and sunken logs. With patience, and willingness to sit quietly on banks at dusk or dawn, you can see large river-dwellers such as otter and beaver. But most people, when they visit fresh water, are more interested in fish.

Even avid fishermen are seldom aware of the many species of fish native to Northwest fresh waters. There are a dozen species of sculpins (*Cottus* spp.) alone. Whether you're out to catch them or not, the looks and life histories of Pacific Northwest fish can be fascinating, even weird.

An example is the largest Pacific Northwest fish (and the largest freshwater fish in North America): the white sturgeon (*Acipenser transmontanus*). As you might expect, these fish are found only in the region's largest rivers: The Columbia River system, including the Snake. (The green sturgeon, *Acipenser medirostis,* of other Northwest rivers are smaller and less desirable for food, but otherwise similar.) With its shovel nose, bearded, toothless mouth, and horny plates, it looks like a living fossil—and it is one. This giant is the only Pacific Northwest genus that dates back to the age of dinosaurs. White sturgeons live peaceful lives, rooting on the bottom for plants, invertebrates, and dead fish, such as spawned-out salmon. Those landlocked behind dams spend their lives in fresh water, while coastal fish come into the Columbia chiefly to spawn. They can live almost as long as a man—80 years or more. Unfortunately, the white sturgeons' huge size—some have been 20 feet long, weighing 1,800 pounds—and their delicious flesh and eggs have made them a favorite prey of man. Their numbers have plummeted, and giant fish are seldom found today.

Some of the Northwest's most mysterious fishes are among its smallest. No one quite knows, for example, why the two-inch-long Olympic mud minnow (*Novumbra hubbsi*) is found only in a few streams of western Washington; why sand rollers *(Percopsis transmontana)* are found only in the Columbia River drainage, or why the Klamath Lake sculpin *(Cottus*

**Figure 8-5.** Hood River Bridge over the lower Columbia River. The Northwest's largest river is home to its largest fish, the white sturgeon.

*princeps)* is found only above Klamath Falls. Probably the once-widespread mud minnows were gradually isolated by the rise of the Rockies and Cascades, and finally by the Ice Age. Sand rollers, closely related to the eastern trout-perches (*Percopsis omiscomaycus*), may have crossed the Continental Divide and then evolved into new species. As for the Klamath Lake sculpins, they seem to be one of many species that developed in isolated Great Basin lakes. Others include the Alvord chub (*Gila alvordensis*) surviving in the desert below Oregon's Steens Mountain, and the Warner sucker (*Catostomus warnerensis*), found only in the small lakes below Hart Mountain further west. Oregon's Upper Klamath Lake was similarly isolated. Only recently, in geologic terms, did the Klamath River erode its way "backward" into it, linking it with Lower Klamath Lake in California, and with the sea.

Burbot or ling (*Lota lota*), the only freshwater codfish, is a fish of the cold lands surrounding the arctic. These long, pointy-nosed fish with blunt fins running half the length of their bodies thrive in deep, cold lakes. They even spawn in midwinter under the ice; writhing masses of males gathered about females who extrude a million or more eggs each.

Another strange-looking Northwest fish is the Pacific lamprey (*Lampetra tridentata*), smooth and round as an eel. Unwelcome followers of salmon on their summer migrations from salt to fresh water, the lampreys inch up riffles, holding onto rocks with their sucker-like mouths. They spend the winter in fresh water. Then, like salmon, they lay their eggs in saucer-like nests, and die.

The larvae hatch blind and toothless. They burrow into stream mud and gravels and stay there for up to five years, filtering microscropic organisms from the water for food. At last, after a series of transformations, the lampreys attain adult form and migrate to the ocean or to a large lake. There, the snake-like creature grasps a trout or salmon with its funnel-like sucking mouth. Its toothed tongue scrapes through scales and skin. The lamprey becomes a vampire, sucking its host's body fluids while injecting an anticoagulant that assures it can continue to feed. This parasitic life lasts a year or two. When the lampreys do at last release their victims, it is to migrate upstream, spawn, and die.

## TROUT AND SALMON

The lives and wanderings of the more familiar game fish—such as trout and salmon—are no less fascinating.

Few sights are as dramatic as big salmon milling below falls, leaping riffles to fall with a heavy splash, or crowding into streamlets to spawn and die. The drama remains although today's runs are not what they once were.

**Figure 8-6.** A migrating salmon leaps a fall on the Soleduck River in Washington's Olympic Peninsula.

Salmon numbers have been reduced by over-fishing, pollution, dams, and disturbance of spawning streams. Cutting natural vegetation, for example, leaves streams vulnerable to floods that wash away eggs. It also removes coverings that the young fish need to hide in and that keep the water cool. (Salmon and trout generally require water below 70° F.) Hatcheries and other forms of artificial assistance have only partly restored the runs.

Today you can best see the drama of salmon spawning where salmon must leap fish ladders, rather than at natural falls. You may know salmon are spawning not because you see the black backs of crowded fish, but because you see bald eagles in the trees, waiting for carcasses.

Salmon lead two lives. The typical life cycle is as follows: The young, hatched in stream or lake gravels, spend as much as a year as plumpish, spotted, bottom-dwelling fish in fresh water. When they reach a critical size, these chubby, shy creatures are transformed. Their bodies slim down. Their swim bladders fill, making them more buoyant. The camouflaging spots disappear, and are replaced by a gleaming dark back and light underside— camouflage for the open sea. The two forms even have different names; *parr* before the transformation, *smolt* afterwards.

Signalled partly by spring's longer days, warmth, and high stream flows, the smolt migrate downstream to the open sea. For a year or two, Pacific Northwest salmon wander the northeastern Pacific. Then, guided by currents, the sun, and the smell of their home stream, they begin their return to the fresh water where they hatched. Besides the physical rigors of an upstream journey of as much as 900 miles (to Idaho's Salmon River, for example), the salmon must evade a wide range of predators, from bear to birds of prey to man. In the stream or the lake edge where they were hatched, females lie on their sides and flip their tails, scooping out a shallow nest called a *redd*. The female lays her eggs in this nest. The male, hovering close by, simultaneously fertilizes them. With more flips of her tail, the female covers the eggs (and often repeats the nesting process). Their reproduction complete, the adults die.

The life cycle is basically the same for all Pacific Northwest salmon, although different species and races migrate at different times and choose different types of spawning sites. Chum and pink salmon (*Oncorhynchus keta* and *gorbuscha)*, for example, usually spawn in the lower reaches of streams. Their young spend only a few weeks in fresh water. Coho, also called silver salmon; chinook, also called king salmon; and sockeye, also called red salmon, mostly make longer journeys, going well upstream to spawn. (Their scientific names are *O. kisutch, tshawytscha,* and *nerka,* respectively.) The young of these three far-journeying salmon spend several months in fresh water before starting the long journey to the sea. Sockeye fry often move first to lakes; some sockeye adults also spend their lives there, migrating only between the lake and the spawning stream. These landlocked populations usually are called *kokanee salmon*, though they differ from other sockeye only in being smaller on the average. Chinook salmon also are divided, into spring and fall races, depending on when they migrate upstream. These races also spend different lengths of time in fresh and salt water.

The lives of Pacific Northwest trout, relatives of salmon, are a variation on this migratory theme. The Northwest has three native trout species— rainbow (*Salmo gairdneri*), cutthroat (*Salmo clarki,*) and Dolly Varden (*Salvelinus malma*)—Dolly Varden are in fact chars, related to the introduced lake trout and brook trout. Some members of all three trout species migrate to salt water and spend their adult lives there. The freshwater and seagoing fish do not seem to be physically different—but they may have different names. Thus, a rainbow trout is the same as a steelhead, the name given seagoing members of its species.

A major difference between the life cycles of trout and salmon is that trout, after laying their eggs, can live to spawn again. (This is one reason why many fishermen who wade into icy winter streams for steelhead release any they catch.)

Seagoing Dolly Varden and cutthroat trout generally do not go as far offshore as steelhead and salmon. Curiously, the longer their journeys, the more precisely fish species tend to home to their native streams. Thus, spawning cutthroat trout, which do not go far to sea or make long journeys inland, quickly explore and colonize new tributaries. This probably is the reason cutthroats were the West's most widespread native trout. Unfortunately, the adventurous fish with the red slashes on their throats now are growing scarce, because they have not thrived in hatcheries.

By contrast with the wandering cutthroats, chinook salmon, though they travel 1,000 miles or more, nearly always return to the stream where they hatched. The very length and difficulty of its journey probably make it important that a fish waste no time or energy exploring if it is to complete its mission to reproduce.

Salmon and trout are not the only anadromous fishes. Small candlefish and smelts as well as giant sturgeons share the habit. Long migrations from salt to fresh water can be looked at as an extreme version of a common pattern. This is the habit of fish moving to smaller streams to lay eggs, probably because this leaves eggs and young safer from large predators. The return of young anadromous fish to the sea similarly is a variation on the theme of young fish moving to larger streams to find more food and stable conditions.

## WHAT YOU CAN LEARN BY LOOKING AT A FISH

Looking thoughtfully at fish usually can teach you something, whether you are a fisherman who sees fish inside and out, or a watcher who sits still and observes life in a pool.

**Figure 8-7.** A trout's streamlined body and his habit of lurking in pools serve to lessen the constant drag of currents (Skykomish River, Washington).

Northwest waters vary from acid peat bogs to alkali ponds and hot springs. But because most precipitation falls in winter and on mountain ranges, most Pacific Northwest streams are fast and cold. The region's native fish are streamlined for easy movement in this environment. Thus, trout, whitefish, and less well-known types such as squawfish and suckers, all have long, slim bodies, pointed fins, forked tails, and small scales. They contrast strikingly with the fish brought by man, that thrive in more still, warmer waters he helped create: Bass, catfish, carp, perch, tench, and sunfish have deeper bodies, rounded fins and tails, and (except catfish) rather large scales.

Currents are a constant drain on the energy of stream-dwelling fish. Their behavior as well as their bodies are designed to minimize this drain. Thus, fish in rapids swim near the bottom where the current is slowest. Fish leaping falls and riffles start from the crest of a standing wave, using the water's upward turbulence.

Fish also "rest" in backwaters behind rocks or other obstacles. As many fishermen know, a big trout in a stream usually stakes out a territory that includes a pool or backwater behind rocks where the fish spends much of his time. Fish seem to choose these territories and stations to get respite from the currents, as much as to get food. Lake fish, in fact, often are not territorial.

Other animals also must adapt to the constant drag of current. Caddisflies and stoneflies fly upstream to lay their eggs, helping to balance the larvae's drift downstream. Crayfish (*Pacificastus klamathensis*) lurk under rocks to avoid the current, and also move upstream to lay eggs.

Fishes' bodies tell other things about their habits. A predatory fish, for example, usually has not only strong teeth in its jaws, but also bony toothed arches in its pharynx, or throat. These help hold, tear, and grind food.

Trout and squawfish eat by lunging at prey above the bottom. Their mouths, at the ends of cigar-shaped bodies, open forward—they look as if they were grinning or frowning. Suckers (*Catostomus* spp.) and dace (*Rhinichthys* spp.), which eat insects and larvae off the bottom, have a hangdog look; Their mouths, set below and behind their noses, open downward toward their food supply. Sculpins ("bullheads"), the often cannibalistic predators of the bottom, have eyes that look upward, and strong spiny fins that can brace them against current as they lie in wait.

The bottom-dwelling fish also have an internal adaptation. Fish stay afloat by means of a swim bladder—basically a gas bag, usually located above other internal organs. Swim bladders of other fish tend to keep them floating. Sculpins and dace, however, sink unless they swim.

Native sturgeon, as well as introduced catfish and carp, get their livings rooting in muddy bottoms. They all have "whiskers"—sensitive projections near the mouth called *barbels*, that help them detect food they cannot see.

The trout or salmon you catch sometimes have pink flesh, sometimes white. The color tells only whether fish have been eating large numbers of animals with reddish pigments. Hatchery-reared trout, for example, tend to be white. Although many fishermen claim otherwise, the color probably doesn't reflect flavor. If you closed your eyes, you probably couldn't tell the difference.

## STILL WATER

"Old man river" is an apt phrase: Rivers shrink, swell, and change their courses, but are continually renewed by the quiet power of water working its way downstream. Many are geologically ancient—older than the hills, as their courses across mountain ranges show.

By comparison, lakes are short-lived and delicate. Imagine a foothill stream as a beaver family builds its dam. As they thrust and weave in more sticks and plaster the barrier with mud, water rises on its upstream side. Some flows over or through the dam. Still, with luck, the beavers create a small lake. Since beavers swim well but move awkwardly ashore, the pond means they can easily transport food (reeds, trees, and bushes on the banks) and escape their enemies, mostly hunters on land. The deepened water enables beavers to build tunnel systems in the bank or offshore lodges, with safely submerged entrances. They also can salt away green sticks as winter food, thrusting them into mud in water deep enough to reach even if the surface freezes.

This safe plenty is short-lived, however. The slowed water drops its load of rock particles and detritus, shallowing the pond and building a fertile soil for reeds and water plants. Stilled, the water grows warm in the sun— especially as bushes and trees no longer overhang the broadened pond. Plants flourish in the warmth. Cattails, reeds, and waterweeds begin to encroach upon and choke the young lake.

The beavers move on well before the pond becomes a shallow swamp, then a moist meadow with a stream meandering through it. Finally, bushes and trees reclaim the land.

This simple life cycle is reflected, with variations, in every lake, from the pool that forms behind a fallen log in a mountain stream to the immense dammed reservoirs that power and irrigate the modern Pacific Northwest.

## PONDS AND SMALL LAKES

Small lakes are like jewels in the landscape—their color and shine enhances their whole setting. These varied gems, scattered from glacial heights to desert basins, are not easily placed into neat categories.

The highest mountain tarns, often filling cirques polished by glaciers, generally are all but barren. Few nutrients wash into them from scant alpine vegetation and soil. Even the little that arrives decays slowly in the cold, or is lost in the rush of snowmelt in late spring. In summer you may find larval salamanders, like small dragons, in such waters. Lakes deep enough to not freeze solid may support trout or other cold-loving fish. But facing near-freezing temperatures year round, with few insects to feed them, such fish are lean and slow-growing.

**Figure 8-8.** Strawberry Lake below Strawberry Mountain, in Central Oregon's Ochoco Mountains, is typical of many peaceful, forest-edged lakes in northwestern mountains.

**Figure 8-9.** The dipper, or water ouzel, catches insects
at the edges of lakes and streams, or walks under water
to find them.

At lower altitudes are green, forest-edged lakes, warm enough—but just barely—for swimming. Their greater wealth of aquatic insects and larvae can be seen in ripples of rising fish, or in a water ouzel or dipper (*Cinclus mexicanus*), a dark, short-tailed little bird, bobbing as he walks along a half-sunken log and then under water to find his prey. Thus, just as in streams, the insects support larger animals—amphibians, birds, fish.

Amphibians—frogs, toads, and salamanders—are among the more interesting animals around lake edges.

Salamanders and newts look like lizards, but they lack lizards' scales and claws. Beginning with fall rains in mild areas, and continuing to midsummer, these greenish, brownish, and reddish animals "home" to ponds and other moist places. Large numbers may join in these migrations and in nocturnal courtship "dances," in which males deposit a packet of sperm that the female must pick up and place within her body.

Most often seen is the rough-skinned newt (*Taricha granulosa*), recognizable by its dark grainy skin (except in breeding males, which have smooth skin). These newts shun the light less than other species, and crowds of them sometimes are on the move toward a single pond or stream.

The skin of most salamanders has a waxy, translucent look that matches its real character. Salamanders spend much of their lives hiding under rocks and logs to avoid losing too much moisture through their permeable skins. As a result, larval salamanders probably are seen more often than are adults.

Although they have the adults' lizard shape, they are the equivalent of frog
tadpoles—they are water dwellers, breathing through gills. This phase can
last for two years or more. In high, cold lakes, where the growing season is
short, gilled "larvae" reach sexual maturity and breed.

Water is not the only substance that passes through salamander skin. A
startled salamander is likely to assume a rigid, "swaybacked" pose, with head
and tail raised. This shows the brighter belly colors, and may warn other
animals about these apparently defenseless animals' protection system:
poison glands in their skin.

A large group of salamanders (family Plethodontidae) actually have no
lungs. They breathe through their delicate skins instead. These lungless
salamanders spend their lives out of water. Skipping the gilled larval stage,
their young hatch tiny, but fully developed, from eggs.

Another mass phenomenon at pond edges in early spring is the mating
of toads. Most commonly, these are western toads (*Bufo boreas*), warty,
brownish to grayish toads about two to five inches long, that walk more than
they hop. Sandy and drier areas are more likely to be homes to Woodhouse's
toad (*Bufo woodhousei*), similar but with a bony "crest" across its forehead,
and more likely to hop than walk.

**Figure 8-10.** Mass matings of Western toads, and the
almost simultaneous transformation of their tadpoles
into tiny frogs, make them a common sight in
mountains and moist places.

In late winter to midsummer, depending on conditions, male "true" toads (genus *Bufo*) develop rough "nuptial pads" on their feet. Both sexes gather in lakes or slow-moving waters. In the shallows, males embrace females, the rough pads helping them grip slippery skin. Couples and even trios splash and roll for hours, so entranced you can get within inches of them. (Touching toads won't give you warts, but some species have chemicals in their skins that irritate eyes or nasal membranes. So if you pick up a toad, wash your hands afterwards.) During the watery orgy, the females extrude eggs that the males fertilize. Tadpoles of such mass matings often metamorphose to small adults at almost the same time. Hundreds, even thousands, may hop away from marshy shores at once.

Frogs are less sociable—rather than joining in mass matings, males generally "sing" or croak to distance rival males as much as to attract females. (Nevertheless, a singing frog will provoke others to join in, and the overall effect is to promote many matings.)

A greenish, brownish, or yellowish frog less than two inches long, singing in a high voice, probably is *Hyla regilla*, the Pacific tree frog. This most common of northwest frogs actually spends little time in trees, though its feet have sticky discs for climbing.

A somewhat larger (two to five inches), spotted but smooth-skinned frog at a pond edge is one of several members of the genus *Rana*, the "true" frogs. The natives have slightly different markings and habitat preferences: The red-legged frog (*Rana aurora*), for example, likes damp lowlands, and is particularly common west of the Cascades. The Cascades frog (*Rana cascadae*) is a species of the Olympics and Cascades above about 3,000 feet. The northern leopard frog (*Rana pipiens*), common across the country, is another lowland species, but in the Northwest is found mostly on the edges of the interior Rocky Mountain ranges. The spotted frog (*Rana pretiosa*), the mountain species of interior ranges, joins the vertical migrations so common in mountains. Frogs hop to uplands soon after snowmelt, but return as these areas begin to dry out in midsummer.

The introduced bullfrog (*Rana catesbeiana*), however, has upset these established divisions. For example, this larger frog (up to eight inches) with the deep "jug-of-rum" call, has driven the red-legged frog to mountain country in many areas.

Reptiles are seen less often than amphibians around Northwest waters. Reptiles—snakes, turtles, and lizards—come out of hibernation later than the frogs, toads, and salamanders. Snakes and turtles also are less common and less varied in the Pacific Northwest than in warmer parts of the country. The turtles you do see, unless they are escaped pets, will be one of two species. Painted turtles (*Chrysemys picta*), most common east of the Cascades, have yellow lines on their head and feet. Western pond turtles (*Clemmys marmorata*), most common west of the Cascades, lack these yellow lines.

**Figure 8-11.** Painted turtles inhabit slow-moving waters east of the Cascades. They can be identified by the yellow lines on head and feet.

Snakes you see swimming in the Pacific Northwest are most likely to be harmless garter snakes (*Thamnophis* spp.), recognizable by the yellow stripe down the center of the back. (Rattlers are the Northwest's only native poisonous snake.) Other Northwest snakes sometimes swim. One is the rubber boa (*Charina bottae*), the region's only native member of the python family, which kills its prey by coiling and strangling. If this stout, plain little snake has a distinguishing feature, it is that his tail looks much like his head—a feature that may deceive enemies into attacking the wrong end.

Fish and frogs in lakes draw still larger birds to hunt them. On mountain lakes, for example, you may meet handsome diving ducks like the rakish, orange-crested American mergansers, common loons with their ghost-like laughter, and great blue herons—dignified stalkers found from the seashore to desert ponds.

As you move lower, the variety of birds increases. Kingfishers, ospreys, and eagles hunt lakes as well as rivers.

Bitterns skulk in reeds. Yellowlegs bob on logs and mud. Both of these long-billed birds keep an eye out for snails, small fish, and unwary frogs.

Canada geese, whistling and trumpeter swans, coots, four kinds of grebes, and more than a dozen colorful kinds of ducks visit or breed on Northwest lakes. Even without knowing the names of all these water birds, you can divide them by the way they seek food. Dabblers—including teal, pintails, and wigeons—"tip up" comically, sterns in the air as they root on the bottom with broad bills. An extreme adaptation to this kind of life is the bill of the shoveller, broadened at its tip to a spoon-like shape. These dabbling ducks, which also graze on land, walk easily—their legs are set in about the middle of their bodies. Their wings are long and powerful—they can take off from a pond no larger than a puddle, springing directly into the air.

Diving birds, by contrast, have narrower and sometimes shorter bills. They have short wings, useful as paddles when they swim underwater, but requiring them to run and splash along the water before they can take off. Their legs are set well back for underwater locomotion—on land they waddle awkwardly. Examples are the dignified western grebes and canvasback ducks, and the rather comical little ruddy ducks and buffleheads.

Some lowland lakes too warm for trout and other native fish have been stocked with nonnatives, such as sunfish, perch, bass, and catfish. Some of these introduced fish need not be looked on as aliens—The Northwest had native catfish and sunfish, for example, before the Ice Age wiped them out. Most of the newcomers have harmlessly filled niches created by man. For example, bass, catfish, sunfish, and perch thrive in water that civilization has made too warm, too turbid, or too low in oxygen for native trout, whitefish, and salmon.

Other introduced fish, though, clearly are harmful. For example, schools of carp, splashing and jumping as they feed and mate, can muddy the water so badly that other fish cannot use it.

**Figure 8-12.** The violence of carp as they spawn or root for food can make water too muddy for other fish (Potholes Reservoir, Washington).

# LARGE LAKES AND RESERVOIRS

Deeper lakes sometimes pose a complex set of problems for life. In a shallow lake, for example, wind, inflow, and outflow mix the water thoroughly. But larger, deeper lakes usually develop a layered structure. In summer, for example, sun warms the top layers of water. But warm water, like warm air, rises above cold. A layer of warm water (called the *epilimnion*) thus tends to form, extending from the lake's surface down to the lowest level at which water is frequently mixed by wind and waves. This water can become too warm for native fish.

Meanwhile, in the lake's cold, dense, bottom layer, another danger can develop. Big, deep lakes have few bottom-dwelling insect larvae or rooted plants. Instead, their food chain, like the ocean's, starts with plankton—tiny floating plants and animals. Again, as in the ocean, you cannot see the individual floaters, but you often can see them as a mass, when their periodic "blooms," or rapid multiplications, cloud the water.

As these organisms die and sink to the bottom, their decay uses up oxygen. The cold bottom waters of the lake (called the *hypolimnion*) can become fatally airless. Fish that need cold water can be trapped in a narrow transitional zone (called the *thermocline*), driven from the lake, or even killed by such conditions.

Fall brings relief, as the surface water grows colder than the bottom water. The resulting turnover also "fertilizes" the lake, bringing up nutrients in the form of dead and decaying organisms that had sunk to the bottom, and so had been temporarily lost to swimming creatures.

Just before water freezes, its density declines. This is why ice floats. Thus, in the dead of winter, ice and the coldest water rise to the surface, trapping and insulating life-saving warmer water beneath them. Spring brings another mixing, as meltwater sinks and warmer water rises again.

Today, the Pacific Northwest's big rivers have largely been bridled, backed up behind dams that harness them for power and irrigation. For fish, these dams and reservoirs have been deadly. Sea-running fish, for example, are barred from thousands of square miles where they once spawned by such dams as Chief Joseph Dam on the Columbia, Hells Canyon Dam on the Snake, and smaller ones like Pelton on Oregon's Deschutes River.

Many other dams can be crossed on fish ladders—essentially stepped riffles low and slow enough for fish to swim or leap. Still, the warm reservoirs, low in oxygen, sap fishes' strength. (Salmon need water below about 70° F and about 80 percent saturated with oxygen.) Young smolt moving downstream are swept over dam spillways, and in the airy pools below dams, "nitrogen sickness"—absorbing too much air—kills fish horribly—bubbles burst in their blood; their eyes explode from their heads.

**Figure 8-13.** Despite aids like this fish ladder on the Oregon side of Bonneville Dam, on the Columbia River, salmon runs are declining, due partly to conditions in the huge reservoirs behind the dams.

The Northwest's strong conservation movement, and alarm over dwindling salmon and steelhead runs, have increased efforts to lessen the effects of dams. But despite hatcheries, trucking young fish around spillways, even dynamiting dams, the future of sea-running fish in many Northwest rivers remains shaky.

## SWAMPS AND BOGS

In a lake's old age, or at its shallow margins, swamps often appear. Typically they have a thick edging of tall, thin-bladed plants: cattails (*Typha latifolia*), rushes (*Juncus* spp.), or bullrushes (*Scirpus* spp.).

Water in marshes also may be all but hidden by glossy broad leaves of such plants as water plantain (*Alisma plantago-aquatica*, wapato (*Sagittaria latifolia*), or native yellow water lilies (*Nuphar polysepalum*). Air pockets in stems and leaves keep them afloat, and help compensate for the sometimes airless condition of stagnant water.

In both streams and lakes, plants must have have tough, flexible stems, but in moving water leaves must be fine and streamlined. Where water is still, broad leaves can float on the surface without constant drag. Some plants compromise: the white-flowered watercrowfoot buttercup (*Ranunculus aquatilis*), for example, has tendril-like underwater leaves, but broad, lobed ones floating on the surface.

Lowland swamps were bread baskets in Indian days. The rich, oily seeds of waterlilies were a staple for tribes of the Klamath Lake marshes, who also depended heavily on fish and wildfowl of the lakes. Many tribes harvested wapato tubers—women waded, holding onto the sides of canoes, and dug out the potato-like tubers with their toes. Cattail and rush leaves made mats, clothing, temporary lodges, and torches.

Swamps are an ideal habitat for shore birds and grazing and dabbling water birds. William Clark, having completed the first overland journey across North America, found he could not sleep at the marshy mouth of the Columbia River "for the noise kept up by Swans, Geese, White and black brants, Ducks, etc. on the opposite bank, and sandhill Cranes, they were emencely numerous and their noise horrid."

**Figure 8-14.** Sandhill cranes in Bear Valley, Oregon. The Northwest's largest bird is rare partly because of draining and filling of marshes.

Because of draining and filling, such swamps are among the "endangered habitats" of the wetter areas of the Northwest. Wapato, for example, is considered a threatened species in Oregon. Some swamp users, such as sandhill cranes and swans, are rare and carefully protected in the small areas they still frequent.

In the dry interior, however, the area of year-round wetlands has increased as irrigation has raised the water table, filling many low spots and potholes that once were wet only in the spring. The result is discussed in the next section, on desert surprises.

You also find another, more barren kind of swamp in Northwest forests. Your feet squish through a fine-leaved cushion of sphagnum moss, edging or covering cold brown water. If you look around, you may find that the surrounding forest looks starved and dry despite the water. Trees are likely to be lodgepole pines, familiar from poor soils of the seacoast and interior. The stunted undergrowth generally is made up of distinctive acid-loving plants: creeping wild cranberries (*Vaccinium oxycoccus*), shrubs like Labrador tea (*Ledum groenlandicum* or *glandulosum*), swamp laurel (*Kalmia occidentalis*), and sweet gale (*Myrica gale*). Brown-water bogs often are edged by cotton grass (*Eriophorum* spp.), waving soft white bristly seed heads.

**Figure 8-15.** Insect-eating Darlingtonias, or cobra plants, near Florence, Oregon.

Bogs also are homes to strange plants—the meat-eaters of the vegetable world. Little sundew (*Drosera rotundifolia*) traps insects in sticky secretions on its disc-like leaves. Longer hairs then bend to tie the victim down until the plant digests and absorbs the insect's nutrients. Pitcher plant (*Darlingtonia californica*) lures insects into its hooded, tubular stems. (The red "forked tongue" hanging from the opening gives the plant its alternate name of "cobra plant.") Downward-pointing hairs guide the hapless nectar-seeker into a trap: a sticky pool where the insect drowns and is digested.

Such bogs, typical of northern latitudes, are born when water stands so long that plants and decay rob it of its oxygen. The environment thus created is airless, cold, and acid. In such conditions, decay and the resultant cycling of nutrients from dead plants to living ones all but stop. (Peat bogs preserve organic matter so well that they are a major source of pollens that make it possible to characterize prehistoric plant communities.)

Only a few plants can survive such conditions. This is the reason for the bogs' limited, specialized plant community. To survive, such plants must be particularly well-adapted to acidity and lack of nutrients. The insects digested by carnivorous bog plants, for example, supply them with badly needed nutrients.

## DESERT SURPRISES

The dry sage-and-grass country of the Pacific Northwest is dotted with lakes. Some of these are old; remnants of much larger Ice Age lakes, surviving now on meager snowmelt and scant rainfall trapped in enclosed basins. Many more of these surprising lakes are young and manmade. The immense canyons, or coulees, carved by ice-age rivers, were easily dammed to make reservoirs for irrigation and water power. Grand Coulee is the most famous. As already mentioned, many of the smaller ponds are manmade accidents: potholes filled with irrigation water that seeps from fields or reservoirs.

Some older desert lakes are salty, particularly in the dry basins of Eastern Washington and Oregon. Such lakes' salt content slowly increases as trapped water evaporates, leaving its minerals behind. These lakes' mineral contents differ, depending largely on the surrounding rock and the degree of saltiness. Their layered structure often is not the same as that of ordinary lakes, where warm water floats above cold. In salt lakes, light, fresh water can float above denser, saltier layers that trap heat because they cannot evaporate or diffuse.

The more dilute salt lakes, such as Moses Lake in Washington, support communities of fishes not very different from those in other lakes. A few salt lakes are airless and dead. Most, though, support a distinctive though limited community of small creatures, some descended from marine ancestors, others remarkably adapted. For example, brine shrimp (*Artemia* spp.) in some life stages can be dried to a state of suspended animation. Given water, even after months or years, the apparently lifeless creatures thrive again.

Salt or fresh, the desert lakes are among the Northwest's most important homes for wildlife—particularly water birds. Perhaps the most fascinating wildlife refuges of the Northwest are the lakes of the dry Columbia Plateau, Snake River Valley, and eastern Oregon's desert.

Life here is crowded and intense, a sharp contrast to the silent dry country nearby. In spring and early summer, gulls and terns migrate hundreds of miles inland to nest on these beaches—and scream and dive at intruders. The abundant willows and reeds are nesting cover for equally noisy and aggressive blackbirds. Larger yellow-heads appropriate the deeper, safer waters, forcing red-wings to nest in more vulnerable areas near shore. A hawk, raccoon, or coyote that invades the harems of brownish females is likely to be driven off by a mob of males, dive-bombing and calling raucously.

Cottonwoods on the shore are pressed into service. They support nesting colonies of great blue herons—or at least of magpies, handsome scavengers and predators on eggs. Marsh hawks flap and glide low over fields and cattails. Red-tailed hawks scream above partly-flooded canyons. Both of these are more interested in mice than birds, but they are "mobbed" by angry nesters nonetheless.

Shore birds of all sizes walk on stilt-like legs and probe the mud with long bills. Among them are the big black-and-white avocets, touched with salmon, and with curious up-curved bills. They, too, protest noisily against trespassers.

Snipe are on the wing, diving in ritual courtship flights, ghostly from the sound of air rushing through their feathers. Grebes court on the water's surface, now splashing comically, now circling one another in graceful water ballet. The little Wilson's phalarope is a nonconformist in courting: the female wears the colorful plumage, and the male rears the young.

The ground-nesting birds lay speckled, earth-colored eggs, well-camouflaged on the ground. One end is narrowed, so that if the egg rolls, it moves in a circle. The eggs are large, and from them hatch youngsters that are able to walk and are covered with camouflaging down—by contrast, young song birds are hatched naked and helpless. While species that nest on the open ground tend to distract enemies with noise and motion, geese and ducks incubate their eggs quietly in thicker vegetation, and lead their broods from feeding spots to hiding places in reeds.

One of the largest of the desert breeding grounds, now the Malheur National Wildlife Refuge, played a key role in the nation's first great conservation movement. Just as a vogue for men's felt hats decimated the beaver, demand for plumes for fanciful ladies' hats all but wiped out many of

(a)

(b)

**Figure 8-16.** A few of the birds
common at watery breeding
grounds in dry country: (a) Infant
red-wing blackbirds in a nest hung
from cattail leaves. (b) A great
blue heron nesting in a waterside
tree. (c) and (d) Killdeer and their
camouflaged eggs. (e) A Western
grebe with eggs on her nest of
floating waterweeds.

(c)

(d)

(e)

**Figure 8-17.** Avocets, with their curious upturned bills, probe for food on the edges of ponds in the arid Northwest.

the country's loveliest birds. Plume hunters discovered Oregon's Harney and Malheur Lakes in the late 19th century, and slaughtered their terns, herons, gulls, and shore birds mercilessly. The protests of naturalists and wildlife lovers led, just in time, to outlawing such hunting, as well as mass killing of wildlife for markets. Today this refuge also shelters flocks of rare sandhill cranes, the Northwest's largest birds.

In fall and winter, the desert lakes and marshes are key resting places for geese and ducks on the Pacific Flyway. This is a somewhat misnamed collection of migration routes. Some geese and ducks do follow the ocean coast, and many British Columbia birds take a short migration loop to the mild winters and sheltered waters of western Washington. More, though, travel to and from the immense breeding grounds of the far north by flying east of the Canadian Rockies roughly to the U.S.-Canadian border. They then turn southwest into northwestern Montana and the Yellowstone Lake country. The rare trumpeter swans winter here. Most birds, though, go on, crossing the low mountains of northern Idaho or following the Snake River Valley to the Columbia. From there, these water birds fly south across East-Center Oregon into their main wintering grounds. These stretch from marshy Goose and Lower Klamath Lakes, on the Oregon-California border, south through California's interior valleys. Thus, paradoxically, the Northwest's desert may be more important to waterfowl than the damp country west of the Cascades, and even the ocean itself.

## DOING IT YOURSELF

Analyze a stream or lake to see if you can guess what, besides fish, lives in and near it. Look for evidence of that life. Look for insects on and near the water. Turn over rocks and logs—replacing them carefully. Look for polliwogs and larval salamanders. Or go on a nighttime "amphibian hunt." (Salamanders are most active at night, and so are lowland frogs. In mountains, though, where nights are colder, frogs are diurnal.) A headlamp conveniently leaves your hands free. Turn it off, though, when trying to get to a frogs' general location by the sound of his voice.

Before collecting polliwogs, frogs, toads, salamanders, snakes, turtles, or fish, consult experts and manuals on the conditions you need to keep them alive. Even after you meet these conditions, take only very few representatives of very common species.

If you fish, you probably are already accustomed to analyzing where fish lurk in lakes or streams. If not, try this exercise, and see if you can confirm your findings by looking down through clear waters, or watching where fish rise and jump. Lower a thermometer to various depths in a lake, and try to guess which kinds of fish may live at various levels. (Trout and salmon need temperatures below about 70° F.)

If you live near a lake or stream, figure out what could be done to improve it as habitat for fish or birds. Would plants stabilize the banks? Would they help provide more cover and food? Would shade keep the water cooler? Would more vegetation on areas that feed the lake or stream help slow runoff, so that the water's speed and level fluctuated less widely?

Get to know waterside life by looking at tracks on the streambank. Early morning is ideal, as most visitors come from dusk to dawn, and tracks are best seen when the is sun casting shadows from a low angle.

Float trips in any kind of motorless craft are ideal ways to see streamside and lake animals. These can range from paddling your own kayak or canoe—or even floating in an inner tube—to commercial trips on big rivers such as the Snake or Rogue.

Most state and federal fish hatcheries are open to the public, and many offer interesting interpretive displays and literature as well as a look at how trout and salmon are raised. Still more interesting are fish ladders when salmon and trout are running. Many Northwest dams have them—the most accessible, and one of the most interesting, is at the Ballard Locks in Seattle.

Crane Prairie Reservoir Osprey Area, near Bend, Oregon, is in a class by itself. Snags in the flooded reservoir are ideal nesting sites for ospreys, making this one of the few places you can feel almost sure of seeing these

**Figure 8-18.** An osprey and an osprey nest (with Mt. Hood in background), Crane Prairie Reservoir, Oregon. Trees killed when the waters were backed up made ideal homes for the fishing hawks.

fishing hawks. Contact the U.S. Forest Service Bend Ranger Station for information.

Good places to see bald eagles are the San Juan Islands, Washington, in summer; the McDonald River area in Glacier National Park in early fall; and the Skagit River near Marblemount, Washington, or Tule Lake, near the Oregon-California border, in winter.

The federal wildlife refuges and state wildlife areas of Eastern Oregon and Washington are ideal places to get to know water birds and shore birds. The federal refuges generally are larger, and most have interesting small museums and leaflets explaining local plants and animals. Spring and fall generally are the best seasons. As areas sometimes are closed for breeding or open to hunters, check with headquarters before you go.

For scenery, perhaps the most attractive areas are Columbia National Wildlife Refuge (headquarters in Othello, Washington) and Turnbull National Wildlife Refuge (headquarters in Cheney, Washington). The largest numbers of birds probably are found in Umatilla Reservoir behind John Day Dam on the Columbia. Umatilla National Wildlife Refuge, with headquarters in Umatilla, Oregon, is the largest refuge here, but the area also includes and Cold Springs and McKay Creek National Wildlife Refuges plus nearby state wildlife areas and the Army Corps of Engineers McNary Wildlife Park. Malheur National Wildlife Refuge in central Oregon offers a 42-mile driving tour including glimpses of Oregon's volcanic geology, wild-West history, and rarities such as trumpeter swans and sandhill cranes. (Information is available from the U.S. Fish and Wildlife Service at Burns, Oregon.)

# 9
# City and Suburbs

Threads of the wilds are woven through every northwestern city. True, asphalt and concrete weigh down strips and scars of earth, but even the region's largest cities are still patterned with green, and edged or cut by creeks, rivers, lakes, and sometimes ocean. In parks, yards, and vacant lots, water and waterside, wild things find homes and resting places. Even such large animals as deer, foxes, coyotes, and beavers are no farther than the outer rim of suburbs.

The round of the seasons is muted in cities. Still, it is sung to anyone who tends a garden, walks in parks, or encourages and watches wild visitors to ordinary yards.

That is why, although you can follow nature's seasonal changes anywhere, this chapter, more than others, describes them. You can observe and enjoy the same cycle, of course, in countryside and wilderness.

Cities have other treasures for nature lovers: They have museums (like Portland's Oregon Museum of Science and Industry) and aquariums (like Seattle's Aquarium) where you can spend rainy afternoons, taking a close and leisurely look at things you may only glimpse in the wild. They have a wide variety of nature walks, classes, and group activities sponsored by parks departments, colleges and universities, and conservation organizations such as the Sierra Club and Audubon Society, among others. These are among the most pleasant and sociable ways to learn about nature.

**Figure 9-1.** Who needs wilderness? Despite a freeway ramp in the background, the edge of Lake Washington in Seattle's Arboretum has become an "old swimming hole."

## HERALDS OF SPRING

Every Pacific Northwest city has fragments of woods and brush. The undergrowth in these spots usually includes escaped garden plants, like aptly-named English holly and ivy; and nonnative weeds, like the familiar dandelion. But much of what grows in abandoned places is almost the same as what the Indians saw, when nearby streets were their foot trails. Thus, in parks and vacant tracts as well as in remote mountains, you can get to know native cone-bearing trees; large deciduous natives like alders, maples, ashes, and aspens; the smaller flowering trees like dogwood, crabapple, and wild cherries and plums; and wild shrubs and herbs.

In such woods, the sheltered underbrush comes to life in early spring, while tree limbs are still bare. As early as February, in the mild country west of the Cascades, you will find rosy fingers of flowering wild currant (*Ribes sanguineum*), and showers of falling-star flowers of Indian plum. Lemony catkins of wild hazelnuts and furry pussy willows dust your nose with pollen if you get close. In swampy places, tissuey magenta flowers of salmonberry, bright against the yellow bark, attract the early returning hummingbirds. Skunk cabbage stands erect in its dignified yellow cloak—a reminder of how, in Indian legend, skunk cabbage won its dress as a reward for keeping the people from starvation, before the coming of salmon.

**Figure 9-2.** Skunk cabbage, a life-saver in Indian
legend, brightens soggy spots in city parks.

These early footfalls of spring show you small climates. If your town is
hilly, you can see that spring comes to sunny south slopes before shady
north-facing ones. In cities edging salt water, like Seattle and Tacoma, buds
usually open first near the shore, because of the moderating influence of the
water.

Although we think of spring as the season of love, the first sign you see
of it in the animal kingdom is likely to be an increase in fighting. While the
trees are still bare, robins start to squabble and jeer in yards. The resident song
sparrow, who practices his repertoire from your corner telephone pole most

216

of the year, drives out an intruder by puffing up his feathers and waving a wing. This increased aggressiveness is, in fact, a prelude to courtship: These and other male birds are staking out territories where they can attract mates and rear young.

If you live near trees, a less-than-welcome sign of spring may be eastern gray squirrels (*Sciurus carolinensis*), transplated to almost every Northwest city. They gallop noisily over roofs in the early morning. Three or four join in a chase that goes on for hours, with occasional breathers. The squirrels are "courting," if you can call it that: Several males join in chasing a female through the trees. The most nimble or aggressive eventually wins the chase, mates quickly—and loses interest almost immediately, leaving the female to go through pregnancy and rearing the young alone.

These squabbles are a signal to you to set out, or clean out, birdhouses, if you want to try to attract birds to your yard. Robins generally are easily contented with the crotch of a limb or bush, though a roofed-over shelf in a leafy spot may attract them. The birds for whom nesting spots usually are in short supply, in cities as in the wilds, are those that lay their eggs in crannies and holes. You can help them by providing a simple box with a base of four to six inches on a side and six to nine inches deep, with a hole 1 1/8 to 1 1/4 inches in diameter. (A gourd or hollowed-out log can serve the same function more picturesquely.) Ventilation holes in the sides will help keep the birdhouse cool. A hinged top will make your yearly cleaning job easier.

Secure the house at least five feet from the ground, in shade, but facing an open space if possible. Fastening it to a tree is fine, but a pole at least six feet from limbs or other launching points will keep nestlings safer from cats and squirrels.

Such a house could become a home for tree or violet-green swallows, downy or hairy woodpeckers, Bewick's or house wrens, chickadees, nuthatches, or others, depending on where you live and the kinds of plants in your yard. To welcome these native birds, though, you will have to stand ready to evict rivals, such as house sparrows and starlings, especially if the entry to your birdhouse is larger than 1 1/4 inches. One reason these nonnative birds have done so well in cities is their aggressiveness—they may even take over an already occupied nesting spot.

## MIGRATION AND RITUAL

As new leaves begin to uncurl, chartreuse and silver, spring becomes more obvious. Migrant birds pass through towns in waves; on the move, even birds that prefer remote wilderness are likely to pass through cities.

First, varied thrushes, birds of mountain forest, may flute their haunting, single note in park woods. Another day, the swallows reappear.

Particularly along waterfronts, they twinkle in the air, wings beating irregularly as they course and wheel after insects. (After you watch birds awhile, you can recognize many simply by their manner of flying.) For a time, leafy parks and yards seem full of warblers, flecks of yellow with dry little songs. Then come the flycatchers, brownish birds that perch upright and loop out from limbs or telephone wires to catch insects.

Knowing where you are in nature's calendar—at the times of early or late migrants, for example—ties you to a cycle that is slower and less demanding than the hands on your watch. In addition, you can begin to compare years—were the swallows late this year because of cold weather further south, or some other condition?

**Figure 9-3.** As trees leaf out, American goldfinches take on bright summer plumage.

Some of the migrants, of course, stay to nest. They join spring's complex counterpoint of song, a daily round that begins with the robins before dawn, reaches a peak in early morning, dwindles as the sun climbs high, and then swells again in late afternoon. The singing males, perched in characteristic spots within established territories, are easy to spot. Thus this season may be best for beginning bird watchers.

Birds whose plumage changes seasonally are wearing courtship plumage. Male goldfinches, common in vacant, weedy spots, have gone from fall's olive drab to lemon yellow. Audubon's warbler left in black and white, but returns with yellow trim.

If you have binoculars or a bird-watching telescope, and the patience to sit quietly, you can watch courting rituals themselves. If Steller or blue jays pass raucously through your yard, keep an eye on them. You may see a male feed a suppliant female as though she were an infant—Humans are not the only creatures to whom a mate is "my baby." In last-year's cattails and still-bare shrubs at water's edge, male red-winged blackbirds hunch their wings to display their bright chevrons, and bow so deeply to the brown females that they almost fall over. The ceremonies of red-shafted flickers are likely to remind us most of our own courting follies. These adaptable woodpeckers are easily recognized by their white rumps and reddish underwings and "moustaches." They are common in cities, at the seacoast, in the desert, and in the mountains. In the spring, two perch opposite one another on limbs or on the ground and "dance." They bob from side to side and bow comically. After awhile, they "whicker" loudly and fly to a new spot—and often a new partner.

If you see a bird making repeated trips past your window with something in its beak, you have a good chance of seeing nest architecture. By following, you can watch robins matting together sticks, mud, and lacy old leaves; bushtits or orioles weaving hanging stockings from moss; and chickadees or nuthatches excavating, casting beakfuls of sawdust to the winds at the entrances to holes in trees.

Such nest watching must be done at a distance. Disturbance can cause parents to abandon nest and eggs, or can frighten young into plunging to their deaths. Getting too close to nests also can be unpleasant for you. Parent birds' alarm attracts others. Soon you are likely to be surrounded by a flock of crows or blackbirds, or a mix from jays to chickadees, all calling and swooping near your head. Appropriately, this behavior is called "mobbing."

As described in the last chapter, newts and salamanders "home" to moist places, where they join in nocturnal courtship dances. In the exuberance of spring courtship, even some snakes wrestle in friendly combat, trying to Indian wrestle their partner's head to the ground. But few see these activities.

**Figure 9-4.** A bushtit peeks from a stocking of moss and a house wren prepares to enter her hollow tree. Both birds have adapted well to city life.

# FLOWER SHOWS

One way to get to know wildflowers is to grow them in your garden. Specialized nurseries and fund-raising sales of garden organizations commonly sell seeds, bulbs, and small plants. Gathering seed from the wild takes considerable expertise, and digging any but the most common species robs the wild, probably without enriching you, for many will not survive the transplant. If you must dig wild plants, choose places about to be logged or cleared for development, so that you will save rather than destroy.

Native wildflowers generally fared less well than larger native plants as civilization disturbed soil, climate, and runoff in towns and cities. Wild lady's slipper or calypso orchids, for example, generally vanish when something upsets the balance of organic matter and fungus they need for nutrition. Plants with corms or bulbs, and those that spread by underground runners, cannot easily retake an area once they have been driven out.

Nevertheless, anyone who walks in less-developed parks or bits of left-over suburban woods is likely to find native wildflowers. Formal western trillium and friendly little yellow violets (*Viola glabella*) are among the early deep-woods bloomers.

Mid-spring flowers commonly surviving in city woods include dangling pink bleeding hearts (*Dicentra formosa*), with lacy, almost fern-like leaves; vanilla leaf (*Achlys triphylla*) waving a white wand above three-parted, sweet-smelling leaves; wild lily of the valley (*Maianthemum unifolium*). Several lilies with small white flowers and large shiny leaves along a succulent stem are often confused: Oregon fairy bells (*Disporum oregonum*), twisted stalk (*Streptopus amplexifolius*), star-flowered Solomon's seal (*Smilacina stellata*), and false Solomon's seal (*Smilacina amplexicaulis*).

Late spring and summer are the best times to enjoy wildflowers surviving in waste places. Plumes of ocean spray and goat's beard (*Aruncus sylvester*) wave from the edges of woods. East of the Cascades, the white-flowering shrubs are more likely to be mock orange (*Philadelphus lewisii*) and service berry. Thickets of pale-pink wild roses (mostly *Rosa nutkana*) are in bloom. In dry, grassy spots you may find pioneering magenta fireweed; pink vetches or wild peas; purple to blue lupine; and red Indian paintbrush. Even in the hottest months, vacant lots are likely to have tansy (*Tanacetum douglasii*), thistle (*Cirsium* spp.), goldenrod (*Solidago* spp.), yarrow (*Achillea millefolium*), and pearly everlasting (*Anaphalis margaritacea*), as well as many white, pinkish, and yellow daisy-like flowers (*Erigeron* spp., *Aster* spp., *Senecio* spp., and *Happlopappus* spp.)

A clue to the survival of tough "weeds" in disturbed areas is that many have abundant seeds carried by the wind. These seeds often are fertile without cross-fertilization—thus, an isolated pioneer plant could reproduce itself.

**Figure 9-5.** Western trillium, vanilla leaf (opposite), and bleeding heart (below): three native wildflowers still found in city woods.

Finally, weed seeds often can remain dormant for widely different periods, until the right conditions come along. While the weeds may be pests, their seeds have one advantage, from our point of view—several, including tansy, thistle, and pearly everlasting, leave behind dried pods that make excellent material for dried arrangements.

As the rush of spring begins to shift to the leisurely heat of summer, nearly all the Northwest's species of butterflies are on the wing. (A few, like the hibernating mourning cloak butterfly, *Nymphalis antiopa*, have been out since March.) Butterflies in the Northwest are not so varied and numerous as they are farther south, but still there are dozens of species in each major region of the Northwest, and close to 200 in all. Even a single butterfly is a delight to see. Watching and photographing their unpredictable movements is an interesting and challenging hobby.

Although they skip away from you, butterflies' behavior with one another can be aggressive. For example, they dog-fight in the air above a few choice plants. Attracting them also is less than poetic. These airy winged creatures are almost as likely to be drawn to mud and manure in your garden as to flowers. Really encouraging butterflies, too, requires something few gardeners like: helping their larvae, caterpillars. This means providing the plants they need as food. These needs can be quite specific. The showy

**Figure 9-6.** A western tiger swallowtail with wings damaged, perhaps by an attacking bird.

Western tiger swallowtail (*Papilio rutulus*) and Lorquin's admiral (*Liminitis lorquini*), for example, lay their eggs on aspen, willow, and cottonwood. Monarchs (*Danaus plexippus*) demand milkweed. Other special diets range from nettles to violets.

## SUMMER YOUNGSTERS

In mid-summer, flowering and the chorus of mating birds subside. June and July are times to watch awkward youngsters, as the offspring of spring courtships begin to explore on their own.

Squirrels conceived in spring's chases, born blind and helpless, now oegin to venture out of their nests, in hollow trunks or basketball-shaped balls of brush high in trees. They are not hard to spot in city parks. At first they nose cautiously around the home tree only, sticking close to their mothers. But soon the siblings chase and play-fight on their own. Such play is practice for autumn and adult life, when they must win rank or territory on their own.

On city ponds ducklings string along behind their mothers, or scoot for cover when they are alarmed. In brushy vacant lots, California quail families

**Figure 9-7.** Midsummer is the time to enjoy cities' wild youngsters, such as these mallard ducklings in Seattle's Arboretum.

carry on soft clucking conversations as they peck insects and seeds. Alarm them, and they take cover, the youngsters silent and the adults calling a spare, occasional "cut." (If you always dreamed of talking with animals, you will find quail and mallard-duck conversation rather easy to learn. Their vocabularies of alarm, mating, moving, and other calls are fairly easily distinguished.)

Summer's fledgling birds often can be recognized by their puffy downiness or camouflaging plumage—young robins, to use a familiar example, have speckled, not red, breasts in their first summer. Behavior also betrays the presence of youngsters. Their parents may scold you (or your dog or cat) raucously for getting too close. Birds just out of the nest flutter awkwardly. For a time they may beg with open mouths and parents may continue to feed them an occasional beakful. (Young gulls will beg for as long as a year—and from any adult, not just their parents.) The length of childhood and adolescence varies: Young swallows take to the air easily, seeming to play winged tag, then perching in a neat line on a telephone wire. Young song sparrows, as if less sure of themselves, explore by following their fathers on feeding trips.

The emergence of young goes on beyond August. Some birds, including goldfinches and pied-billed grebes, are late nesters. Many successful city animals, including robins, song sparrows, and gray squirrels, raise two sets of young a year.

## WILD NEIGHBORHOODS

In the dry interior Northwest, bird baths, or simply lawn sprinklers, will attract grateful birds to your yard. Summer's fine weather also makes it a good time to explore your town, seeing it as the wild things do. Like natural landscapes, cities and suburbs supply food and shelter that animals adapt to in surprising ways.

A good example is the swallow family, most of whose members have taken readily to manmade structures. Tree and violet-green swallows, both with darkly irridescent backs and white undersides, nest in holes in houses and pilings along waterfronts. Barn swallows, handsome blue, cinnamon, and buff birds with forked tails, got their common name from their readiness to build their mud-cup nests in barns. Nowadays the choice is more likely to be under a freeway bridge. A concrete abutment protected by an overhang may be home to a colony of cliff swallows, quarreling over status and position like social climbers.

One swallow species, by a twist of history, is not thriving: The purple martin took to the wooden buildings in Northwestern coastal cities the way its kindred took to manmade "martin houses" in the Midwest. But as the older, crannied buildings were torn down and replaced, the martins dwindled. They do not seem to be making a second change in their habits, even when bird lovers supply them with custom-built apartments. As a result, these big dark swallows, once common in the Northwest, now are rather rare.

Many animals are most active in early mornings or at dusk. These hours also give you your best chance of seeing nocturnal animals. Thus, late and early walks are likely to tell you what kinds of rabbits survive in your city, hiding from dogs and cats in daytime, eating succulent greens and tender brush at night.

Deer, foxes, and coyotes wander into most large suburban parks. If you are a regular visitor, sooner or later you will see their tracks (though those of foxes and coyotes are difficult to distinguish from dog tracks). With luck, at odd hours, you may see the animals themselves.

Less shy animals let you know they're in woodsy neighborhoods— skunks, for example, by their raids on garbage and their smell, if a local dog is foolish enough to chase them. Raccoons just raid garbage. Those that encourage these masked, ring-tailed little bandits because they're cute sometimes regret it. Start feeding one raccoon and you're soon feeding half a dozen, who all but come to your door to knock. If you must feed raccoons, don't lure them to eat from your fingers. You're likely to end up with a nasty bite.

**Figure 9-8.** Not all city wildlife gets along well with man. Feed the "cute" raccoons and you may be all but beseiged by the masked bandits.

A problem with feeding wild animals in general is that unless the feeding place is carefully designed, much of the handout ends up in the bellies of mice and rats.

For many city dwellers and suburbanites, the difficulty is not attracting wild animals, but getting rid of them. Squirrels, for example, are cute—but not when they're living in your attic. Rabbits, moles, and pocket gophers can ruin gardens overnight. Problems can come from unexpected sources. Pheasants, introduced game birds that flourish in many grassy suburban areas, have a special fondness for tulip bulbs. Families living on waterfronts sometimes wake to find that beavers have dammed their drainage ditches or gnawed down their waterfront trees.

Such problems usually can be solved without killing the animals. Appropriate fences can protect most gardens (though not from burrowers). Trimming trees away from houses can keep animals from deciding to share living quarters with the family. If an unwanted visitor does move into your attic or basement, mothballs may discourage him. Or you can wait until he is likely to be out (nighttime in the case of skunks or raccoons), then block up the entrance hole.

Local animal-control offices or state game departments supply advice and sometimes live traps. You or the officials can then transport the animals to a more suitable home.

## GETTING READY FOR FALL AND WINTER

As wild harvest-time begins, city (and countryside) wildlife again is on the move, with a new urgency. You become suddenly aware of squirrels and chipmunks quarrelling and scolding noisily over summer's bounty. Their chases, their bird-like calls, flicking tails, and bobbing heads, may seem comic to us. But they are in a serious competition over who will store enough food to survive the lean winter.

The native Douglas and red squirrels trill and chase to establish territories in the conifers. Piles of cone scales beneath a tree show you their locations. Look up, and you may see a squirrel pulling off scales and turning the cone as he nibbles it like an ear of corn. A cone being cut for buried storage may bounce down on your head.

Watching your town carefully, you may find that squirrels have it "segregated" into neighborhoods occupied by different species, depending on the local trees. The woods of needled evergreens, similar to natural forests, probably are still held by the small natives—orange-bellied Douglas squirrels from the Cascades west, and whitish-bellied red squirrels farther east. Landscaped parks and yards, however, are more likely to support eastern gray squirrels, and, in some towns, big, cinnamon-bellied fox squirrels (*Sciurus niger*). Both were brought to the Northwest by man. Unlike the smaller native squirrels, they do not establish territories. This may be because in their native East and Midwest the seeds and nuts they needed were scattered in a diverse hardwood forest. You may see several in and beneath a park sycamore, horse chestnut, or oak, cutting and burying nuts. Among them, face-offs and chases establish rank, and thus access to food.

Late summer sometimes brings a wave of excitement to local bird-watchers, as a member of some seldom-seen species appears in town. These wanderers are usually adventurous adolescents. They are extreme examples of the late-summer dispersal that keeps populations from becoming too dense, and locates suitable but unused habitats.

These wandering youngsters and unmated males also become the nuclei of fall flocks, which begin to form as soon as nesting ends in June. Watch for flocks of small birds tinkling through your yard. Some species drift south as early as August—terns, for example, course and dip like swallows on Northwest waterfronts, on their way south from the Arctic. By September you will notice plumage changes and the absence of some familiar summer residents of Northwest towns. For example, a half-dozen kinds of warblers, flecks of summer yellow, move south. Only Audubon's warbler stays year-round, its winter dress of sedate black and white brightened only by a yellow rump patch.

**Figure 9-9.** Canada geese flying in Vs are common sights over most Northwest cities.

Geese flying in high Vs and flocks of ducks making restless short flights on the waterfront at dawn give you a good idea that migration is underway. (Don't be deceived, though, by the Canada geese that live year-round in coastal cities.)

Except among water birds, one seldom sees actual migration. Most species are fly-by-nights—that is, they migrate in darkness. (Birds use an amazing variety of clues to navigate, from the earth's magnetic fields to sound and cloud patterns.)

What you can see is how these nighttime waves of movement replace the summer visitors with waves of birds "just passing through," and with others seeking winter shelter. In cities west of the Cascades, the little winter wren of deep mountain woods moves into shady fern clumps that will remain snow-free. The water pipit, that patrolled alpine lakes in summer, bobs and walks on city waterfronts. In parks and yards, flocks of juncos and kinglets from colder areas join local bushtits and chickadees, in flocks that tinkle through woods and brush. Pine siskins buzz through the treetops. Waves of western meadowlarks, singers of the desert, settle briefly on vacant lots and then move on.

The variety of autumn visitors points up birds' physical adaptations to their lifestyles. Some are obvious—hummingbirds' long, narrow beaks, adapted to sucking nectar, for example. Not visible is the fact that these smallest of birds can let their body temperatures drop drastically in cold weather and at night, cutting the amount of food they must consume to produce energy to keep warm.

Birds that perch have slim feet and legs, and the hind toe is long for grasping. Birds that find their food while walking have larger, stronger legs and feet, with widespread toes. The grasping hind toe, though, is shortened, or, as in killdeer, absent.

The hooked claws and beaks of meat-eating birds, such as shrikes, hawks, and owls, serve to grasp and impale prey. Birds that hunt insects on the wing, though, such as swallows, usually have short, broad bills and wide-gaping mouths. Those that probe for insects, such as woodpeckers, have long, strong beaks. Short, deep bills, like those of sparrows and finches, easily grasp and shell seeds.

Autumn and winter give you your best chance of seeing hawks and owls in cities and suburbs. Though some of these hunters live and raise young in surprisingly populated areas, fall migration and the search for winter shelter increase their numbers.

The smallest of the hawks is the American kestrel (commonly called *sparrow hawk*), a dapper, bright-colored little hawk that hunts open places, eating mostly insects caught on the wing. His long pointed wings, like those of falcons, are adapted for speed with their rapid, shallow beats.

In woods you may see a crow-sized Cooper's hawk loop after a flock of chickadees. This hunter's short wings and long tail are adapted for tight

**Figure 9-10.** The short, deep beaks of house finches make it easy for these common birds to hold and crack seeds.

steering and quick braking among branches. His prey, you will notice, get a fair chance by having a similar shape.

Hawks with rounded tails and broad wings, like the common red-tailed hawk or the bald or golden eagle, are built for soaring and wheeling. Look for red-tails over wide open spaces, including freeways and airports. Marsh hawks, too, come into cities that have reedy or grassy lakefronts.

As owls are mostly night-time hunters, you are less likely to see them than hawks. Some of the smaller owls, however, are daytime hunters. Occasionally, too, a population crash of lemmings in the Arctic brings snowy owls south, seeking food.

Most owl enthusiasts, though, enjoy the birds on night-time walks, listening for cries or trying to get the owls to answer tape-recorded calls. These are not just "hoots"—owls whistle, bark, and yap as well. Check local park departments, the Audubon Society, and other outdoor groups if you are interested.

**231**

# BERRIES, NUTS, LEAVES, BARK

Northwest residents are lucky to have a bounty of wild berries available in town and country. Almost every city has tangles of domestic blackberries (*Rubus laciniatus* and others), escaped from cultivation and become pests. The fruit is not as good as the rarer and more rural native blackberries, blackcaps, and raspberries (*Rubus vitifolius*, *leucodermis*, and *idaeus*, respectively). But the escapees are abundant, and they ripen as early as July. So do the soft, raspberry-like fruits of thimbleberry, a common pioneer in shady places; and the rather insipid salmonberries, found in damp spots west of the Cascades.

Blue-berry elder (*Sambucus glauca*), a smallish tree with sprays of compound leaves and a flat-topped cluster of edible blue berries, often grows wild in dry places in and near towns. It is easily distinguished from red-berry elder (*Sambucus callicarpa*), which has rounded clusters of red, poisonous fruit, and prefers moister locations.

Two easily found berries used by Indians, but seldom eaten today, are Indian plum west of the Cascades and serviceberry, or amelanchier, in the interior. The many species of wild currant and gooseberry also are of little value on the table, though some make good preserves. (Gooseberry plants have thorns; currants do not.)

Wild cranberry, once common in coastal bogs, is rare today because civilization dredged or filled so many of its homes. "High-bush cranberry" (*Viburnum trilobum*—not a cranberry at all) probably was always rare in the Northwest—it is a plant of the far north, common in Alaska.

Most of the Northwest's abundant, tasty, and varied huckleberries are mountain plants or have disappeared from populated areas. An exception is the evergreen huckleberry (*Vaccinium ovatum*), still easily found west of the Cascades, especially in southern Washington and Oregon. These are among the later-ripening fruits, along with salal and Oregon grape, generally sought only for jelly-making.

In contrast to wild berries, edible wild nuts are uncommon in the evergreen Northwest. One exception is the wild hazelnut. The shrubby tree is common, but you seldom will get many nuts, with their rough, long-tailed husks. Chipmunks and squirrels eat or store most while they are still green.

As trees drop their leaves, winter reveals new, subtle tones. Many woodsy places are red-brown and green, rather than gray, through the winter. They are warmed by the cinnamon-colored bark of cedars, Douglas firs, and ponderosa pine, and by wine-colored young alder twigs. Here and there are brighter tones. Willow twigs, used by Indians to make string and as a toothache remedy, glow orange to gold in swampy places. West of the Cascades, madrona sheds much of its orange-red bark in late summer and fall, revealing a new layer, satin-smooth and greenish ochre. Woods of the dry

**Figure 9-11.** Flowers of thimbleberry, left, and salal, common edible berries that grow in and near cities.

interior often have striking contrasts. Aspens and paper birches are white; young twigs of birch and wild cherry are glossy bronze—they were favorites for decorating Indian baskets.

## YOUR OWN WINTER SANCTUARY

All you need is a windowsill to feed pigeons, house sparrows, and, in coastal cities, gulls. The fallout from your sill, though, may make you unpopular with people living below you.

If you have a yard you can create something of a wildlife sanctuary there, especially during hard times in winter. One of the best ways to do this is by thinking ahead when you landscape. Leafy evergreens provide cover and warmth. Bushes with berries that cling to the branches, such as pyracantha and holly; and flowers that keep their seeds, such as sunflowers, will help feed birds without extra effort on your part.

If you do put out food for birds, squirrels, or other wild things, remember that you are taking on a responsibility. The supply must be regular, and it cannot be cut off in mid-winter. Otherwise, creatures that have become dependent on you may starve. For your sake as well as your neighbors', you also should have a feeding platform that cannot be reached by rats. The best bird feeder is:

- at least a foot square, so that several birds can feed at once;
- roofed, to keep out rain and snow;
- walled on its windiest sides, or at least equipped with a rim to prevent birds kicking much of the food on the ground (glass walls let birds see in and you see out);
- away from limbs that cats, rats, and squirrels could leap from; and
- at least five feet from the ground and equipped with a circular collar about two feet in diameter, to keep marauders from climbing its supporting post.

Different species like different foods. Birds, like children, relish peanut-butter and jam—but you may find providing them rather expensive. Commercial bird feed is fine, but chicken scratch from farm-supply stores may be cheaper. You also can make your own mixtures, experimenting to see which seeds your local birds like. Stale crumbs are not a balanced bird diet, but they will be welcome, especially if dipped in leftover grease for insect-eating birds, such as chickadees and jays. Such "carnivorous" birds also enjoy suet or any scraps of trimmed-off fat. Put it in a mesh pocket to be pecked at by many birds, rather than hogged by one. To be decorative, soak open pine cones, or sticks with

**Figure 9-12.** A bushtit, left, and a red-breasted nuthatch, right, are happy with seed and suet in a simple bird feeder. Both are common in mixed flocks of birds that winter in Northwest cities.

short horizontal holes, in melted grease. Then hang them out for pecking when the fat has hardened.

In the mild coastal cities of the Northwest, winter blends into spring. Tree frogs begin to peep about the time alders are dropping their leaves, in December.

Nevertheless, the leanest time for animals generally is late winter. In about February you may see signs of real hunger in city parks. Squirrels nose out the remains of their buried stores and gnaw bark, particularly that of maples, in which the sweet sap already is rising. Half-tame geese and ducks all but peck the legs of visitors as they beg for food.

Animals' death rates normally rise in winter. Snow and ice can cover food supplies. Small birds may not be able to eat enough to replace energy used to keep warm. Rabbits and other brush eaters, including elk and deer, can die of starvation with full stomachs if the available vegetation does not supply enough nutrition or cannot be converted by the stomach bacteria on

**Figure 9-13.** The harmless common garter snake, sunning in a garden or on a log, is a sign of another spring.

which they depend for digestion. Even if an animal is only weakened, it becomes easier prey for predators, including city cats and dogs.

Thus it is not only we human beings who welcome spring. Squirrels in parks relish the first green shoots and emerging insects, and climb high to eat cottonwood's red-plush catkins. Spider webs again glisten in the mornings—a sign that it is warm enough for insects to hatch and get caught. Snakes wriggle out of holes to sun themselves. So the year's round goes on—waiting for you to join, at least as a spectator.

## DOING IT YOURSELF

Many activities suggested in previous chapters can be carried out as well in the city as in the countryside.

Find out what's available from local museums. Most universities have interesting displays on regional wildlife, geology, and so on. The University of Washington's Burke Museum in Seattle and the Oregon Museum of Science and Industry in Portland are examples. Check the Northwest collection of your local public library to find books worth reading—and worth buying.

Look at a schedule of activities from the local parks department and from outdoor and conservation groups such as the Audubon Society, Sierra Club, Washington's Mountaineers, and Oregon's Mazamas. You may want to join in. Check adult education courses offered by university extensions, community colleges, and many school districts, among others. Through such courses you can become an expert on anything from identifying mosses to surviving in the wilderness. Some newspapers list outdoor activities. In addition, bulletin boards in stores that sell outdoor equipment often are a good place to find out about privately offered activities.

To be in touch with nature's calendar, keep a chart or diary of when things bloom, when you see certain animals or activities, and so on. Year-to-year variations often are interesting. Get to know the ecology of your yard or of a local park. Where do the birds roost at night? What do they eat? What insects live where?

If you want to encourage wildlife in your own yard, try planting cover and food plants, and setting out bird houses if you have the right conditions. If you feed animals, remember your responsibilities to them—that is, you must feed steadily—and to your neighbors—that is, don't attract mice and rats.

Become familiar with the larger city, county, and state parks in your area. This is great when children are too young to take long hikes, and in early mornings and in winter, when parks are often all but deserted. Most people are surprised at the many wild things they find once they start to look.

Find out whether the policies of local parks departments and other agencies needlessly discourage native plants and animals. You may want to get involved in matters such as land purchasing and land use, landscaping, and use of pesticides.

# For Further Reading

## NATURAL HISTORY AND GENERAL

BROWN, G.W., JR., ed. *Desert Biology*, Vols. I and II. New York: Academic Press, 1968 and 1974. Technical and complete collection of papers.

BURROUGHS, R.D., ed. *The Natural History of the Lewis and Clark Expedition.* Lansing: Michigan State University Press, 1961. Quotations on plants and animals from first-person accounts of the expeditions.

CLARK, ELLA E. *Indian Legends of the Pacific Northwest.* Berkeley: University of California Press, 1953. Indian legends in close to the original versions.

HIGHSMITH, R.M., JR., ed. *Atlas of the Pacific Northwest: Resources and Development.* Corvallis: Oregon State College, 1953. Good basic reference.

JACKMAN, E.R., and R.A. LONG. *The Oregon Desert.* Caldwell, Idaho: Caxton Printers, Ltd., 1964. Charming account of a pioneer rancher, with natural history.

KIRK, RUTH. *Exploring Mt. Rainier.* Seattle: University of Washington Press, 1968. This and other books in Kirk's "Exploring" series (*Exploring Yellowstone*, 1972, and *Exploring Olympic Park*, 3rd ed., 1980) are knowledgeable, interesting guides to popular areas.

KOZLOFF, E.N. *Plants and Animals of the Pacific Northwest.* Seattle: University of Washington Press, 1976. Excellent introduction to plants, animals, and ecology west of the Cascade Range.

MAYR, E. *Populations, Species, and Evolution: An Abridgement of "Animal Species and Evolution."* Cambridge, Mass.: Belknap Press of Harvard University Press, 1970. Short version of a standard text on basic principles of evolution.

MOUNTAINEERS. *Mountaineering: The Freedom of the Hills.* Seattle: Mountaineers, 1974. One of the best basic guides to basic techniques and safety of hiking and climbing.

OSOLINSKI, STAN. *Nature Photography: A Guide to Better Outdoor Pictures.* Englewood Cliffs, N.J.; Prentice-Hall, Inc., 1981. Easy-to-read guide.

SCHWARTZ, S., B. SPRING and E. SPRING. *Cascade Companion.* Seattle: Pacific Search, 1976. Brief basic natural history of the Washington Cascades.

SPRING, B., I. SPRING, and MANNING, H. *102 Hikes in the Alpine Lakes, South Cascades, and Olympics.* Seattle: Mountaineers, 1971. This and other books in the Mountaineers' "Hikes" series are excellent tour guides for backpackers.

# WEATHER

SCHROEDER, M.J. and C.C. BUCK. *Fire Weather: A Guide for Application of the Meteorological Information to Forest Fire Control Operations.* U.S. Forest Service Agriculture Handbook 360, 1970. Despite the title, an excellent summary of mountain weather, in simple language with clear illustrations.

# GEOLOGY

ALT, DAVID D., and D.W. HYNDMAN. *Roadside Geology of Oregon.* Missoula, Mont.: Mountain Press Publishing Co., 1978. Easy-to-understand, up-to-date guidebook.

FLINT, R.F. *Glacial and Quarternary Geology.* New York: John Wiley & Sons, 1971. Technical and detailed.

GREELEY, RONALD, and JOHN S. KING. *Geologic Field Guide to the Quarternary Volcanics of the South-Central Snake River Plain, Idaho.* Moscow, Idaho: Idaho Bureau of Mines and Geology Pamphlet 160, 1975. Nontechnical, informative guide.

HALLIDAY, W.R. *Caves of Washington.* Olympia, Wash.: Washington State Division of Mines and Geology Information Circular 40, 1963. Brief, thorough guide.

HARRIS, STEPHEN L. *Fire and Ice; The Cascade Volcanos.* Seattle: Mountaineers, 1976. Nontechnical and informative natural history, somewhat out of date (new findings on continental drift make geology books obsolete quickly).

HUBBS, C.L. *Zoogeography.* Washington, D.C.: American Association for the Advancement of Science, 1958. Technical papers on origins of modern animal life.

JOHNSTON, D.A., and J. DONNELLY-NOLAN, eds. *Guides to Some Volcanic Terranes in Washington, Idaho, Oregon, and Northern California.* Washington, D.C.: U.S. Geological Survey Circular 838, 1981. Excellent free guide.

LIVINGSTON, VAUGHN E. *Fossils in Washington.* Olympia, Wash.: Washington State Division of Mines and Geology Information Circular 33, 1959. Beginning guide for fossil hunters.

MCKEE, BATES. *Cascadia: The Geologic Evolution of the Pacific Northwest.* New York: McGraw Hill Book Co., 1972. Fairly nontechnical explanation, somewhat out of date.

*Ore Bin,* magazine of the Oregon Department of Geology and Mineral Industries. Interesting articles on landforms, geology, and history, understandable to nonspecialists.

PARSONS, W.H. *Middle Rockies and Yellowstone.* Dubuque, Iowa: Kendall/Hunt Publishing Co., 1978. Clear, up-to-date field guide covering Yellowstone, the Tetons, and eastern Idaho.

RANSOM, J.E. *The Rock-Hunter's Range Guide.* New York: Harper & Row, 1962. Tells beginning rockhounds where and how to look.

ROSS, SYLVIA H. *Introduction to Idaho Caves and Caving.* Moscow, Idaho: Idaho Bureau of Mines and Geology Earth Sciences Series 2, 1969. Brief, thorough guide.

SHELTON, J.S. *Geology Illustrated.* San Francisco: W.H. Freeman & Co., 1966. Beautifully illustrated, easy-to-read explanations of western landforms.

TABOR, R.W. *Guide to the Geology of Olympic National Park.* Seattle: University of Washington Press, 1975. Clear and up-to-date.

VANDERS, I., and P.F. KERR. *Mineral Recognition.* New York: John Wiley & Sons, 1967. Well-illustrated guide with explanations.

WRIGHT, H.E., JR., and D.G. FREY, eds. *The Quarternary of the United States.* Princeton, N.J.: Princeton University Press, 1965. Complete and technical collecticn of papers.

# TREES AND FLOWERING PLANTS

CRONQUIST, A. et al. *Intermountain Flora.* New York: Hafner Publishing Co., 1972. Rather technical guidebook to Great Basin plants.

DAUBENMIRE, R. *Plant Geography.* New York: Academic Press, 1978. Condensed, fairly technical explanation of why plants live where they do.

HITCHCOCK, D.L. and A. CRONQUIST. *Flora of the Pacific Northwest.* Seattle: University of Washington Press, 1973. Complete, well-illustrated, and technical.

HOSKIN, L.L. *Wildflowers of the Pacific Coast.* Portland: Binfords and Mort, 1934. Charming guidebook with lots of lore.

LYONS, C.P. *Trees, Shrubs, and Flowers to Know in Washington.* Toronto; J.M. Dent & Sons, Ltd., 1956. Excellent guide for beginners.

MOHNEY, R. *Why Wild Edibles? The Joys of Finding, Fixing, and Tasting—West of the Rockies.* Seattle: Pacific Search Books, 1975. Useful guide to what you can eat from the wilds.

MUNZ, P.A. *Shore Wildflowers of California, Oregon and Washington.* Berkeley: University of California Press, 1964. Useful brief guide.

PECK, M.E. *A Manual of the Higher Plants of Oregon*, 2nd ed. Portland: Binfords & Mort, 1961, useful manual.

PEATTIE, D.C. *A Natural History of Western Trees*. Boston: Houghton Mifflin & Co., Boston, informative and good reading.

WATTS, T. *Pacific Coast Tree Finder*. Berkeley: Nature Study Guild, 1973. Handy pocket-sized guide.

## MUSHROOMS, FERNS
## MOSSES, LICHENS

CONARD, H.S. *How to Know the Mosses and Liverworts*. Dubuque, Iowa: Wm. C. Brown, 1956. Good beginning in a difficult subject.

HALE, M.E., JR. *How to Know the Lichens*. Dubuque, Iowa: Wm. C. Brown, 1969. Good for beginners.

McKENNY, D.E. *The Savory Wild Mushroom*, 2nd ed., revised by D.E. Stuntz. Seattle: University of Washington Press, 1971. Excellent field guide, useful for beginners.

SMITH, A.H. *A Field Guide to Western Mushrooms*. Ann Arbor: University of Michigan Press, 1975. Another useful field guide in a subject in which more than one book is advisable.

TAYLOR, T.M.C. *Pacific Northwest Ferns and Their Allies*. Toronto: University of Toronto Press, 1970. For beginners and experts.

## BIRDS AND LAND ANIMALS

BENT, A.C. *Life Histories of North American Birds*. Monumental series first published by the United States Government Printing Office; reprinted by Dover Publications, New York, 1962.

CODY, M.L. and J.M. DIAMOND. *Ecology and Evolution of Communities*. Cambridge, Mass.: Belknap Press of Harvard University Press, 1975. Technical basic reference.

*Harper & Row's Complete Field Guide to North American Wildlife*. Western Edition. Assembled by J.E. Ransom. New York: Harper & Row, 1981. As close as you'll come to an all-in-one field guide.

GABRIELSON, I.N., and S.G. JEWETT. *Birds of Oregon*. Corvallis: Oregon State College Press, 1940. Informative, but not a portable field guide.

INGLES L.G. *Mammals of the Pacific States—California, Oregon, and Washington*. Palo Alto: Stanford University Press, 1965. Excellent and informative guide, though bulky for the field.

KORTRIGHT, F.H. *Ducks, Geese and Swans of North America*. Harrisburg, Pa.: Stackpole Co., 1967. Complete guide with life histories.

LARRISON, E.J. *Washington Mammals: Their Habits, Identification, and Distribution*. Seattle: Seattle Audubon Society, 1970. Well-illustrated guide.

LARRISON, E.J., and D.R. JOHNSON. *Mammals of Idaho*. Moscow, Idaho: University Press of Idaho, 1981.

LARRISON, E. J. and K.G. SONNENBERG. *Washington Birds: Their Location and Identification*. Seattle: Seattle Audubon Society, 1968. Informative if used with a better-illustrated field guide.

MURIE O.J., *A Field Guide to Animal Tracks*, 2nd ed. Boston: Houghton Mifflin Co., 1974. Indispensable for getting to know tracks and scats.

NEILL, W.A., and D.J. HEPBURN. *Butterflies Afield in the Pacific Northwest*. Seattle: Pacific Search Books, 1976.

ROBBINS, C.S., et al. *Birds of North America*. New York: Golden Press, 1978. Probably the best field guide for beginners.

ROTH, C.E. *The Wildlife Observer's Guidebook*. Englewood Cliffs, N.J.: Prentice-Hall, Inc., 1982. Excellent guide for serious animal watchers.

PETERSON, R.T. *A Field Guide to Western Birds*. Boston; Houghton Mifflin Co., 1961. Excellent, though the Golden Press guide, by Robbins et al., may be easier for beginners.

PYLE, R.B. *Watching Washington Butterflies*. Seattle; Seattle Audubon Society, 1974. Brief guide.

SCHWARTZ, S., B. SPRING and I. SPRING. *Wildlife Areas of Washington*. Seattle: Superior Publishing Co., 1976. Where to watch wildlife in Washington.

SPRING, B. and I. SPRING. *Oregon Wildlife Areas*. Seattle: Superior Publishing Co., 1978. Where to watch wildlife in Oregon.

STEBBINS, R.C. *A Field Guide to Western Reptiles and Amphibians*. Boston: Houghton Mifflin Co., 1966. Excellent, complete guide.

SWAIN, R.B. *The Insect Guide*. New York: Doubleday & Co., 1948.

# WATER LIFE

BURNER, C.J. *Pacific Salmon*. U.S. Fish and Wildlife Service, Bureau of Commericial Fisheries, Fisheries Leaflet 563. Basic information.

CAREFOOT, THOMAS. *Pacific Seashores; A Guide to Intertidal Ecology*. Seattle: University of Washington Press, 1977. Excellent explanations for nonexperts.

FREY, D.G., ed. *Limnology in North America*. Madison: University of Wisconsin, 1963. Good basic reference.

GUBERLET, M.L. *Seaweeds at Ebb Tide*. Seattle: University of Washington Press, 1956. Useful guide illustrated with drawings.

HYNES, H.B.N. *The Ecology of Running Waters*. Liverpool, England: Liverpool University Press, 1970. Good basic reference.

KOZLOFF, E.N. *Seashore life of Puget Sound, the Strait of Georgia, and the San Juan Archipelago*. Seattle: University of Washington Press, 1974. Easy to read and informative.

MORISAWA, M. *Streams; Their Dynamics and Morphology*. New York: McGraw-Hill, 1968. Good short explanation.

REID, G.K. *Ecology of Inland Waters and Estuaries*. New York: Reinhold Publishing Corp., 1961. Good basic reference.

RICE, T.C. *Marine Shells of the Pacific Northwest*, Rev. ed. Edmonds, Wash.: Ellis Robinson Publishing Co., 1972. Nicely illustrated handbook.

SIMPSON, J. C., and R. L. WALLACE. *Fishes of Idaho*. Moscow, Idaho: University Press of Idaho, 1978. Easy-to-use, thorough handbook.

SMITH, L. S. *Living Shores of the Pacific Northwest*. Seattle: Pacific Search, 1976. Beautifully illustrated guidebook.

Washington (State) Department of Fisheries. *Pacific Northwest Marine Fishes*. Olympia, Wash.: Dept. of Fisheries, 1967. Booklet of basic information.

WILLERS, W.B. *Trout Biology: An Angler's Guide*. Madison: University of Wisconsin Press, 1981. Detailed, readable biology.

WYDOSKI, R.R. and R.R. WHITNEY. *Inland Fishes of Washington*. Seattle: University of Washington Press, 1979. Highly informative guide that serves almost as well for Oregon and Idaho.

# INDEX